MIDRASH AS LITERATURE

The Primacy of
Documentary Discourse

MIDRASH AS LITERATURE

The Primacy of
Documentary Discourse

Jacob Neusner

UNIVERSITY
PRESS OF
AMERICA

LANHAM • NEW YORK • LONDON

Copyright © 1987 by

University Press of America,® Inc.

4720 Boston Way
Lanham, MD 20706

3 Henrietta Street
London WC2E 8LU England

British Cataloging in Publication Information Available

Library of Congress Cataloging-in-Publication Data

Neusner, Jacob, 1932-
Midrash as literature.

(Studies in Judaism)
Includes bibliographical references and index.
1. Midrash—History and criticism.   2. Kugel,
James L.—Views on Midrash.   I. Title   II. Series.
BM514.N48   1987   296.1'406   87-6272
ISBN 0-8191-6307-4 (alk. paper)
ISBN 0-8191-6308-2 (pbk. : alk. paper)

All University Press of America books are produced on acid-free
paper which exceeds the minimum standards set by the National
Historical Publication and Records Commission.

For

HELEN H. VENDLER

a token of appreciation of, thanks to, an old and dear friend who has taught
me the most about literature.

Working on literature deemed, as is Midrash, dense, difficult, and obscure,
she has opened poetry to us all by showing us its human meanings
and displaying the achievement and sheer hard work
that has gone into the act of creation – both the poet's and the critic's.

Her keen eye and cool, courageous intelligence prevent her from
treating as romantic and sentimental what are in fact hard and uncompromising
statements of truth.

She is the one who sets the standard and defines the model of criticism
for all students of all literatures.

The basic unit of the Bible, for the midrashist, is the verse: this is what he seeks to expound, and it might be said that there simply is no boundary encountered beyond that of the verse until one comes to the borders of the canon itself.

James Kugel

"Two Definitions of Midrash," *Prooftexts* 3, 1983, pp. 131-155 = Geoffrey H. Hartman and Sanford Budick, eds., *Midrash and Literature* (New Haven, 1986: Yale University Press), pp. 77-103. Quote: p. 93.

CONTENTS

Part Four
THE PRIMACY OF DOCUMENTARY DISCOURSE

Preface

The basic unit of the Bible, for the midrashist, is the verse: this is what he seeks to expound, and it might be said that there simply is no boundary encountered beyond that of the verse until one comes to the borders of the canon itself.

James Kugel

In this book I conduct a debate with James Kugel about introducing midrash, that is, about the definition and character of midrash, a particular literary genre within Judaism. The issues of the debate will quickly transcend the narrow framework of Judaic religious writing, for at the heart of matters is a much-vexed question. It is whether, and to what extent, we are to read and interpret a work of literature initially within a particular social and historical context. In our reading of the received writings of former times may we ignore questions of circumstance and context, setting and society? In my view, in introducing midrash, Kugel reads Scripture-exegesis out of the determinate past and instead treats it as a statement both deriving from, and directed toward, an indeterminate and eternal present: nothing in particular to whom it may concern. Indeed, his proposed definition of midrash is so encompassing as to include pretty much everything about anything to do with Scripture and much else. The definition signals confusion generated by an ahistorical and anti-contextual approach to interpretation of midrash, in which documents make no difference, and knowledge of the particular time and place and condition of a given authorship contributes in no way to our understanding of the genre in all its specificity.

Let me specify the statements of Kugel subject to discussion here, so that an accurate representation of his views, in his own words, may define the issues for debate. As I see it, in his "Two Introductions to Midrash," he makes these five important points:[1]

---

[1] I shall stipulate that minor errors in the representation of the Hebrew texts, translation, major errors of interpretation and even description, will not impede discourse. It is not about details or misunderstandings or misinterpretations that I conceive a book-length debate to be appropriate, but about a position fundamental to his entire position and, as I shall show, utterly in contradiction to the character of the literature Kugel claims to describe, analyze, and interpret.

1. Midrash stands for Judaic biblical interpretation in general:

> At bottom midrash is not a genre of interpretation but an interpretative
> stance, a way of reading the sacred text...The genres in which this way of
> reading has found expression include ...translations of the Bible such as
> the early Aramaic targumim; retellings of biblical passages and books
> such as the 'Genesis Apocryphon'...; sermons, homilies, exegetical
> prayers and poems, and other synagogue pieces; and of course the great
> standard corpora of Jewish exegesis..., in short, almost all of what
> constitutes classical and much of medieval Jewish writing....for at heart
> midrash is nothing less than the foundation stone of rabbinic Judaism
> and it is as diverse as Jewish creativity itself.[2]

2. Midrash is precipitated by the character of the verse subject to exegesis:

> ...midrash's precise focus is most often what one might call surface
> irregularities in the text: a good deal of the time, it is concerned
> with...*problems*.[3]

3. Midrash is an exegesis of biblical verses, not of books:

> ...midrash is an exegesis of biblical verses, not of books. The basic
> unit of the Bible for the midrashist is the verse: this is what he seeks to
> expound, and it might be said that there simply is no boundary
> encountered beyond that of the verse until one comes to the borders of
> the canon itself.[4]

4. The components of midrash-compositions are interchangeable:

> Our midrashic compilations are in this sense potentially deceiving, since
> they seem to treat the whole text bit by bit; but with the exception of
> certain patterns, these "bits" are rather atomistic, and, as any student or
> rabbinic literature knows, interchangeable, modifiable, combinable – in
> short, not part of an overall exegesis at all.[5]

5. Midrash is the way every Jew reads Scripture:

> Forever after, one cannot think of the verse or hear it recited without
> also recalling the solution to its problematic irritant–indeed,
> remembering it in the study-house or synagogue, one would certainly
> pass it along to others present, and together appreciate its cleverness and

---

[2]*Op. cit.* pp. 91-2.

[3]P. 92.

[4]P. 93.

[5]P. 95.

erudition. And so midrashic explications of individual verses no doubt circulated on their own, independent of any larger exegetical context. Perhaps in this sense it would not be inappropriate to compare their manner of circulating to that of jokes in modern society; indeed, they were a kind of joking, a learned and sophisticated play about the biblical text, and like jokes they were passed on, modified, and improved as they went, until a great many of them eventually entered into the common inheritance of every Jew, passed on in learning with the text of the Bible itself.[6]

We shall pass by in silence the sleight of hand that transforms the *no doubt* of the middle of the paragraph into the factual historical statement at the end, that "a great many of them *eventually entered....*" These minor slips need not detain us; Kugel is an honest scholar.

In Chapters Two and Three I shall construct a null hypothesis to take up the more important of Kugel's definitions, and I shall address all these propositions in Chapter Nine, after I have laid out the traits of midrash-compilations of a representative sample of midrash-exegeses of the Judaism of the dual Torah in late antiquity. Then we may see whether or not Kugel's propositions conform to, or contradict, the evidence in hand. Since, as he says, *any student of rabbinic literature knows* the facts as he represents them, we shall have a chance to ask whether or not what "any student of rabbinic literature" knows is right, that is, knows what he or she is talking about, starting, of course, with Mr. Kugel himself.

Before we enter the debate, however, I have to specify what is at stake. Why should anyone not in a rabbinical school or a synagogue pulpit care about the definition of midrash, on the one side, and the literary traits of the documents subject to description, on the other?[7] The issue at hand, brings us to ask whether and how we see literature in context, and what we may mean by the appropriate arena for discourse. Let me spell out the issue, first in its particularity, then in more general terms.

I maintain that midrash-exegesis of Scripture reaches us in distinctive documents, and the first (though not the last) point of entry into the reading and interpretation of midrash-exegesis finds location in the document: hence, documentary discourse. As he says explicitly and repeatedly in his "Two Definitions," Kugel treats documentary lines as null, just as he treats all data, deriving from all times and all places, as equally valid and wholly undifferentiated evidence for the genre he claims to define. That is how and why

---

[6]P. 95.

[7]Felicities of style do not comprise one of the reasons to read the literary critical essays at hand. The papers assembled in the volume edited by Hartman and Budick seem to me remarkably prolix and verbose, using a great many fancy words to say a few simple things, most of them wrong. But we shall not dwell on trivialities, though, admittedly, it is no joy to read the circle represented by Kugel. Still, his paper is by no means the worst of the lot.

the very broad issue comes to concrete debate in the exchange between James Kugel, cited above, and the argument laid forth in this book as a systematic and detailed response, through the careful description, analysis, and interpretation of the actual sources, to Kugel's position. In the details of this debate, specific and in some ways perhaps remote from commonly known works of literature, a large and general issue may come under illumination. That at any rate is my intent in taking at face value and examining in detail the position outlined above. For if Kugel is right about the documents before us, then, I am inclined to think, we may generalize as follows.

First, we may reasonably ignore the documentary limits pertaining to the very particular literature at hand. Second, even though the midrash-exegeses were formed into compilations of exegesis in circumstances we may identify, for a social group we may describe in detail, in response to issues we may define and describe, we may – so the argument runs – turn directly to the contents of all the books of midrash-exegesis, without paying any attention to the context of any one of them.

And, second, it must follow, then we surely may do so when we read literature not so definitively circumscribed by time, circumstance, and social setting. That conclusion will then permit us to maintain as a general principle of hermeneutics an essentially ahistorical, anti-contextual, and formal reading. In interpreting all literature we may treat as null those considerations of society and history, particular sensibility and distinctive circumstance, to which documents in all their particularity and specificity point.

But it is the documentary definition of discourse – this book and its traits, that books and its aesthetic, its plan and its program – that to the present have guided us in our reading of the received classics of our culture. It will not longer matter, in our understanding of the heritage of the West, that an author lived in one time, rather than some other, and addressed one situation, rather than a different one. Everything is the same as everything else, and no work of writing speaks to anyone in particular. The stakes therefore are high. It is probably unfair to Kugel to impute to him the confusion between mishmash and midrash, but in the approach to midrash exemplified in his circle, there does surface a tendency to put in one's thumb and pull out a plum, with slight regard to the ingredients or even the flavor of the pudding at hand.

Let me now broaden discourse and introduce the still larger issue, one of general intelligibility signaled by the contrast between mishmash and midrash. It concerns the textuality of a text. Kugel's position rests on the prevailing, and wrong, notion that all the canonical writings of Judaism are to be read as a single document: "the one whole Torah of Moses, our rabbi." That hermeneutic derives from the theological conviction that at Sinai God gave the Torah in two media, oral and written, to Our Rabbi, Moses, and, furthermore, everything that a great prophet or sage later on would say forms part of that one and seamless Torah. As believing Jews, Kugel and his religious colleagues maintain these convictions, and, as a believing Jew, so do I. But for the inductive construction of intrinsic evidence, such a theological premise makes no contribution to hermeneutics. When I systematically tested the claims framed within the literary-critical category known as that of "intertextuality," as these theological-literary claims are advanced by Shaye J. D. Cohen, Lawrence Schiffman, and Susan Handelman, I found no sustaining evidence in the canonical literature of Judaism in its formative age, down through the seventh century. Each test that I devised in support of each claim and definition of intertextuality produced negative results.[8] Kugel's treatment of midrash in particular rests upon the same deeply flawed construction of the Judaic canon in general and measured against the limns of actual documents, is equally groundless. It derives as much as do the misconstructions of Schiffman, Cohen, and others, from the received, Orthodox-Judaic reading of the holy books of Judaism. I state the Orthodox-Judaic position, represented in both the State of Israel and in Jewish seminaries in this country, as well as in the few universities possessed or controlled by the Orthodox, e.g., Yeshiva University and Harvard University. *That reading is ahistorical, ignoring all issues of specific time, place, and context; unitary, homogenizing all documents into a single Torah (as Kugel says, reaching out to the limits of the canon); linear and incremental, seeing a single Judaism, in a straight line from Sinai, and, therefore, triumphalist.* It also is – as a matter of fact – wrong.

A debate such as this one, with its large and abstract issues, therefore involves real people, exchanging views (where they choose to address one

---

[8]*Canon and Connection: Intertextuality in Judaism* (Lanham, 1987: University Press of America). That book forms the third, and this book, the fourth, in the sequence from *The Integrity of Leviticus Rabbah. The Problem of the Autonomy of a Rabbinic Document* (Chico, 1985: Scholars Press for Brown Judaic Studies), then *Comparative Midrash: The Plan and Program of Genesis Rabbah and Leviticus Rabbah* (Atlanta, 1986: Scholars Press for Brown Judaic Studies). But these two books just applied to the documents at hand the findings of my *History of the Mishnaic Law of Purities. VII. Negaim. Sifra* (Leiden, 1976: E. J. Brill), which demonstrated the documentary definition of Sifra. (Chapter Four of this book goes over the main results). Kugel simply declines to consider the facts and arguments of those books. When in autumn, 1984, I asked him why he passed in utter silence by my work on many of the problems and texts he deals with in the section on the rabbinic literature of his work in his book on the parallelism of biblical poetry, he stated, "Your name is not on the canon of scholarship, and I do not have to pay attention to your work." Whether he has paid attention to the literary definition and traits of the canon in which midrash-writings take their place is for the reader to determine on the basis of the evidence adduced in Part Three of this book and applied in Part Four to Kugel's allegations of the definition(s) of midrash.

another and not to debate through *Todschweigen*[9]) on deeply held convictions. So we must ask, *cui bono?* Why is the issue raised as it is? Profound theological convictions intervene, and as I said, the issues are not literary nor even religious but narrowly theological. That explains why evidence and rigorous argument play so slight a role in the debate; it explains why episodic citation of self-evidently probative proof-texts takes the place of rigorous reasoning; and it accounts for the deporable fact that books and articles of the other side are not answered but ostentatiously ignored as though they did not exist. The viewpoint represented by Kugel proves particularly attractive to Orthodox Jews and formerly-non-Jewish Jews who have become reversioners to Judaism in what they imagine to be its "traditional" form. A sound theological reason yields that preference.

From the classical perspective of the theology of Judaism the entire canon of Judaism ("the one whole Torah of Moses, our rabbi") equally and at every point testifies to the entirety of Judaism. All documents in the end form components of a single system. Each makes its contribution to the whole. If, therefore, we wish to know what "Judaism" or, more accurately, "the Torah," teaches on any subject, we are able to draw freely on sayings relevant to that subject wherever they occur in the entire canon of Judaism. Guided only by the taste and judgment of the great sages of the Torah, as they have addressed the question at hand, we thereby describe "Judaism." And that same theological conviction explains why we may rip a passage out of its redactional context and compare it with another passage, also seized from its redactional setting. In the same way Kugel and his friends wish to move freely across the boundaries of documents alike, that is to say, ignoring all questions of time and condition in pursuit of the episodes of Torah, one by one, all alike, all equal on a single plane of circumstance and context: the one whole Torah of Moses, our rabbi, timeless and ubiquitous. But the theological *apologia* for doing so has yet to reach expression; and there can be no other than a theological *apologia*. In logic I see none; epistemologically there never was one.

Let me lay out the alternative to the theological reading of the canon. This alternative description forms the premise of this book and explains what I require

---

[9]I look in vain in an article purportedly defining midrash for debate with Gary G. Porton, "Defining Midrash," or to Porton's *Understanding Rabbinic Midrash. Text and Commentary* (N.Y., 1985: Ktav Publishing House) as noted elsewhere in this book. In Kugel's defense I note that his essay originally appeared in 1983, so was compelted in 1982. But in presenting his published paper at the conference of which the Hartman volume is the report, he does not appear to have updating his original paper, nor has he tried to come abreast with current literature. Still, even as of 1983, Kugel appears to have learned very little from a very long list of scholars, whose books he does not cite or dismisses casually and routinely. The same traits of sectarianism characterize other writers in the book edited by Hartman and Budick, and call into question the effectiveness of the referee-system of Yale University Press. Scholarly responsibility requires all of us to debate with those with whom we disagree, not to pretend the other side does not exist and to assassinate through silence entire viewpoints and positions. That is not scholarship, except among orthodoxies, and, in the Judaic setting, within Orthodox Judaism.

in demanding the recognition of the primacy of the definitive boundaries of documentary discourse.

These are three dimensions to a document within the canon of the Judaism of the dual Torah. In fact documents stand in three relationships to one another and to the system of which they form part, that is, to Judaism, as a whole. The specification of these relationships constitutes the principal premise of this inquiry and validates the approach to *the* primacy of documentary discourse in the study of midrash that I offer here.

1. Each document is to be seen all by itself, that is, as autonomous of all others.

2. Each document is to be examined for its relationships with other documents universally regarded as falling into the same classification, as Torah.

3. And, finally, in the theology of Judaism (or, in another context, of Christianity) each document is to be allowed to take its place as part of the undifferentiated aggregation of documents that, all together, constitute the canon of, in the case of Judaism, the "one whole Torah revealed by God to Moses at Mount Sinai."

Simple logic makes self-evident the proposition that, if a document comes down to us within its own framework, as a complete book with a beginning, middle, and end, in preserving that book, the canon presents us with a document on its own and not solely as part of a larger composition or construct. So we too see the document as it reaches us, that is, as autonomous. That is why I spend the shank of this book – Part III – showing the autonomy and integrity of six documents, by demonstrating that each has its distinctive rhetorical, logical, and topical definition and program.

If, second, a document contains materials shared verbatim or in substantial content with other documents of its classification, or if one document refers to the contents of other documents, then the several documents that clearly wish to engage in conversation with one another have to address one another. That is to say, we have to seek for the marks of connectedness, asking for the meaning of those connections. It is at this level of connectedness that I developed my program in *Comparative Midrash*, and that forms the premise of Chapters Four through Eight. For the purpose of definition, as much as of comparison, is to tell us what is like something else, what is unlike something else. We know what something is only when we also know what it is not, hence comparison and definition form twin-procedures. To begin with, we can declare something unlike something else only if we know that it is like that other thing. Otherwise the original judgment bears no sense whatsoever. So, once more, canon defines context, or, in descriptive language, the first classification for the labor of definition as well as for comparative study is the document, brought into juxtaposition with, and contrast to, another document.

Finally, – and this is the correct entry for theological discourse, whether in the philosophical or historical or literary idiom – we take the measure of the dimension of continuity, in which we see all documents together in a single statement. The community of the faithful of Judaism, in all of the contemporary expressions of Judaism, concur that documents held to be authoritative constitute one whole, seamless "Torah," that is, a complete and exhaustive statement of God's will for Israel and humanity, we take as a further appropriate task, if one not to be done here, the description of the whole out of the undifferentiated testimony of all of its parts. These components in the theological context are viewed, as is clear, as equally authoritative for the composition of the whole: one, continuous system. In taking up such a question, we address a problem not of theology alone, though it is a correct theological conviction, but one of description, analysis, and interpretation of an entirely historical order. It is at this third point of entry that Kugel and his associates join discourse. Were they theologians, they would have chosen the right door.

But if they propose to interpret the literature as literary scholars, they should have come in through the first entry. For, in my view the various documents of the canon of Judaism produced in late antiquity demand a hermeneutic altogether different from the one of homogenization and harmonization, the ahistorical and anti-contextual one represented by Kugel. It is one that does not harmonize but that differentiates. It is a hermeneutic shaped to teach us how to read the compilations of exegeses first of all one by one and in a particular context, and second, in comparison with one another.

Let me briefly set forth the order of argument. In Part One, comprising Chapter One, I shall unpack the premises of the position of Kugel as I understand them and spell out the argument and evidence as I shall lay out a contrary position in this book. In Part Two, made up of Chapters Two and Three, I then form and test the null hypothesis. In Part Three, covering Chapters Four through Nine, I display the documentary evidence and analysis, and in Part Four, which is Chapter Nine, I return to Kugel's thesis and show, point by point, where he has erred.

In reading with care and responding to the writings of other circles and parties, the Orthodox and ethnic in particular, in contemporary Judaic scholarship on ancient Judaism, I take up debate within the three disciplines in which I work, literature, history, and religion. This book addresses one circle of literary critics, and, in its companion, just now published, I address a circle of historians. In another work, I plan to deal with a circle of scholars of religion (one cannot call them historians of religion).

Specifically, this book forms a sequel to my *Reading and Believing: Ancient Judaism and Contemporary Gullibility* (Atlanta, 1986: Scholars Press for Brown Judaic Studies), in which I undertake a debate on the *historical* study of ancient Judaism and its sources with some contemporary scholars. It stands alongside *Canon and Connection: Intertextuality in Judaism* (Lanham, 1987: University Press of America Studies in Judaism series). In the present work and in *Intertextuality* the debate is on literature, in *Gullibility* on history. In both cases the debate addresses what I conceive to be the theological premises of secular, academic scholarship.

By debating with Orthodox and other ethnic (that is, non-academic) Jewish scholars engaged in the literary, historical, and religious study of ancient Judaism and its sources, I aim at solving a problem of contemporary scholarship on Judaic studies in the academy in particular. It is the failure of purportedly *academic*, as distinct from sectarian and theological, scholars to confront the ideas of one another. The academy has the right to expect its norms to govern in the newly-arrived field of Judaic studies. But those norms of free and encompassing debate, reasoned discourse, honorable contention among mutually respectful and rational parties to a common debate, have yet to define discourse among Jewish scholars of Judaic studies in universities.

In Judaic studies conducted under not academic but theological and ethnic auspices the tendency is not to argue with, but to ignore what one does not like or understand, or to condemn as worthless work with which one differs, or to pretend that viewpoints other than those of oneself and circle do not warrant discussion at all. Whether or not in that tradition, Kugel and the others in the book in which his paper appears simply ignore systematic and sustained studies of precisely the literature they discuss, efforts at accomplishing exactly the same goal (e.g., introducing and defining midrash, Kugel's project and also that of Gary G. Porton and Addison Wright, to name only two not cited by Kugel and others in Hartman's and Budick's book). If, at this time, in Judaic studies, scholars are to meet the norms of free, open, and honest discourse among honorable women and men, it is only by debates in a sustained and rigorous way, such as, in this book, I undertake with Mr. Kugel. If I did not hold with respect the scholarship and intelligence of Kugel and others of his circle, I should not devote an entire book to the systematic refutation of his views, which represent the premises of the work of them all.

It remains to observe that the approaches outlined here rest on data set forth in a sizable corpus of my own work. My analyses of the documents presented here occur in the following books of mine:

Judaism and Scripture: The Evidence of Leviticus Rabbah . Chicago, 1986: The University of Chicago Press. [Fresh translation of Margulies' text and systematic analysis of problems of composition and redaction.]

Genesis Rabbah. The Judaic Commentary on Genesis. A New American Translation. Atlanta, 1985: Scholars Press for Brown Judaic Studies.

I. *Genesis Rabbah. The Judaic Commentary on Genesis. A New American Translation. Parashiyyot One through Thirty-Three. Genesis 1:1-8:14.*

II. *Genesis Rabbah. The Judaic Commentary on Genesis. A New American Translation. Parashiyyot Thirty-Four through Sixty-Seven. Genesis 8:15-28:9.*

III. *Genesis Rabbah. The Judaic Commentary on Genesis. A New American Translation. Parashiyyot Sixty-Eight through One Hundred. Genesis 28:10-50:26.*

Sifra. The Judaic Commentary on Leviticus. A New Translation. The Leper. Leviticus 13:1-14:57. Chico, 1985: Scholars Press for Brown Judaic Studies.

Sifré to Numbers. An American Translation. I. 1-58. Atlanta, 1986: Scholars Press for Brown Judaic Studies

Sifré to Numbers. An American Translation. II. 59-115. Atlanta, 1986: Scholars Press for Brown Judaic Studies. [III. *116-161:* William Scott Green].

The Fathers According to Rabbi Nathan. An Analytical Translation and Explanation . Atlanta, 1986: Scholars Press for Brown Judaic Studies.

Pesiqta deRab Kahana. An Analytical Translation and Explanation. I. 1-10. Atlanta, 1986: Scholars Press for Brown Judaic Studies.

Pesiqta deRab Kahana. An Analytical Translation and Explanation. II. 11-22. Atlanta, 1987: Scholars Press for Brown Judaic Studies.

Pesiqta deRab Kahana. An Analytical Translation and Explanation. III. 23-28. With an Introduction to Pesiqta deRab Kahana. Atlanta, 1987: Scholars Press for Brown Judaic Studies.

The Integrity of Leviticus Rabbah. The Problem of the Autonomy of a Rabbinic Document. Chico, 1985: Scholars Press for Brown Judaic Studies.

Comparative Midrash: The Plan and Program of Genesis Rabbah and Leviticus Rabbah. Atlanta, 1986: Scholars Press for Brown Judaic Studies.

Canon and Connection: Intertextuality in Judaism. Lanham, 1986: University Press of America. *Studies in Judaism* Series.

The Oral Torah. The Sacred Books of Judaism. An Introduction. San Francisco, 1985: Harper & Row.

Scriptures from the Oral Torah. Sanctification and Salvation in the Sacred Books of Judaism. San Francisco, 1987: Harper & Row.

Judaism and Story: The Evidence of The Fathers According to Rabbi Nathan. Chicago, 1988: University of Chicago Press.

Midrash in Context: Exegesis in Formative Judaism. Philadephia, 1983: Fortress.

Only *Midrash in Context* appears in the bibliography of the book in which Kugel's essay appears, and Kugel does not refer to that book, nor has he learned its lessons. Since he also ignored Gary G. Porton's interesting discussion of the definition of midrash, I have included in the appendix a précis of Porton's principal results, to make certain that future debate will gain the advantage of Porton's contribution.

I enjoyed important counsel and advice from William Scott Green, University of Rochester, which I acknowledge with much gratitude.

Jacob Neusner

Simhat Torah, 5747
23 Tishré 5747
October 26, 1986

Program in Judaic Studies
Brown University
Providence, Rhode Island 02912-1826

Part One

CONTENTS AND CONTEXT
IN MEDIUM AND MESSAGE

There are many recent works that seek to define midrash, and nothing would be gained here by attempting to reduce these efforts to a few sentences; though one might say more pointedly (and paraphrasing what a recent book had to say about definitions of irony) that, since these studies have already not defined midrash in ample detail, there is little purpose in our not defining it again here.

James Kugel

Chapter One

Canon and Context

I

Introducing and Defining Midrash

Kugel's is not the first exercise in introducing, therefore defining midrash, as he himself states:

> There are many recent works that seek to define midrash, and nothing would be gained here by attempting to redce these efforts to a few sentences; though one might say more pointedly (and paraphrasing what a recent book had to say about definitions of irony) that, since these studies have already not defined midrash in ample detail, there is little purpose in our not defining it again here.[1]

Readers interested in a fine survey of the problem of introducing and defining midrash, together with a rigorous definition, will set aside Kugel's judgment as partial and consult Gary G. Porton, "Defining Midrash," in J. Neusner, ed., *The Study of Ancient Judaism* (N.Y., 1981: Ktav Publishing House) I, pp. 55-92, as well as his Understanding Rabbinic Midrash. Text and Commentary (N.Y., 1985: Ktav Publishing House), pp. 1-18. Lee Haas, "Bibliography on Midrash, in J. Neusner, ed., *The Study of Ancient Judaism* (N.Y., 1981: Ktav Publishing House) I, pp. 93-103, lists a fair number of items of enduring interest, for instance, Addison G. Wright, "The Literary Genre Midrash," *Catholic Biblical Quarterly* 1966, 28:105-138, 415-457. Wright's paper is only one among a substantial number of excellent efforts to introduce midrash as that genre of literature occurs in the writings of diverse groups of Jews, from authors of documents now included in the Hebrew Scriptures, e.g., the "midrash" of Chronicles on Samuel and Kings, through the midrash effected by the translators into Greek and Aramaic (to which he refers, but to the scholarly literature on which he scarcely alludes), forward to the end of Judaic writing in late antiquity.

Why Kugel has decided to dismiss this entire scholarly literature as he has I cannot say. How his two introductions and definitions relate to, and even improve upon, the existing scores of introductions and definitions no one knows. The somewhat prolix explanation for Kugel's disinterest in engaging

---

[1]*Op. cit.*, p. 91.

with other scholars should not discourage us from a brief inquiry into how the word, midrash, is used.

The word *midrash* stands for many things. But, in the main, in ordinary usage, the word serves in three ways, to speak of, first, the process or hermeneutic of exegesis of Scripture, second, the content or outcome of that process of exegesis of Scripture in the treatment of a given verse or passage, and, third, the compilation of exegeses of a set of verses of Scripture, e.g., a collection of exegeses of a given biblical book.

First, *midrash* refers to the processes of scriptural exegesis carried on by diverse groups of Jews from the time of ancient Israel to nearly the present day. That use of the word to refer to a supposedly distinctive hermeneutic of exegesis of Scripture – midrash as method or process – is clearly the sense in which Kugel uses the word. Thus people say, "He produced a *midrash* on the verse," meaning, "an exegesis." A more extreme usage produces, "Life is a *midrash* on Scripture," meaning that what happens in the everyday world imparts meaning or significance to biblical stories and admonitions. It is difficult to specify what the word *midrash* in Hebrew expresses that the word *exegesis* or hermeneutic in English does not. It follows that quite how "exegesis" in English differs from *midrash* in Hebrew, or why, therefore, the Hebrew will serve better than the more familiar English, I do not know. Nor – as we shall see – does Kugel tell me, despite the prolixity of his statement.

Some imagine that *midrash* for Jewish exegetes generically differs from *exegesis* for non-Jewish ones. My sense is that Kugel and his colleagues wish to think so, though they do not prove it in concrete ways. What hermeneutics characterizes *all* exegeses produced by Jews (everyone, everywhere, in all Judaisms, all canonical constructions), but *no* exegeses produced by non-Jews (anywhere, in all Christianities and among all their canonical compositions), who presumably do not produce *midrashim* on verses but do produce exegeses of verses, of the same Hebrew Scriptures, no one has said. So as a category, *midrash* meaning simply all "Jewish" or "Judaic exegesis" but no gentile exegesis rests upon self-referential, therefore essentially inherent (that is, racist) lines. Appeals to innate traits, whether of race or religion or ethnic group, settle no important questions for reasonable people.

Accordingly, the first usage seems so general as to add up to nothing, or so racist as to add up to an unacceptable claim to private discourse conducted through inherently ethnic or national or religious modes of sensibility not shared with the generality of humanity. If *midrash* is what Jews do while *exegesis* is what gentiles do when each party, respectively, interprets the same verses of the the same Holy Scripture with (in modern times) essentially the same result as to the meaning of the passage at hand, then in my mind it follows that *midrash*, a foreign word, simply refers to the same thing – the same activity or process of thought or intellectual pursuit – as does *exegesis*, an English word. Then the word *midrash* bears no more, or less, meaning than the word *exegesis*. Though much is made of the uniqueness of *midrash* and its definitive power for Judaism, no method or hermeneutic always characteristic of the processes or methods of Jewish *midrash* but never of those of the Christian exegesis is adduced in evidence.

The other two usages will detain us considerably less, since they bear a precision lacking in the first. The word *midrash* further stands for [2] *a compilation* of scriptural exegeses, as in "that *midrash* deals with the book of Joshua." In that sentence, *midrash* refers to a a document, with a program and an organizing principle, compilation of exegeses, hence the statement means, "That compilation of exegeses deals with the book of Joshua." The book of Joshua supplies the organizing principle and holds together – even imparts cogency to – the contents of the document. *Compilation* or composite in the present context clearly serves more accurately to convey meaning than *midrash*. I use both words in this book.

The word *midrash*, finally, stands for [3] the written composition (e.g., a paragraph with a beginning, middle, and end, in which a completed thought is laid forth), resulting from the process of *midrash*. In this setting *a midrash* refers to a paragraph or a unit of exegetical exposition, in which a verse of the Hebrew Scriptures is subjected to some form of exegesis or other. In this usage one may say, "Let me now cite the *midrash*," meaning, a particular passage of exegesis, a paragraph or other completed whole unit of exegetical thought, a composition that provides an exegesis of a particular verse. I use the word component of a document, or *composition*, in this sense.

Accordingly the word bears at least three distinct, if related, meanings. If someone says "the *midrash* says," he or she may refer to [1] a distinctive *process* of interpretation of a particular text, thus, the hermeneutic, thus, this mode of interpretation yields the result that follows; or to [2] a particular compilation of the results of that process, thus, a book that is the composite of a set of exegeses, or to [3] a concrete unit of the working of that process, of scriptural exegesis, thus the write-up of the process of interpretation as it applies to a single verse, the exegetical composition on a particular verse (or group of verses).

It follows that for clear speech the word *midrash*, standing by itself, bears no meaning. In place of the word *midrash*, I prefer to use these words:

[1] *exegesis*, for *midrash* in the sense of the method or process of explaining the meaning (of indeterminate character) of a verse of Scripture. Proponents have yet to show that midrash stands for a specific and distinctive hermeneutic of scriptural interpretation – and, as I said, Kugel's definitions seem to point to the meaning of hermeneutic in general, that is, simply, reading Scripture and interpreting it. Unless we can make the case that the process of midrash in particular materially differs from the process or method of hermeneutics in general, I see no compelling reason to make a point of introducing into a sentence in which either *exegesis* or *hermeneutic* serves the word *midrash*, in the

sense of an allegedly distinctive process for the interpretation of Scripture in general or for the exegesis of a given verse of Scripture.

[2] composite, or *compilation of exegeses* (or occasionally, compilation of *midrashim*), for *midrash* in the sense of a sustained and sizable set or sequence or group of exegeses or even for a whole book made up of exegeses of Scripture. (My sense is that this usage plays slight role in Kugel's writing, and that is for good reason.)

[3] and a piece of writing, a paragraph, *a unit of exegetical discourse*, that is, a whole or completed unit of thought, composition, or similar expressions, for *midrash* in the sense of a single paragraph or a single fully spelled out essay of exegesis of a given verse or group of verses.

We may now move from the definition of the literature under discussion to the issue at hand. Contemporary Jewish literary critics represented by Kugel and those others published in the book edited by Hartman (and his colleagues in the sectarian literary journal, *Prooftexts*), draw upon the genre of writing in Judaism called *midrash* for probative examples of the larger propositions of literary criticism subject to debate in the academy. In doing so, they enjoy an unfair advantage over their gentile colleagues, both allies and otherwise, who, not being Jewish, assume both that the literature at hand has been accurately represented ("Jews know those things, we don't" – another kind of racism), and also that they cannot know the inherited writings that Jews know. In this book I shall right the balance. Let me now frame the issues for debate as I see them.

II

The Canonical Context of Midrash

Since I wish to argue for the primacy, in interpreting the literature of midrash-compilations and their contents, of the document, let me next introduce the documents to which I make reference here.

All midrash-documents under discussion derive from the Judaism in particular that appeals to the Torah, which God revealed to Moses at Mount Sinai, in two media, written and oral. The written component of this "one whole Torah of Moses, our rabbi" is made up of the Pentateuch, Prophetic Books, and Writings. Because midrash-documents form components of the oral part of the Torah, it is by reference to the unfolding of the canon of the Oral Torah that we establish the context in which these writings are to be described, analyzed, and interpreted. The oral part of the dual Torah reached its first literary expression in ca. 200 C.E. and its last in ca. 600 C.E. The appeal to books of passages of Scripture as the organizing principle of documents began mid-way in the unfolding of the canon; prior to that time, documents were organized around tractates of the Mishnah, the first component of the Oral Torah. A brief review of the sequence in which the several canonical books originated will place into the correct context the composition of midrash-compilations.

The Oral Torah of the Mishnah and its Companions: The first document, the Mishnah, drew together teachings of authorities of the period beginning in the first century, before 70, when the Temple was destroyed and autonomous government ended, and ending with the publication of the code in ca. 200. The last, the Talmud of Babylonia (Bavli) provided the authoritative commentary on thirty-seven of the sixty-two tractates of the Mishnah as well as on substantial portions of the Hebrew Scriptures. In joining sustained discourse on the Scriptures, called, in the mythic of the present system, the Written Torah, as well as on the Mishnah, held to be the Oral, or memorized Torah, the Bavli's framers presented a summa, an encyclopaedia, of Judaism, to guide Israel, the Jewish people, for many centuries to come.

In-between ca. 200, when autonomous government was well established again, and ca. 600 the continuous and ongoing movement of sages, holding positions of authority in the Jewish governments recognized by Rome and Iran, as political leaders of the Jewish communities of the Land of Israel (to just after 400 C.E.) and Babylonia (to about 600 C.E.), respectively, wrote two types of books. One sort extended, amplified, systematized, and harmonized components of the legal system laid forth in the Mishnah. The work of Mishnah-exegesis produced four principal documents as well as an apologia for the Mishnah.

This last – the rationale or apologia – came first in time, about a generation or so beyond the publication of the Mishnah itself. It was tractate Abot, ca. 250 C.E., a collection of sayings attributed both to authorities whose names occur, also, in the Mishnah, as well as to some sages who flourished after the conclusion of the Mishnah. These later figures, who make no appearance in that document, stand at the end of the compilation. The other three continuators of the Mishnah were the Tosefta, the Talmud of the Land of Israel (the Yerushalmi), and the Bavli. The Tosefta, containing a small proposition of materials contemporaneous with those presently in the Mishnah and a very sizable proportion secondary to, and dependent, even verbatim, on the Mishnah, reached conclusion some time after ca. 300 and before ca. 400. The Yerushalmi closed at ca. 400. The Bavli, as I said, was completed by ca. 600. All these dates, of course, are rough guesses, but the sequence in which the documents made their appearance is not. The Tosefta addresses the Mishnah; its name means "supplement," and its function was to supplement the rules of the original documents. The Yerushalmi mediates between the Tosefta and the Mishnah, commonly citing a paragraph of the Tosefta in juxtaposition with a paragraph of the Mishnah and commenting on both, or so arranging matters that the paragraph of the Tosefta serves, just as it should, to complement a paragraph of the Mishnah. The Bavli, following the Yerushalmi by about two centuries, pursues its own program, which, as I said, was to link the two Torahs and restate them as one.

The Written Torah of Scripture and its Continuators: The stream of exegesis of the Mishnah and exploration of its themes of law and philosophy flowed side by side with a second. This other river coursed up out of the deep wells of the written Scripture. But it surfaced only long after the work of Mishnah-exegesis was well underway and followed the course of that exegesis, now extended to Scripture. The exegesis of the Hebrew Scriptures, a convention of all systems of Judaism from before the conclusion of Scripture itself, obviously occupied sages from the very origins of their group. No one began anywhere but in the encounter with the Written Torah. But the writing down of exegeses of Scripture in a systematic way, signifying also the formulation of a program and a plan for the utilization of the Written Torah in the unfolding literature of the Judaism taking shape in the centuries at hand, developed in a quite distinct circumstance.

Specifically, one fundamental aspect of the work of Mishnah-exegesis began with one ineluctable question. How does a rule of the Mishnah relate to, or rest upon, a rule of Scripture? That question demanded an answer, so that the status of the Mishnah's rules, and, right alongside, of the Mishnah itself, could find a clear definition. Standing by itself, the Mishnah bore no explanation of why Israel should obey its rules and accept its vision. Brought into relationship to Scriptures, in mythic language, viewed as part of the Torah, the Mishnah gained access to the source of authority by definition operative in Israel, the Jewish people. Accordingly, the work of relating the Mishnah's rules to those of Scripture got under way alongside the formation of the Mishnah's rules themselves. Collecting and arranging exegeses of Scripture as these related to passages of the Mishnah first reached literary form in the Sifra, to Leviticus, and in two books, both called Sifré, one to Numbers, the other Deuteronomy. All three compositions accomplished much else. For, even at that early stage, exegeses of passages of Scripture in their own context and not only for the sake of Mishnah-exegesis attracted attention. But a principal motif in all three books concerned the issue of Mishnah-Scripture relationships. Among these, for the purposes of the discussion in this book I deal with Sifra and Sifré to Numbers, in Chapters Four and Five.

A second, still more fruitful path also emerged from the labor of Mishnah-exegesis. As the work of Mishnah-exegesis got under way, in the third century, exegetes of the Mishnah and others alongside undertook a parallel labor. It was to work through verses of Scripture in exactly the same way – word for word, phrase for phrase, line for line – in which, to begin with, the exegetes of the Mishnah pursued the interpretation and explanation of the Mishnah. To state matters simply, precisely the types of exegesis that dictated the way in which sages read the Mishnah now guided their reading of Scripture as well. And, as people began to collect and organize comments in accord with the order of sentences and paragraphs of the Mishnah, they found the stimulation to collect and organize comments on clauses and verses of Scripture. As I said, this kind of work got under way in the Sifra and the two Sifrés. It reached massive and magnificent fulfillment in Genesis Rabbah, which, as its name tells us, presents a line-for-line reading of the book of Genesis. I take up Genesis Rabbah in Chapter Six.

Beyond these two modes of exegesis and the organization of exegesis in books, first on the Mishnah, then on Scripture, lies yet a third. To understand it, we once more turn back to the Mishnah's great exegetes, represented to begin with in the Yerushalmi. While the original exegesis of the Mishnah in the Tosefta addressed the document under study through a line by line commentary, responding only in discrete and self-contained units of discourse, authors of units of discourse gathered in the next, the Yerushalmi, developed yet another mode of discourse entirely. They treated not phrases or sentences but principles and large-scale conceptual problems. They dealt not alone with a given topic, a subject and its rule, but with an encompassing problem, a principle and its implications for a number of topics and rules. This far more discursive and philosophical mode of thought produced for Mishnah-exegesis, in somewhat smaller volume but in much richer contents, sustained essays on principles cutting across specific rules. And for Scripture the work of sustained and broad-ranging discourse resulted in a second type of exegetical work, beyond that focused on words, phrases, and sentences.

Discursive exegesis is represented, to begin with, in Leviticus Rabbah, a document that reached closure, people generally suppose, sometime after Genesis Rabbah, thus in ca. 400-500, one might guess. Leviticus Rabbah presents not phrase-by-phrase systematic exegeses of verses in the book of Leviticus, but a set of thirty-seven topical essays. These essays, syllogistic in purpose, take the form of citations and comments on verses of Scripture to be sure. But the compositions range widely over the far reaches of the Hebrew Scriptures while focusing narrowly upon a given theme. They moreover make quite distinctive points about that theme. Their essays constitute compositions, not merely composites. Whether devoted to God's favor to the poor and humble or to the dangers of drunkenness, the essays, exegetical in form, discursive in character, correspond to the equivalent, legal essays, amply represented in the Yerushalmi. The framers of Pesiqta deRab Kahana carried forward a still more abstract and discursive mode of discourse, one in which verses of Scripture play a subordinated role to the framing of an implicit syllogism, which predominates throughout, both formally and in argument. I deal with Leviticus Rabbah in Chapter Seven.

So in this other mode of Scripture-interpretation, too, the framers of the exegeses of Scripture accomplished in connection with Scripture what the Yerushalmi's exegetes of the Mishnah were doing in the same way at the same time. We move rapidly past yet a third mode of Scriptural exegesis, one in which the order of Scripture's verses is left far behind, and in which topics,— syllogisms, commonly left implicit but vastly overstated – and not passages of Scripture, take over as the mode of organizing thought. Represented by Pesiqta deRab Kahana, Lamentations Rabbati, and some other collections conventionally assigned to the sixth and seventh centuries, these entirely discursive compositions move out in their own direction, only marginally relating in mode of discourse to any counterpart types of composition in the Yerushalmi (or in the Bavli). I discuss Pesiqta deRab Kahana in Chapter Eight.

A work that falls into the middle range between Scripture-exegesis and Mishnah-exegesis is The Fathers According to Rabbi Nathan. This provides an extended account of the Mishnah tractate, the Fathers. Strictly speaking, The Fathers According to Rabbi Nathan does not fall into the category of a midrash-compilation. It serves as an amplification of Mishnah-tractate Avot, The Fathers. But the framers pursue many avenues of interest important to midrash-compilers and writers, with in particular in amplifying the narratives of Scripture, on the one side, and in employing narrative in the form of parables and tales about sages, on the other. For the sake of a complete account of the documentary issues at hand, I provide an entry into The Fathers According to Rabbi Nathan in my *Judaism and Story: The Evidence of The Fathers According to Rabbi Nathan* (in press), and I do not summarize the results here.

The Babylonian Talmud in Conclusion: At the end of the extraordinary creative age of Judaism, the authors of units of discourse collected in the Bavli drew together the two, up-to-then distinct, modes of organizing thought, either around the Mishnah or around Scripture. They treated both Torahs, oral and written, as equally available in the work of organizing large-scale exercises of sustained inquiry. So we find in the Bavli a systematic treatment of some tractates of the Mishnah. And within the same aggregates of discourse, we also find (in somewhat smaller proportion to be sure, roughly 60% to roughly 40% in the sample I made of three tractates) a second principle of organizing and redaction. That principle dictates that ideas be laid out in line with verses of Scripture, themselves dealt with in cogent sequence, one by one, just as the Mishnah's sentences and paragraphs come under analysis, in cogent order and one by one. But the Bavli is not a compilation of midrash-exegeses, nor do its composites of midrash-exegetes ordinarily serve to state (however implicitly) and then to demonstrate syllogisms of any kind. So I have not devoted attention to the problem of the Bavli's documentary definition of discourse on midrash-exegeses.

The several documents' dates, as is clear, all constitute guesses. But the sequence Mishnah, Tosefta, Yerushalmi, Bavli for the exegetical writings on the Mishnah is absolutely firm and beyond doubt. The dates for the exegetical collections on Scripture are still less certain. But the sequence I follow – the Sifra and the two Sifrés at the head, followed by Genesis Rabbah, then Leviticus Rabbah, then Pesiqta deRab Kahana and Lamentations Rabbati and beyond – is entirely sure. We have no well-argued date for either of the Mekhiltas to Exodus, and I do not know how to deal with those documents.[2]

The Documentary Context of Analysis: What then constitutes the context and therefore also the history of an idea in formative Judaism? We trace what references we find to a topic in accord with the order of documents just now spelled out. In this study we learn the order in which ideas came to expression in the canon. We begin any survey or study of the context of a kind of writing or interpretation, e.g., midrash, with the Mishnah, the starting point of the canon. We proceed systematically to work our way through tractate Abot, the Mishnah's first apologetic, then the Tosefta, the Yerushalmi, and the Bavli at the end. In a single encompassing sweep, we finally deal with the entirety of the compilations of the exegeses of Scripture, arranged, to be sure, in that order that I have now explained.

Let me expand on the matter of my heavy emphasis on the order of the components of the canon. The reason for that stress is simple. We have to ask not only what documents viewed whole and all at once ("Judaism") tell us about our theme. In tracing the order in which ideas make their appearance, we ask about the components in sequence ("history of Judaism") so far as we can trace the sequence. Then and only then shall we have access to issues of *history*, that is, of change and development. If our theme makes its appearance early on in one form, so one set of ideas predominate in a document that reached closure in the beginnings of the cannon and then that theme drops out of public discourse or undergoes radical revision in writings in later stages of the canon, that fact may make considerable difference. Specifically, we may find it possible to speculate on where, and why a given approach proved urgent, and also on the reasons that that same approach receded from the center of interest.

Since the various compositions of the canon of formative Judaism derive not from named, individual authors but from collective decisions of schools or academies, we cannot take for granted attributions of sayings to individuals provide facts. We cannot show that if a given rabbi is alleged to have made a statement, he really did say what is assigned to him. We do not have a book or a letter he wrote such as we have, for example, for Paul or Augustine or other important Christian counterparts to the great rabbis of late antiquity. We also do not know that if a story was told, things really happened in the way the story-teller says, in some other way, or not at all. Accordingly, we cannot identify as historical in a narrow and exact sense anything that comes down to us in the canon of Judaism. What is absolutely firm and factual, by contrast, is that these books represent views held by the authorship behind them. At the point at which a document reached conclusion and redaction, views of a given group of people reached the form at that moment of closure in which we now have them

---

[2]I take very seriously the arguments of Ben Zion Wacholder, "The date of the Mekilta deRabbi Ishmael," *Hebrew Union College Annual* 1968, 39:117-144. But the argumentation is slovenly and the article therefore at best suggestive.

(taking account of for variations of wording). That is why I do not allege we know what people were thinking prior to the point at which, it is generally assumed, a given document was redacted. Accordingly, if I wish to know the sequence in which views reached their current expression, I have recourse to the conventional order and rough dating assigned by modern scholarship to the several documents, from the Mishnah through the Bavli.

Still more critical, in knowing the approximate sequence of documents and therefore the ideas in them (at least so far as the final point at which those ideas reached formal expression in the canon), a second possibility emerges. What if – as is the case – we find pretty much the same views, treated in the same proportion and for the same purpose, yielding the same message, early, middle, and late in the development of the canon? Then we shall have to ask why the literature remains so remarkably constant. Given the considerable shifts in the social and political condition of Israel in the land of Israel as well as in Babylonia over a period of more than four hundred years, that evident stability in the teachings for the affective life will constitute a considerable fact for analysis and interpretation.

The Primacy of Documentary Discourse: The reason that the foregoing, somewhat protracted theory of the development and organization of the sources of formative Judaism requires attention is simple. If we are to conduct public argument about the character of Midrash, we must focus our attention not on snippets that may or may not be representative, retailing impressions we cannot validate or share, arguing by appeal to examples of we know not what, proposing to to prove propositions pertinent to a provenance we cannot specify. We must conduct discourse through appeal to the facts and the evidence deriving from the documents at hand, which, are all, we purport to describe, analyze, and interpret as literature. *What we cannot show we do not know.*

The midrash-documents derive from the Judaism of the dual Torah and form part of its canon. The generative context, therefore, which defines the interpretation of these writings finds definition in a religious comunity, that constituted by the authorship of the writings at hand. That community defined its Judaism, that is to say, its religious system – way of life, world-view, addressed to an Israel, a distinctive social group – and in so doing dealt with those questions it deemed urgent by giving answers it held self-evidently true. In working out its system, the framers of the Judaism of the dual Torah drew upon those books or verses of the received Scripture, which it called the Written Torah ("the Hebrew Bible," "the Old Testament") which it found useful, neglected others. The system therefore defined the canon, that is to say, the authoritative writings, beginning with those works of the Hebrew Scriptures that it deemed useful and worthy of systematic study. The selection of particular verses of the Written Torah for study follows in sequence upon the identification of the passages or books of the Written Torah to be studied. The sequence then is, first, the system, then the canon, and, within the canon, third, the selection of topics of special interest, which yields, fourth, identification of those books of the Written Torah to be subjected to close reading, and that produces, finally, the attention to the specific verse or verses found to be probative. We come now to the argument at hand.

III

The Primacy of Documentary Discourse and the Debate with Kugel

Let me begin with the issue of general intelligibility. Framing the question as we must see it here, I ask how we know that a given book in the canon of Judaism is something other than a scrapbook. The choices are clear. One theory is that a document serves solely as a convenient repository of prior sayings and stories, available materials that will have served equally well (or poorly) wherever they took up their final location. In accord with that theory it is quite proper in ignorance of all questions of circumstance and documentary or canonical context to define and interpret midrash=exegesis of verses of Scripture. The other theory is that a composition exhibits a viewpoint, a purpose of authorship distinctive to its framers or collectors and arrangers. Such a characteristic literary purpose – by this other theory – is so powerfully particular to one authorship that nearly everything at hand can be shown to have been (re)shaped for the ultimate purpose of the authorship at hand, that is, collectors and arrangers who demand the title of authors. In accord with this other theory the document – that is to say, the context and circumstance of exegesis of a verse of Scripture – form the prior condition of inquiry, the result, in exegetical terms, the contingent one.

To resort again to a less than felicitous neologism, I thus ask what signifies or defines the "document-ness" of a document and what makes a book a book. I therefore wonder whether there are specific texts in the canonical context of Judaism or whether all texts are merely contextual. In framing the question as I have, I of course lay forth the mode of answering it. We have to confront a single rabbinic composition, and ask about its definitive traits and viewpoint. The propositions subject to debate, among the five presented in the preface, are these in particular:

> ...midrash's precise focus is most often what one might call surface irregularities in the text: a good deal of the time, it is concerned with...*problems*.[3]

> ...midrash is an exegesis of biblical verses, not of books. The basic unit of the Bible for the midrashist is the verse: this is what he seeks to expound, and it might be said that there simply is no boundary

---

[3]P. 92.

encountered beyond that of the verse until one comes to the borders of the canon itself.[4]

Our midrashic compilations are in this sense potentially deceiving, since they seem to treat the whole text bit by bit; but with the exception of certain patterns, these "bits" are rather atomistic, and, as any student or rabbinic literature knows, interchangeable, modifiable, combinable – in short, not part of an overall exegesis at all.[5]

Specifically, I shall show that nearly every sentence in the passage of James Kugel cited above is false as to the evidence at hand, which derives from the initial formation of the midrash-compilations in late antiquity, from the second through the sixth centuries. Whether there are writings produced in medieval times that accord with his description I cannot say. I can only claim to demonstrate that within the sample at hand, which I claim to be probative for the Judaism of the dual Torah of late antiquity concerning the writings of which he claims to speak, he is simply, completely, and totally wrong – and with him, all those associated with this subdivision of the literary critical circle at hand. For those literary critics who appeal for probative examples of the principles of literary criticism they espouse to midrash, salvation is not of the Jews, even when some Jews claim it is.

The reason is that Kugel, and those for whom he speaks, cites wholly out of context all midrash, meaning exegeses of verses. That is why he can treat each item as equivalent to all others, and appeal to the whole for proof of the characteristics of the parts. There are no intervening lines of structure, from the beginning to the end. Consequently, – in Kugel's explicit statement – everything is the same everywhere, there are no lines of order and demarcation, and, it follows, we need pay no attention to context and circumstance, e.g., a particular time, a specific place and condition of a concrete and discrete authorship. Only the end product – the midrash=exegesis of a verse of Scripture – matters.

IV

The Argument of this Book

Let us proceed with a brief survey of my program of debate, then spell out the premises of my position. I begin with an exercise in the proof of the null hypothesis, then proceed to display the evidence in favor of the thesis at hand.

Chapter Two: We begin in Chapter Two with false proposition I, concerning exegesis and comparison: *The verse, not the document, is the generative category.* I shall show the opposite. Concretely, Kugel imagines that the verse of Scripture forms the precipitant and the generative category of

---

[4]P. 93.

[5]P. 95.

what he calls midrash. Everything starts (he maintains) from the character and contents of the particular verse under discussion. I can show that *nothing* starts from the character and contents of the verse under discussion, since different people read the verse out of a different set of questions to produce different results for different groups, then we cannot impute to the base-verse a determinative role in midrash-exegesis. Traits of the base-verse may or may not play a role in dictating what people say about the verse. But if they do, it is after the fact. *All exegesis is eisegesis, simply because the selection of one verse, rather than some other, expresses a prior program of inquiry: different people talking about different things to different people.*

Chapter Three: False proposition II, dealt with in Chapter Three, concerning pattern and proposition maintains the following: *modes of rhetoric transcend documentary lines.* Kugel treats as null, that is, as lacking all indicative power and differentiating capacity, diverse formal traits of syntax, language, the organization of the rhetorical elements of discourse. These principles of rhetoric he treats as adventitious and not to be differentiated, rather than as suggestive and even indicative. He does not imagine that on rhetorical grounds, that is, through form-analysis, we may differentiate one document – and its "midrash"-components – from some other document. In Kugel's definition(s) all documents serve equally as mere receptacles for "midrash" and make no mark upon their contents. Only on the foundation of the premise that formal traits, characteristic of one document and not some other, make no difference in defining "midrash" can Kugel utterly ignore the documentary dimension of discourse. That premise that documentary limits effect no boundaries of medium or message alike permits Kugel to treat as of no account the fact that a story or saying appears in one document, brought to closure at one time and under one set of circumstances (whether political, whether theological), rather than in some other. Indifference to the traits of literary style and form – what we call rhetoric – forms an odd trait in a literary critic.

What is all the more surprising is that form-analysis yields significant differences when we compare what looks like the same form in two closely related documents. In Chapter Three, therefore, I compare a single rhetorical pattern as it appears in materials shared between two documents to a pattern of essentially the same formal traits that occurs in only one of the same two documents. I show the differences, and *I furthermore explain them in terms of the modes of syllogistic discourse characteristic of each of the two documents respectively.* In this way in the exploration of the null hypothesis I again demonstrate the primacy of documentary discourse. Formal traits constitute an independent variable in differentiating one midrash-exegesis from another, and in maintaining the contrary premise by ignoring the documentary context of discourse as he does, Kugel is wrong.

Chapters Four through Eight: From the investigation of the null hypothesis, I turn in the presentation of my side of the debate to the demonstration of the opposite: the hypothesis that documents define the initial (not the sole or final) limits of interpretation of their contents. Specifically, in the six chapters of Part Three I display the actual character of the midrash-literature, so far as that literature took written form in late antiquity, the age of its origination within the Judaism that has flourished from then to now.

Chapter Nine: In Part Four I further compare the documents to Kugel's representation of midrash, such as we find collected in those same documents. His claim to characterize "midrash" – encompassing the character and probative uses of midrash-writings – therefore can now be assessed by all who appreciate the literary mode of rational discourse. Statements as to the character of midrash and as to how that kind of writing exemplifies the doctrines of certain literary critics – I here show – conflict with the literary character of midrash in its classic forms.[6] Indeed, when the reader has reviewed, in Part Three, samples of the midrash-documents of late antiquity, the reader is very likely to share my astonishment at the blatant misrepresentation of the literature, midrash, in its classical form. Let us now turn to the history of the canon of the Judaism of the dual Torah, of which midrash forms an important part.

The Appendix: Since Kugel fails to refer not only to my sustained investigation of the definition of midrash, deriving from a concrete analysis of texts, but also to the equally rigorous work of Gary G. Porton, I have included a statement of his definition of midrash as well.

Now let me state the case as I shall lay it out. I shall prove, in reading midrash as literature, that *context* – this setting, documentary discourse – in fact is determinative and probative of meaning. This I shall show by an analysis of six of the midrash-compilations of the classical and formative period of the literature. In each case I shall demonstrate that the document at hand possesses integrity. That is in three definitive dimensions.

First, its discrete components follow a cogent outline and an intelligible principle of ortganization.

Second, its discrete components conform, in their large aggregates, to a limited and discernible rhetorical plan.

Third, the discrete components also contribute to the demonstration of propositions that recur through the document, indeed that the authorship of the document clearly wishes to make.

And fourth, that means that the document takes priority over its details, and that the initial discourse of the document takes place within the documentary setting, viewed whole and within a broad perspective of balance, order, and

---

[6]The medieval midrash-compilations tend to imitate the received forms, and the diversity of manuscript evidence pertaining to the ancient compilations testifies that medieval copyists contributed to the evidence their own compositions as well. Much that I shall show characterizes the ancient midrash-documents pertains to the medieval and early modern ones as well. But I shall restrict my comments to the literature I know first hand.

proportion – there, and not solely, or primarily, within the smallest whole units of discourse of which the document is made up, of which the authorship has made use in proving its broader propositions.

Hence taking *midrash-meaning-exegesis* out of *the midrash-meaning-a-document* that organizes and presents midrash, turns *midrash* into *mishmash*. Kugel's definitions violate the lines of structure, order, and meaning, exhibited by the internal evidence of the documents, inductively construed. To say matters plainly, Kugel and those he represents therefore misrepresent the literature they purport to adduce in evidence of their hermeneutic and heuristic program, and that misrepresentation affects not merely a minor detail, the spelling or the translation of a phrase, but their fundamental grasp of the literature, midrash. Their picture of midrash as literature does more than beg the question by imposing on the data the theory for demonstration of which the data are adduced. That picture drastically and blatantly misconstrues the data, beginning, middle, and end, by reading only in bits and pieces what originated whole and complete. At stake is whether or not an authorship intervenes in the formation of a composite. If it does, then the authorship plays an active role in the display of the selected items of their composition, and they give us not a mere scrapbook but a carefully crafted text, a book, a document. If it does not, then what we have is not a collage but an accident, a hodgepodge, a junk heap, this and that about nothing in particular to no one. At stake in the debate conducted in this book, therefore, is the character of a literature. My proposition is that midrash constitutes a literature, and the appropriate limits of discourse derive from the documents of which a literature is composed: the document, in our terms, the book, as the generative unit of the cogent syllogism, therefore of intelligible discourse.

That is why I argue for the primacy of documentary discourse, by which I mean that discourse must first start with the definition of the documentary context, the whole of a compilation of exegeses. The documentary context in the case of midrash, that is, exegesis of Scripture in the Judaic context, stands first in line because it it is what we know for sure.

V
The Document as the Generative Category of Midrash

When we describe a document, we know as fact that [1] a given method of exegesis has yielded [3] a given exegetical comment on a verse of Scripture, the result of which is now in [2] *this particular document*. Since we know the wonderfully simple facts of what is found in which document, we can begin the work of describing the traits imparted *by* [2] that document *to* the [3] exegetical result *of* [1] the exegetical method at hand. Traits characteristic of [2] the documentary setting likewise emerge without a trace of speculation. To state matters more concretely, if a document routinely frames matters in accord with one repertoire of formal conventions rather than some other, and if it arranges its formal repertoire of types of units of discourse in one way, rather than some other, and if its compilers repeatedly propose to make one point, rather than some other, we can easily identify those traits of the passage under study that derive from the larger documentary context.

Accordingly, we begin with the document because it presents the first solid fact. Everything else then takes a position relative to that fact. What then are some of the documentary facts? Here are some: this saying or story occurs here, bears these traits, is used for this larger redactional and programmatic purpose, makes this distinct point in its context (or no point at all). One may readily test these allegations and determine their facticity. These facts therefore define the initial context of interpretation. The facts deriving from the documentary setting define the context in which a given trait shared or not shared among the two discrete items to be compared. In laying emphasis on the document as the correct initial and generative point of interpretation, I exclude as the appropriate point of departure for hermeneutics two others, namely, [1] modes of exegesis, hence, comparative hermeneutics, and [3] results of exegesis, hence, the focus on the characteristics of a given verse in interpreting the message an exegete claims to discover in that verse. That matter, which has predominate in the received exegetical tradition of the midrash-compilations and (rather talmudically) continues to predominate today in the writings that Kugel and his allies do cite, yields mere formalities. The result is to describe in our own words, what the midrash-writer says, and then to claim that the midrash-writer says what he says because of inherent traits in the verse under discussion – as though that made any difference, as if there were anything at stake other than a theological apologetics for Judaism of a certain kind. And beside, how shall we ever know whether we are right – or wrong – in imputing to the midrash-exegete the reason we discover in the verse subject to exegesis? Lacking a test of falsification, we have nothing but the good guess of the literary critic. That, standing by itself, does not seem to me worth much attention, being an essentially political statement in the end.

Having explained why this, let me specify, why not that. That is to say, what do we miss when we treat as null the documentary limits of discourse? If we ignore as unimportant the characteristic traits of the documentary locations of an exegesis of a verse of Scripture or of a story occurring in two or more documents, or if we treat as trivial the traits characteristic of those locative points, we establish no context that imparts meaning to the work of interpretation.

Let me spell this matter out. Everything we propose to interpret finds its original place in some document, rather than in some other (or in two or three documents and not in ten or twenty others). Have the framers or compilers of one document selected an item merely because that item pertains to a given verse of Scripture? Or have they chosen that item because it says what they wish to say in regard to a verse of Scripture they have identified as important? Have they framed matters in terms of their larger program of the formalization of language, syntax and rhetoric alike? Have their selection and formalization of the item particular relevance to the context in which they did their work, the purpose for which they composed their document, the larger message they planned to convey to those to whom they planned to speak? These questions demand answers, and the answers will tell us the *"what else,"* that is, what is important about what people say in common or in contrast about the verse at hand. Without the answers provided by analysis of circumstance and context, plan and program, of the several documents one by one and then in comparison and contrast with one another, we know only what people said about the verse. But we do not know why they said it, what they meant by what they said, or what we learn from the fact *that* they said what they said about the verse in hand. The answers to these questions constitute that "what else?" that transforms catalogues of pointless facts into pointed and important propositions – hermeneutics.

VI

The Independent Variable:
The Verse of Scripture or the Midrash-Compilation?

The question about the precipitant of exegesis, namely, whether it is the literary and systemic (theological) context, as I maintain, or principally the verse subject to exegesis, as Kugel and his friends hold, brings us to the crux of the matter. The premise of all that I have said is that Scripture serves diverse purposes and therefore cannot establish a single definitive plane of meaning, the frame of reference against which all other things constitute variables. Scripture constitutes the neutral background, not the variable. Exegetes tell us what verses of Scripture matter and what we should learn from those verses. Scripture dictates nothing but endures all things. What people tell us about the meaning of Scripture (points [1] and [3] in what has gone before) represents the outcome of the work of exegetes, not the inexorable result of the character or contents of Scripture.

The issue for debate as I think it should be argued is this:

1. Does the character e.g., the wording, of a verse of Scripture dictate the substance of exegesis? As I said, that has been the position of all exegetes of midrash-compilations for a thousand years and remains the premise of the reading of midrash-compilations and midrash-exegeses by Kugel and his colleagues.

2. Or do exegetes bringing to their task the givens of the Judaism of which they form a part dictate the sense they wish to impart to (or locate in) Scripture? That is the position that emerges when we recognize the primacy of documentary discourse in the reading of midrash-compilations and interpretation of midrash-exegeses.

If the former, then the ground for comparison finds definition in a verse of Scripture. What X said, without regard to circumstance or even documentary context, compared with what Y said, viewed also with slight attention to canonical context and concrete literary circumstance, matters. As I noted, Chapter Two provides a refutation of the former of the two possibilities through a single example of what is, in fact the ubiquitous datum of Western biblical interpretation: it is that people make of Scripture anything they wish, choosing the passage they deem important to prove the proposition they bring to that passage for validation. Claims to the contrary represent theological apologetics, that alone. They derive from an inner-facing reading of the received literature, from the stance of the faith and for the hearing of the faithful. Those judgments have no independent hermeneutical bearing – and those that make them scarcely pretend otherwise. The paramount fact of the history of the Bible (both Testaments) in the West – the amazing diversity of meanings "discovered" by exegetes precisely where they wish to find them in the workings of either divine grace or wonderful serendipity – imparts to the position espoused by Kugel and his friends a certain piquance. They imitate Canute, sweeping back the oceans of facts that will turn to sand and dust for beaches we know no where the detritus – the scriptural pebbles – of their certainty.

Since the facts of the entire history of biblical interpretation in the West support the latter proposition, it follows that the canon and its components take pride of place, defining the primary arena of discourse and interpretation. What diverse persons said about a given verse of Scripture defines only a coincidence, unless proved on the basis of circumstance and context to constitute more than mere coincidence. Then, and only then, will the intrinsic traits of the verse come to the fore as candidates for the generative role of precipitating discourse. One systematic example out of which the answers to be framed therefore is given in Chapter Two: comparison, specifically, of midrash-exegesis to midrash-exegesis of a single verse of Scripture. What we see is different people talking about different things to different people. But if the verse were determinative, then different people ought, even when talking to different people, to be talking at leaset *about* the same thing – even though reaching different conclusions!

The answer to the question transcends the case presented here. It lies spread across the surface of the reading of Scripture in the history of the scriptural religions of the West, the Judaisms and the Christianities in perpetual contention among and between themselves about which verses of Scripture matter, and what those that matter mean. That remarkably varied history tells the story of how diverse groups of believers selected diverse verses of the Hebrew Scriptures as particularly important. They then subjected those verses, and not other verses, to particular exegetical inquiry. The meanings they found in those verses answer questions they found urgent. Scripture contributed much but dictated nothing, system – circumstance and context– dictated everything and selected what Scripture might contribute in *midrash*. In this context, *midrash* means the whole extant repertoire of exegeses of verses of Scripture we possess in [2] various compilations of exegeses of Scripture, made up of [3] compositions of exegesis of verses of Scripture, guided by [1] diverse hermeneutical principles of interpretation of Scripture. Since in *midrash* as just now defined, system, *hence canon*, comes first, prior to exegeses of particular verses of Scripture, all the more so prior to the hermeneutics that guides the work of exegesis, the documents that constitute the canon and contain the system form the definitive initial classification for comparative *midrash*. In addressing midrash as literature, the primacy of documentary discourse requires that system be interpreted, that is, compared to system, not detail to detail, and, therefore, to begin with, we compare [2] compilation of exegeses to the counterpart, thus document to document.

Before we know the answers, we have to understand the questions people addressed to Scripture. Why so? Because a group chose a repertoire of verses distinctive to itself, rarely commenting on, therefore confronting, verses important to other groups. When we deal with different groups talking about different things to different groups, what difference does it make to us that, adventitiously and not systematically, out of all systematic context, we discover that someone reached the same conclusion as did someone else, of some other group? What else do we know if we discover such a coincidence? Parallel lines never meet, and parallel statements on the same verse may in context bear quite distinct meaning. Scripture itself (and therefore, the discrete verses of Scripture) forms the undifferentiated background. It is the form, not the substance, the flesh, not the spirit. The fact that a single verse of Scripture generates diverse comments by itself therefore forms a statement of a merely formal character. It is a sequence of facts that may or may not bear meaning.

Now Kugel and the many who share the position that we may utterly ignore documentary lines of discourse appeal to an acknowledged fact of the canon of Judaism, exegetical and legal alike. That trait is that a given saying or story may float from one document to another. The proportion of sayings and stories not unique to a given document varies. For Leviticus Rabbah it is under 10%, for Pesiqta deRab Kahana it is over 18%. The volume of floating materials – peripatetic sayings and stories – has been vastly overstated, its definitive character within the documents in which it is found substantially exaggerated. But for the generality of interpreters of the received canon of Judaism, it follows from the fact that some materials float from document to document that for all materials we may ignore the documentary lines of definition and structure, because everything is everywhere anyhow. That is why we have also to confront the issue of the "sources"[7] upon which the redactors of a given document have drawn. By "sources" I mean simply passages in a given book that occur, also, in some other rabbinic book. Such "sources" – by definition prior to the books

---

[7]I use that word only because it is commonplace. In fact it is a misleading metaphor. In *Integrity* I pursued the possibility of characterizing the shared stories in such a way as to claim, as a matter of hypothesis, that they derive from a source, that is, a single common point of origin. The materials I examined in no way suggest that there was a single point of origin.

in which they appear – fall into the classification of materials general to two or more compositions and by definition not distinctive and particular to any one of them. In Chapter Three we confront that issue head on, and we see that what occurs in two documents can be shown on purely formal and intrinsic literary grounds to be primary to one document and derivative for the other, to conform to the formal preferences of the primary document *and to violate the formal preferences and also the syllogistic method of the second one.* That result again calls into question Kugel's notion that anything anywhere is pretty much the same thing as everything else, what I call Kugel's *mishmash-theory of midrash,* to which I shall return at the end of Chapter Ten.

The word "source" therefore serves as an analogy to convey the notion that two or more sets of authors have made use of a single, available item. About whether or not the shared item is prior to them both or borrowed by one from the other at this stage we cannot speculate. These shared items, transcending two or more documents and even two or more complete systems or groups, if paramount and preponderant, would surely justify the claim that we may compare exegeses of verses of Scripture without attention to context. Why? Because there is no closed context defined by the limits of a given document and its characteristic plan and program. All the compilers of documents did is collect and arrange available materials. Therefore we must ask – again, as I do in Part Three once I have established the null nypothesis in Part Two – about the textuality of a document – is a compilation of midrashim-exegeses a composition or a scrap book? – so as to determine the appropriate foundations for discourse. We ask about whether the materials unique to a document also cohere, or whether they prove merely miscellaneous. If they do cohere, we may conclude that the framers of the document have followed a single plan and a program. That would in my view justify the claim that the framers carried out a labor not only of conglomeration, arrangement and selection, but also of genuine authorship or composition in the narrow and strict sense of the word. So we may solve for the case at hand the problem of the rabbinic document, exegetical ("midrashic") or legal: do we deal with a scrapbook or a cogent composition? A text or merely a literary expression, random and essentially promiscuous, of a larger theological context? That is the choice at hand. In Part Three, for six midrash-documents, I once more demonstrate the primacy of documentary discourse.

In conclusion the argument of the book may be briefly summarized. In Part Two I take up two fundamental premises of the position contrary to the one argued here. I set up two components of the null hypothesis, that is, I take two premises of Kugel's position and show that, in two representative test-cases, they contradict the character of the evidence. In Part Three I lay out the evidence sustaining the positive hypothesis, that documents define the primary and initial (though not complete and final) framework of discourse. In Part Four I review the verbatim statements of Kugel and refer to the documentary evidence of Part

Three to refute them. That, sum and substance, is the argument laid forth here. At Part Four I simply explain where and why I think Kugel has reached the false position he has taken in introducing midrash. I need hardly underline the motive of this exercise. If I did not recognize the learning and honor the initiative of Kugel and his allies, I should not have composed a full-scale reply to their position and demonstration that the premises of that position rest solidly upon the theology of Orthodox Judaism but somewhat infirmly upon historical, literary, and religious scholarship.

Part Two

TOPIC AND RHETORIC:
TWO PROPOSITIONS AND THEIR REFUTATION

...midrash's precise focus is most often what one might call surface irregularities in the text: a good deal of the time, it is concerned with...problems.[1]

James Kugel

False Proposition I: Concerning Exegesis and Comparison:
The verse, not the document, is the generative category

...midrash is an exegesis of biblical verses, not of books. The basic unit of the Bible for the midrashist is the verse: this is what he seeks to expound, and it might be said that there simply is no boundary encountered beyond that of the verse until one comes to the borders of the canon itself.[2]

Our midrashic compilations are in this sense potentially deceiving, since they seem to treat the whole text bit by bit; but with the exception of certain patterns, these "bits" are rather atomistic, and, as any student or rabbinic literature knows, interchangeable, modifiable, combinable – in short, not part of an overall exegesis at all.[3]

James Kugel

False Proposition II: Concerning Pattern and Proposition:
Modes of rhetoric transcend documentary lines because documents of midrash-compilations make no mark on midrash-exegesis

---

[1] P. 92.

[2] P. 93.

[3] P. 95.

Chapter Two

Exegesis and Comparison: Different People Talking about Different Things to Different People

...midrash's precise focus is most often what one might call surface irregularities in the text: a good deal of the time, it is concerned with...problems.[1]

James Kugel

False Proposition I: Concerning Exegesis and Comparison:
The verse, not the document, is the generative category

The importance of the present proposition derives from its theological usefulness in Judaic apologetics. The proposition is that to account for the interpretation of a given verse of Scripture supplied by a Judaic exegete (the proponents sometimes use the rather odd word, *midrashist,* once more invoking a foreign word for a common noun, e.g., exegete, or, if Kugel prefers, "Jewish exegete"), we turn initially (and solely) to the traits of the verse under discussion. We expect to find in the wording, spelling, juxtaposition, or some other indicative aspect of that verse the reason or precipitant for the position taken by the exegete. The upshot is that the meanings imputed to verses of Scripture in the midrash-compilations enjoy the standing of – if not the plain and obvious sense of the verses – at least the implicit meaning. Then the larger system of the Judaism that draws upon the midrash-compilations, the Judaism of the dual Torah, rests squarely and firmly, symmetrically and solidly, upon Scripture – there alone.

It follows that the Judaism under discussion – the apologists know it as the only Judaism, or The Torah – simply states in its way the original and legitimate message of The Torah. Since, it is commonly recognized, the meanings imputed to Scripture by Christian exegesis impose upon Scripture categories and issues not "originally" present, it must follow, upon a purely factual basis, that Judaism states the original, the historical meaning of Scripture, and Christianity does not. Then Christians believe things, but Jews only affirm facts, and, within the positivistic framework of nineteenth-century

---

[1]P. 92.

religious disputation, which up to now has defined the categories and proportions of Judaic scholarship, including theology and apologetics, appeals to fact enjoy probative value, while (obviously, self-evidently) appeals to faith cannot and do not. It follows that a critical apologetic for Judaism in modern times imputes to the claims of Judaism sheer exegetical facticity, and to those of Christianity, mere eisegetical fantasy. Part of the apologetic that claimed for Judaism the status of positive fact simply carries forward the received hermeneutic of the exegetes of the midrash-compilations who for a thousand and more years have turned first and finally to the indicative traits of the verse under discussion to discover the origin of the exegetical outcome: the midrash-exegesis. But another part of the apologetic appeals to the "mere facticity" of Judaism (in its Orthodox form, to be sure) by demonstrating that pretty much whatever our side says about Scripture is what Scripture says anyhow.[2]

The first false proposition therefore follows. It is that the verse forms the generative, the initial, and the precipitating category of interpretation of Judaic biblical interpretation. My citation of Kugel shows that I do not misrepresent his position. What the midrash-exegete says simply solves problems of the text, therefore derives from the (mere) facts of the case, and, it must follow, the outcome of the exegesis bespeaks not a prior system (as extrinsic and imposed as the system that appeals to the New Testament for the meaning of the Old, in Christian theological categories), but – I cannot overstress – the mere facts of the case. The apologetic resting on positivism, on the facts mainly of history, then follows, gaining strength from the encounter (even) with the fanciful reading of Scripture in the service of the faith. That is why we take as our stance the issue inherent in the allegation that midrash-exegesis begins with the original verse of Scripture.

I test that proposition through a simple exercise of comparison, specifically, drawing side by side two treatments of precisely the same verse. That comparison permits us to ask this simple question: do traits or characteristics inherent in the verse itself precipitate the reflection of the diverse authorships? We shall know that traits of the verse govern, if diverse parties respond to the same facts of the verse at hand – even though they find different things to say about those facts. Or do those authorships arrive at their definition of what is important about the chosen verse with distinctive programs of inquiry, each particular to its own broader interests, perspectives, and context? We shall know that the traits of the verse mean little if two distinct authorships turn out to be talking about different things to different people and discern in the verse at hand not a single trait of common interest. Then the midrash-exegeses are precipitated not by the verse but by the prior program and interest of diverse authorships, which may or may not have any interest at all in the "problem(s)" of the verse.

---

[2]The hostility toward biblical criticism displayed by Reform Judaism for its first century forms part of the same polemic in favor of Israel's reading of Scripture, building solid foundations in historical fact for propositions of the faith (whatever they might be).

If the former, then the verse forms the generative category, if the latter, then the system does. And, if it is the system, then it is the document that brings to expression an important proposition or component of the (prior, generative) system. The apologetic choice follows. If we may interpret the textual meaning within the *out-there* of the verse, its merely factual traits, of a positive character, we may simply ignore the *in-here* of the authorship and its concerns, the beliefs and convictions of faith-imposed-upon-fact. The test of the first of our two false propositions, the one on topic, the other on rhetoric, requires us therefore to compare and contrast midrash-exegesis to midrash-exegesis: two interpretations of the same verse of Scripture. In terms of the meanings of the word midrash given in Chapter One, I compare one *midrash* to another *midrash*, meaning, how a verse of Scripture is treated in one compilation of exegeses, its plan and program, with how that same verse is treated in another compilation of exegeses, its plan and program.

I

Comparative Midrash

On the day when Moses had finished setting up the tabernacle...
Numbers 7:1

When we compare what one authorship thinks important about a verse of Scripture, such as that just cited, with what another authorship, of the same religious world and of approximately the same period, chooses to emphasize in that same verse of Scripture, we must conclude that in hand are the results of the exegesis of different people talking about the same verse, but with an interest in utterly different things, to different people.[3] When we compare what one document and its authorship have to say about a given verse with what another composition and its writers find interesting and probative in that same verse, we must ask ourselves whether we have compared comparable entities. For prior to comparison comes the process of establishing grounds for comparison, and that demands that we show likeness. Once groups are demonstrated to be alike, then the points of difference become significant. If entities are utterly unlike, then what difference to us does the differences between them make?

In taxonomic terms, what is required is that we show two specimens belong in a single genus, and then, only then, do we undertake the work of speciation. These simple rules of logic govern, also, in the field of comparing exegeses of verses of a common Scripture, as I shall now show in a striking case. When we examine what two authorships within the canon of Judaism say about one verse, we call into question the meaning of comparison of exegesis. For, as we shall now note, nothing in the reading of the verse produced by one group intersects

---

[3]Compare my "The Jewish Christian Argument in the First Century. Different People Talking about Different Things to Different People," *Crosscurrents*, 1985, 35:148-158.

with anything in the reading of the same verse yielded by the other: different people addressing a single thing but talking about different things to different people.

Comparative midrash[4] – that is, comparing exegeses of the same theme or verse of Scripture among the same circles of exegetes – can rest on solid foundations in logic.[5] These follow the outlines of the primacy established by documentary discourse, as I shall now explain. The basis of comparison and contrast is established by points in common. Once we know that two things are like one another, then – and only then – do the points of difference become consequential. Two documents in the same canon surely bear broad affinities, having been selected by the consensus of the sages or the faithful as authoritative. They rely upon the opinion or judgment of sages of the same circle. They have been preserved and handed on by the same institutions of the faith. They presumably present basically cogent convictions upon the meaning of Scripture. Accordingly, a variety of indicators justifies the judgment that the documents form a solid fit, bearing much in common. Then, it must follow, the work of comparison yields to the exercise of contrast. Being alike, the documents, in their treatment of precisely the same verse of Scripture, produce differences, and these differences make a difference. They tell us how one authorship wishes to read Scripture in one way, another in a different way. In the case at hand, however, the differences prove so profound and far-reaching that they call into question the very act of comparison.

In the present exercise we compare the treatment of precisely the same verse by exegetes within the same religious world, that of the sages of the Judaism of the dual Torah, written and oral, who flourished between the third and sixth centuries A.D. So that all who wish to follow the debate at hand may enjoy equal status, I present the entire chapter of each of two documents pertinent to the verse before us. In their reading of Numbers 7:1, *"On the day when Moses had finished setting up the tabernacle...,"* we see strikingly different approaches to what is important in the verse at hand in the minds of two authorships. One group of exegetes, that behind Sifré to Numbers, a close reading of selected passages of the book of Numbers concluded at an indeterminate point but possibly by about ca. 400, asks one set of questions, the other, the authorship of Pesiqta deRab Kahana, possibly within the fifth century, finds a quite different point of interest in the same verse. Indeed, as we shall see, it is difficult to relate the message of the one to that of the other. And that is a surprising result,

---

[4]See my *Comparative Midrash: The Plan and Program of Genesis Rabbah and Leviticus Rabbah* (Atlanta, 1986: Scholars Press for Brown Judaic Studies).

[5]Compare Jonathan Z. Smith, "What a difference a difference makes," in *Take Judaism for Example* (Chicago, 1983: University of Chicago Press), ed. Jacob Neusner, and his equivalent paper in *"To See Ourselves as Others See Us:" Jews, Christians, "Others" in Late Antiquity* (Atlanta, 1985: Scholars Press: Studies in the Humanities), ed. by Jacob Neusner and Ernest S. Frerichs.

since we have every reason to expect people who read Scripture within pretty much the same framework to seek in the same passage similar points of stress. But that is not what we shall now see. Indeed, were the theory to take shape that within the circles of the sages of the dual Torah were profound differences on what required stress and what did not, the following comparison of exegeses – comparative midrash – would provide solid evidence. Quite how to sort out the amazing differences in approach, emphasis, and inquiry, that separate the authorship of Sifré to Numbers from that of Pesiqta deRab Kahana remains a puzzle. I mean at this point only to raise the question of how both documents belong within the same canon and to ask what we can mean by canon when the authoritative writings relate so slightly as do these. The relevance to false proposition 1 is self-evident. If the verse formed the generative category, we should find in the exegeses of the respective documents points of intersection or at least thematic congruence. But we find neither. One authorship – that is, the group that selected and arranged the materials in a given document – reads the verse in one context of meaning, the other, in an utterly different and unrelated framework. Since I can multiply examples of the same phenomenon for one pair of documents after another, or for one verse of Scripture after another read in a broad selection of canonical compilations of exegeses, the weight of evidence accumulates against the proposition I have labelled as false. The translations in both cases are my own.

II

Sifre to Numbers 44 on Numbers 7:1

The text I translate is *Sifré debe Rab. Sifré al sefer Bammidbar veSifré Zuta*, ed. by Haim Shaul Horovitz (Leipzig, 1917) [series title: *Schriften, herausgegeben von der Gesellschaft zur Foerderung der Wissenschaft des Judentums. Corpus Tannaiticum. Sectio Tertia: Continens Veterum Doctorum ad Pentateuchum Interpretationes Halachicas. Pars Tertia. Siphre d'Be Rab. Fasciculus primus: Siphre ad Numeros adjecto Siphre Zutta. Cum variis lectionibus et adnotationibus. Edidit* H. S. Horovitz]. There is no complete English translation of the document prior to mine.[6] We do not know when the document came to closure. All the named authorities belong to the age of the Mishnah, but we have no way of identifying the authentic from the pseudepigraphic attributions. In the model of the Tosefta,[7] a demonstrably Amoraic document, a large portion of which cites verbatim and comments on the

---

[6]Jacob Neusner and William Scott Green, *Sifré to Numbers. An American Translation* (Atlanta, 1986: Scholars Press for Brown Judaic Studies). I-III. I and II are now in print, covering *Pisqaot* 1-116, and III is expected in 1987.

[7]I have demonstrated that fact in my systematic comparison of the Tosefta to the Mishnah in my *History of the Mishnaic Law* (Leiden, 1974-1986: E. J. Brill) I-XLIII, and in my *Tosefta. Translated from the Hebrew* (N.Y., 1977-1986: Ktav) I-VI.

Mishnah and so is post-mishnaic, we may hardly assign the present composition to a period before the end of the fourth century.[8]

The authorship of Sifré to Numbers makes use of two basic approaches to the presentation of a cogent statement, e.g., an argument. The first is the syllogistic composition, resting on the premise that Scripture supplies hard facts, which, properly classified in lists of like-facts (hence an instance of *Listenwissenschaft*), generate syllogisms. By collecting and classifying facts of Scripture, therefore, we may produce firm laws of history, society, and Israel's everyday life. The second maintains the fallability of reason unguided by scriptural exegesis. Scripture alone supplies reliable basis for speculation. Laws cannot be generated by reason or logic unguided by Scripture. That is the recurrent polemic of the document – a point of interest completely outside of the imagination of the framers of Pesiqta deRab Kahana, as we shall see. They are arguing about different things, presumably with different people. For nothing in the program of questions addressed to the book of Numbers draws one group into alignment with the other: they simply do not raise the same questions or produce congruent answers. Whether or not the exegetical-eisegetical results can be harmonized is a separate question.[9]

XLIV:I

1. A. *On the day when Moses had finished setting up the tabernacle [and had anointed and consecrated it with all its furnishings and had anointed and consecrated the altar with all its utensils, the leaders of Israel, heads of their fathers' houses, the leaders of the tribes, who were over those who were numbered, offered and brought their offerings before the Lord, six covered wagons and twelve oxen, a wagon for every two of the leaders, and for each one an ox, they offered them before the tabernacle. Then the Lord said to Moses, "Accept these from them, that they may be used in doing the service of the tent of meeting, and give them to the Levites, to each man according to his service." So Moses took the wagons and the oxen and gave them to the Levites]* (Num. 7:1-6):

   B. Scripture indicates that for each of the seven days of consecrating the tabernacle, Moses would set up the tabernacle, and every morning he would anoint it and dismantle it. But on that day he set it up and anointed it, but he did not dismantle it.

   C. R. Yose b. R. Judah: *Also on the eighth day he set it up and dismantled it, for it is said, "And in the first month in the second year on the first*

[8]Moses David Heer, *Midrash*, *Encyclopaedia Judaica* (Jerusalem, 1971: Keter Publishing Co), s.v. I have found no more authoritative statement on the present view of the dates of all midrash-compilations than Heer's. It is a question that will have in time to be reopened.

[9]That question demands attention in a far wider context than the present one. For it is the issue that when addressed will require us to ask what we mean by the canon, and, more important, what meanings inhere within the canon as a whole but not in some one of its parts: what holds the whole together that is not stated in any one component? I have no doubt whatever that that Judaism behind the systems of the several components of the canon of the dual Torah awaits systematic and rigorous definition; but at this writing I am uncertain about how to proceed.

*day of the month the tabernacle was erected" (Ex. 30:17). On the basis
of that verse we learn that on the twenty-third day of Adar, Aaron and his
sons, the tabernacle and the utensils were anointed.*

This is the focus of interest: the meaning of the word KLH, that is, completed, and the same point will be made in Pesiqta deRab Kahana. But here it is the main point, since the exegete proposes to say what he thinks the simplest sense of the verse is. The second compilation of exegeses, by contrast, treats the matter in a much richer and more imaginative way.

XLV:I

2. A. On the first day of the month the tabernacle was set up, on the second the red cow was burned [for the purification rite required at Num. 19], on the third day water was sprinkled from it in lieu of the second act of sprinkling, the Levites were shaved.

   B. On that same day the Presence of God rested in the tabernacle, as it is said, "Then the cloud covered the tent of meeting, and the glory of the Lord filled the tabernacle, and Moses was not able to enter the tent of meeting, because the cloud abode upon it" (Ex. 40:34).

   C. On that same day the heads offered their offerings, as it is said, *He who offered his offering the first day...* (Num. 7:12). Scripture uses the word "first" only in a setting when "first" introduces all of the days of the year.

   D. On that day fire came down from heaven and consumed the offerings, as it is said, *And fire came forth from before the Lord and consumed the burnt-offering and the fat upon the altar* (Lev. 9:24).

   E. On that day the sons of Aaron offered strange fire, as it is said, *Now Nadab and Abihu, the sons of Aaron, each took his censer and put fire in it...and offered unholy fire before the Lord, such as he had not commanded them* (Lev. 10:1).

   F. *And they died before the Lord...* (Lev. 10:2): they died before the Lord, but they fell outside [of the tabernacle, not imparting corpse uncleanness to it].

   G. How so? They were on their way out.

   H. R. Yose says, *An angel sustained them, as they died, until they got out, and they fell in the courtyard, as it is said, "And Moses called Mishael and Elzaphan, the sons of Uzziel the uncle of Aaron, and said to them, 'Draw near, carry your brethren from before the sanctuary out of the camp'"* (Lev. 10:4). What is stated is not, "From before the Lord," but, "from before the sanctuary."

   I. R. Ishmael says, "The context indicates the true state of affairs, as it is said, 'And they died before the Lord,' meaning, they died inside and fell inside. How did they get out? People dragged them with iron ropes."

The exegete draws together a broad range of events which, in his view, all took place on one day. But what is interesting – as the contrast will show in a moment – is what he does not say. He does not introduce the issue of Israel and Israel's redemption. Rather, he focuses upon the here and the now of what happened long ago. There is a perceived difference between the one-time historical event of the setting up of the tabernacle and the eternal and paradigmatic character of the event: its continuing meaning, not its one-time character at all. The tabernacle is not the paradigm of the natural world, and Israel's salvation simply plays no role in the passage. Now to the matter at hand.

The expansion and amplification of the base-verse runs through No. 1. From that point, No. 2, we deal with the other events of that same day, surveying the several distinct narratives which deal with the same thing, Ex. 40, Lev. 9-10, and so on. This produces the effect of unifying the diverse scriptural accounts into one tale, an important and powerful exegetical result. One of the persistent contributions of our exegetes is to collect and harmonize a diversity of verses taken to refer to the same day, event, or rule.

XLIV:II

1. A. "...and had anointed and consecrated it with all its furnishings and had anointed and consecrated the altar with all its utensils":
   B. Might I infer that as each utensil was anointed, it was sanctified?
   C. Scripture says, "...and had anointed and consecrated it with all its furnishings and had anointed and consecrated the altar with all its utensils," meaning that not one of them was sanctified until all of them had been anointed.   [The process proceeded by stages.]

Once more we shall see that the second exegesis – that of Pesiqta deRab Kahana – makes precisely this point. But it is swallowed up in a much different range of interest. The later document covers nearly everything in the earlier one, but makes nothing of what is constitutive of the received writing.

XLIV:II

2. A. "...and had anointed and consecrated it with all its furnishings and had anointed and consecrated the altar with all its utensils":
   B. The anointing was done both inside and outside [of the utensil].
   C. R. Josiah says, "Utensils meant to hold liquids were anointed inside and outside, but utensils meant to hold dry stuffs were anointed on the inside but not anointed on the outside."
   D. R. Jonathan says, "Utensils meant to hold liquids were anointed inside and not outside, but utensils meant to hold dry stuffs not anointed.
   E. "You may know that they were not consecrated, for it is said, *You shall bring from your dwellings two loaves of bread to be waved, made of two tenths of an ephah* (Lev. 23:17). Then when do they belong to the Lord? Only after they are baked." [The bread was baked in utensils at home, so the utensils have not been consecrated.]

The exegetes at Pesiqta deRab Kahana have no interest whatever in the details at hand. Theirs is not a search for concrete details.

XLIV:II

3. A. Rabbi says, "Why is it said, ...*and had anointed and consecrated it* ? And is it not already stated, '...and had anointed and consecrated it'?
   B. "This indicates that with the anointing of these utensils all future utensils were sanctified [so that the sanctification of the tabernacle enjoyed permanence and a future tabernacle or temple did not require a rite of sanctification once again]."

No. 1 clarifies the rite of sanctification, aiming at the notion that the act of consecration covered everything at once, leading to the future conclusion, at the end, that that act also covered utensils later on to be used in the cult. No. 3 goes over that same ground. No. 2 deals with its own issue, pursuing the exegesis of the verse at hand. Its interest in the consecration of the utensils is entirely congruent with No. 3, because it wants to know the status of utensils outside of the cult, and, while they serve the purpose of the cult as specified, still, they are not deemed to have been consecrated. That, sum and substance, is the message of the passage: this and that about not very much, apart from the sequence of events that took place on one and the same day, an effort to harmonize and unify diverse tales into a single set of cogent events.

III

Pesiqta deRab Kahana 1 on Numbers 7:1

My translation of the critical text of Pisqta deRab Kahana published by Bernard Mandelbaum, *Pesikta de Rab Kahana. According to An Oxford Manuscript. With Variants from All Known Manuscripts and Genizoth Fragments and Parallel Passages. With Commentary and Introduction* (N.Y., 1962: The Jewish Theological Seminary of America) I-II. I have further followed Mandelbaum's notes and commentary. I also consulted William G. (Gershon Zev) Braude and Israel J. Kapstein, *Pesikta de-Rab Kahana. R. Kahana's Compilation of Discourses for Sabbaths and Festal Days* (Philadelphia, 1975: Jewish Publication Society of America).[10]

---

[10]Theirs is not a translation but a an eisegetical rendition, more of a literary paraphrase than an academic translation. Moreover, the Hebrew text on which Braude's and Kapstein's translation is based appears to be eclectic, one that they appear to have chosen for the occasion, therefore is not readily available to scholars in general, rather than systematic and commonly accessible. Finally, because they have not analyzed the text into its constitutive components, they have translated (eisegetically) as though one clause derived from the last and led to the next, when, in fact, each component was worked out within its own framework and is not necessarily cogent with the others fore and aft. Consequently, their translation harmonizes constantly what seem to me discrete components of discourse. Their penchant for translating not the text but what they (not necessarily without reason) conceive to be its meaning makes the translation attractive and engaging, but in no way reliable as an account of what is there in the Hebrew. It has to be checked at every point, though I would not dismiss it as without value, even as a translation of the Hebrew. Its lack of accuracy on minor points makes little material difference as to its usefulness. I certainly would not discard or dismiss their translation, but I am in the process of replacing it with something more useful to learning.

The formal traits of the second compilation differ radically. The authorship of Pesiqta deRab Kahana approaches the exegesis of the verse of primary interest, which I call the base-verse, by means of a secondary and superficially unrelated verse, which I call the intersecting-verse. The latter will be treated entirely on its own.[11] Then the exegete will move from the intersecting-verse to the base-verse, showing how the verse chosen from some other passage in fact opens up the deeper meaning of the verse of primary concern. In what follows the intersecting-verse, Song 5:1, is chosen because it refers to "bride," and the word for " had finished" is formed of the letters KLH, which can be read as bride. So in the mind of the exegete, an appropriate intersecting-verse will speak of the same matter – KLH = finish or bride – and the rest follows.

But, as we shall see, that intersecting-verse imparts its deepest meaning on the base-verse, and, in the present instance, the tabernacle on that account is taken as the place in which Israel entered the bridal canopy of God. The clear purpose of the authorship emerges in their treatment of the base-verse, Num. 7:1: teleological-eschatological, beginning, middle and end. The one thing important about the base-verse is the opposite of the main thing that struck the authorship of Sifré to Numbers: its interest in a one-time event on a particular day. To the authorship of Pesiqta deRab Kahana, Scripture presents eternal paradigms and not one-time history.

I:I

1. A. *I have come back to my garden, my sister, my bride* (Song 5:1):

B. R. Azariah in the name of R. Simon said, "[The matter may be compared to the case of] a king who became angry at a noble woman and drove her out and expelled her from his palace. After some time he wanted to bring her back. She said, 'Let him renew in my behalf the earlier state of affairs, and then he may bring me back.'

C. "So in former times the Holy One, blessed be He, would receive offerings from on high, as it is said, *And the Lord smelled the sweet odor* (Gen. 8:21). But now he will accept them down below."

2. A. *I have come back to my garden, my sister, my bride* (Song 5:1):

B. Said R. Hanina, "The Torah teaches you proper conduct,

C. "specifically, that a groom should not go into the marriage canopy until the bride gives him permission to do so: *Let my beloved come into his garden* (Song 4:16), after which, *I have come back to my garden, my sister, my bride* (Song 5:1)."

---

[11] We return to this matter of the rhetorical patterns of the midrash-compositions and compilations in the next chapter, where I shall differentiate the intersecting-verse/base-verse form as used in Pesiqta deRab Kahana from the counterpart formation as used in Leviticus Rabbah and further show that the formal differences represent differences in the principles of logical discourse characteristic of the two authorshiops, respectively. The one, we shall see, aims at a more severely economical statement of an implicit syllogism than does the other, and, further, the same difference in economic of syllogistic expression permits us to differentiate the way in which each authorship reads and interprets the components of the base-verse, read on their own and in isolation from the intersecting-verse.

As we shall see, the intersecting-verse is fully exposed entirely in its own terms, before we are able to recover the base-verse and find out what we learn about that verse from the intersecting one.

3 . A. R. Tanhum, son-in-law of R. Eleazar b. Abina, in the name of R. Simeon b. Yosni: "What is written is not, 'I have come into the garden,' but rather, *I have come back to my garden.* That is, 'to my [Mandelbaum:] canopy.'

B. "That is to say, to the place in which the the principal [presence of God] had been located to begin with.

C. "The principal locale of God's presence had been among the lower creatures, in line with this verse: *And they heard the sound of the Lord God walking about* (Gen. 3:8)."

4 . A. [*And they heard the sound of the Lord God walking about* (Gen. 3:8):] Said R. Abba bar Kahana, "What is written is not merely going,' but 'walking about,' that is, 'walking away from.'"

B. *And man and his wife hid* (Gen. 3:8):

C. Said R. Aibu, "At that moment the first man's stature was cut down and diminished to one hundred cubits."

5 . A. Said R. Isaac, "It is written, *The righteous will inherit the earth* (Ps. 47:29). Where will the wicked be? Will they fly in the air?

B. "Rather, the sense of the clause, *they shall dwell thereon in eternity* is, they shall bring the presence of God to dwell on the earth."

6 . A. [Reverting to 3.C,] the principal locale of God's presence had been among the lower creatures, but when the first man sinned, it went up to the first firmament.

B. The generation of Enosh came along and sinned, and it went up from the first to the second.

C. The generation of the flood [came along and sinned], and it went up from the second to the third.

D. The generation of the dispersion...and sinned, and it went up from the third to the fourth.

E. The Egyptians in the time of Abraham our father [came along] and sinned, and it went up from the fourth to the fifth.

F. The Sodomites..., and sinned, ...from the fifth to the sixth.

G. The Egyptians in the time of Moses...from the sixth to the seventh.

H. And, corresponding to them, seven righteous men came along and brought it back down to earth:

I. Abraham our father came along and acquired merit, and brought it down from the seventh to the sixth.

J. Isaac came along and acquired merit and brought it down from the sixth to the fifth.

K. Jacob came along and acquired merit and brought it down from the fifth to the fourth.

L. Levi came along and acquired merit and brought it down from the fourth to the third.

M. Kahath came along and acquired merit and brought it down from the third to the second.

N. Amram came along and acquired merit and brought it down from the second to the first.

O. Moses came along and acquired merit and brought it down to earth.

P. Therefore it is said, *On the day that Moses completed the setting up of the Tabernacle, he anointed and consecrated it* (Num. 7:1).

The selection of the intersecting-verse, Song 5:1, rests, as I said, on the appearance of the letters KLT, meaning completed, but yielding also the word KLH, meaning bride. The exegete wishes to make the point that in building the tabernacle, Moses has brought God down to earth, 6.P. This he accomplishes by bringing the theme of "garden, bride" together with the theme of the union of God and Israel. The parable at 1.B then is entire apt, since it wishes to introduce the notion of God's having become angry with humanity but then reconciled through Israel in the sacrificial cult. 1.B then refers to the fall from grace, with Israel as the noble spouse who insists that the earlier state of affairs be restored. C then makes explicit precisely what is in mind, a very effective introduction to the whole. No. 2 pursues the exegesis of the intersecting-verse, as does No. 3, the latter entirely apropos. Because of 3.C, No. 4 is tacked on; it continues the exegesis of the proof-text but has no bearing on the intersecting-verse. But No. 5 does – at least in its proposition, if not in its selection of proof-texts. No. 6 then brings us back to 3.C, citing the language of the prior component and then making the point of the whole quite explicit. Even with the obvious accretions at No. 4, 5, the whole hangs together and makes its point – the intersecting-verse, Song 5:1, the base-verse Num. 7:1 – in a cogent way.

I:II

1. A. *King Solomon made a pavilion for himself* (Song 3:9) [The New English Bible: *The palanquin which King Solomon had made for himself was of wood from Lebanon. Its poles he made of silver, its head-rest of gold; its seat was of purple stuff, and its lining was of leather]:*

   B. *Pavilion* refers to the tent of meeting.

   C. *King Solomon made a ...for himself* he is the king to whom peace (*shalom/shelomoh*) belongs.

2. A. Said R. Judah bar Ilai, "[The matter may be compared to the case of] a king who had a little girl. Before she grew up and reached puberty, he would see her in the market place and chat with her, or in alleyways and chat with her. But when she grew up and reached puberty, he said, 'It is not fitting for the dignity of my daughter that I should talk with her in public. Make a pavilion for her, so that I may chat with her in the pavilion.'

   B. "So, to begin with: *When Israel was a child in Egypt, then in my love of him, I used to cry out* (Hos 11:1). In Egypt they saw me: *And I passed through the land of Israel* (Ex. 12:12). At the sea they saw me: *And Israel saw the great hand* (Ex. 14:31). At Sinai they saw me: *Face to face the Lord spoke with you* (Deut. 5:4).

   C. "But when they received the Torah, they became a fully-grown nation for me. So he said, 'It is not appropriate to the dignity of my children that I should speak with them in public. But make me a tabernacle, and I shall speak from the midst of the tabernacle.'

D. "That is in line with this verse: *And when Moses entered the tent of the presence to speak with God, he heard the voice speaking from above the cover over the ark of the tokens from between the two cherubim: the voice spoke to him* (Num. 7:89)."

3. A. *[The palanquin which King Solomon had made for himself was of wood from Lebanon. Its poles he made of silver, its head-rest of gold; its seat was of purple stuff, and its lining was of leather]* ...*was of wood from Lebanon. Make for the tabernacle planks of acacia-wood as uprights* (Ex. 26:25).

B. *Its poles he made of silver:* The hooks and bands on the posts shall be of silver (Ex. 27:10).

C. ...*its head-rest of gold:* Overlay the planks with gold, make rings of gold on them to no hold the bars (Ex. 26:29).

D. ...*its seat was of purple stuff:* Make a veil of finely woven linen and violet, purple, and scarlet yarn (Ex. 26:31).

E. ...*and its lining was of leather:*

F. R. Yudan says, "This refers to the merit accruing on account of the Torah and the righteous."

G. R. Azariah in the name of R. Judah bar Simon says, "This refers to the Presence of God."

4. A. Said R. Aha bar Kahana, "It is written, *And there I shall meet with you* (Ex. 25:22),

B. "to teach that even what is on the outside of the ark-cover is not empty of God's presence."

5. A. A gentile asked Rabban Gamaliel, saying to him, "On what account did the Holy One, blessed be He, reveal himself to Moses in a bush?"

B. He said to him, "If he had revealed himself to him in a carob tree or a fig tree, what might you have said? It is so as to indicate that there is no place in the earth that is empty of God's presence."

6. A. R. Joshua of Sikhnin in the name of R. Levi: "To what may the tent of meeting be compared?

B. "To an oceanside cave. The sea tide flows and engulfs the cave, which is filled by the sea, but the sea is not diminished.

C. "So the tent of meeting is filled with the splendor of the presence of God."

D. Therefore it is said, *On the day that Moses completed the setting up of the Tabernacle, he anointed and consecrated it* (Num. 7:1).

Seen by itself, No. 1 has no bearing upon the larger context, but it does provide a good exegesis of Song 3:9 in terms of the theme at hand, the tabernacle. The point of No. 2 is that the purpose of the tabernacle was to make possible appropriate communication between a mature Israel and God. Then the two items are simply distinct workings of the theme of the tabernacle, one appealing to Song 3:9, the other, Num. 7:89.

The introduction at **I:II** of Song 3:9, with the explanation that palanquin refers to the tent of meeting, accounts for the exposition of No. 3, which reads each phrase of that intersecting-verse in line with the proof-texts concerning the tent of meeting. Had **I:II.1** been continued by No.3, we should have a smoother statement of the main point. No. 4 seems to me to flow from No.3's interest in the tent of meeting; the point of contact is with the viewpoint that God's presence was in the tent. Then No. 5 is tacked on for obvious reasons, a story that makes the same point as the exegesis. No. 6 goes over the matter yet again. The force of 6.D is derived only from its redactional function, which is to direct our attention back to our base-verse. But while the theme – the tent of meeting or tabernacle – has been worked out, the base-verse in its own terms has not been discussed. Tacking it on is only for purpose of marking the finish of the discourse at hand.

I:III

1. A. [Continuing the exegesis of the successive verses of Songf 3:9ff.] *Come out, daughters of Jerusalem, you daughters of Zion, come out and welcome King Solomon, wearing the crown with which his mother has crowned him, on his wedding day, on his day of joy* (Song 3:11) [Braude and Kapstein: *Go forth, O younglings whose name Zion indicates that you bear a sign*]:
   B. Sons who are marked [a play on the letters that stand for the word, *come out*] for me by the mark of circumcision, by not cutting the corners of the head [in line with Lev. 19:27], and by wearing show-fringes.
2. [*...and welcome] King Solomon:*
   B. The king to whom peace belongs.
3. A. Another interpretation: *and welcome King Solomon:*
   B. The King [meaning God] who brings peace through his deeds among his creatures.
   C. He made the fire make peace with Abraham, the sword with Isaac, the angel with Jacob.
   D. It is the king who brings peace among his creatures.
   E. Said R. Yohanan, "*Merciful dominion and fear are with him* (Job 25:2) [that is, are at peace with him]."
   F. Said R. Jacob of Kefar Hanan, "*Merciful dominion* refers to Michael, and *fear* to Gabriel.
   G. "*With him* means that they make peace with him and do not do injury to one another."
   H. Said R. Yohanan, "The sun has never laid eyes on the blemished part of the moon [the black side], nor does a star take precedence over another one, nor does a planet lay eyes on the one above it."
   I. Said Rabbi, "All of them traverse as it were a spiral staircase."
4. A. It is written, *Who lays the beams of your upper chambers in the waters, who makes the flaming fires your ministers* (Ps. 104:2-3):
   B. R. Simeon b. Yohai taught, "The firmament is of water, the stars of fire, and yet they dwell with one another and do not do injury to one another."
   C. "The firmament is of water and the angel is of fire, and yet they dwell with one another and do not do injury to one another."
   D. Said R. Abin, "It is not the end of the matter [that there is peace between] one angel and another. But even the angel himself is half fire and half water, and yet they make peace."
   E. The angel has five faces – *The angel's body was like beryl, his face as the appearance of lightning, his eyes as torches of fire, his arms and feet*

like in color to burnished brass, and the sound of his words like the sound of a roaring multitude (Dan. 10:6) – [yet none does injury to the other].

5. A. *So there was hail and fire flashing continually amid the hail* (Ex. 9:24):

   B. R. Judah says, "There was a flask of hail filled with fire."

   C. R. Nehemiah said, "Fire and hail, mixed together."

   D. R Hanin said, "In support of the position of R. Judah is the case of the pomegranate in the pulp of which seeds can be discerned".

   E. R. Hanin said, "As to Nehemiah's, it is the case of a crystal lamp in which are equivalent volulme of water and oil, which together keep the flame of the wick burning above the water and the oil."

6. A. *[So there was hail and fire flashing continually amid the hail* (Ex. 9:24)]: What is the meaning of *flashing continually?*

   B. Said R. Judah bar Simon, "Each one is dying in their [B&K, p. 10:] determination to carry out their mission."

   C. Said R. Aha, "[The matter may be compared to the case of] a king, who had two tough legions, who competed with one another, but when the time to make war in behalf of the king came around, they made peace with one another.

   D. "So is the case with the fire and hail, they compete with one another, but when the time has come to carry out the war of the Holy One, blessed be He, against the Egyptians, then:*So there was hail and fire flashing continually amid the hail* (Ex. 9:24) – one miracle within the other [more familiar one, namely, that the hail; and fire worked together]."

7. A. *[Come out, daughters of Jerusalem, you daughters of Zion, come out and welcome King Solomon,] wearing the crown with which his mother has crowned him, on his wedding day, [on his day of joy]* (Song 3:11):

   B. Said R. Isaac, "We have reviewed the entire Scripture and have not found evidence that Beth Seba made a crown for her son, Solomon. This refers, rather, to the tent of meeting, which is crowed with blue and purple and scarlet."

8. A. Said R. Hunia, "R. Simeon b. Yohai asked R. Eleazar b. R. Yose, 'Is it possible that you have heard. from your father what was the crown with which his mother crowned him?'

   B. "He said to him, 'The matter may be compared to the case of a king who had a daughter, whom he loved even too much. He even went so far, in expressing his affection for her, as to call her, "my sister." He even went so far, in expressing his affection for her, as to call her, "my mother."

   C. "'So at the outset, the Holy One, blessed be He, expressed his affection for Israel by calling them, "my daughter": *Hear, O daughter, and consider* (Ps. 45:11). Then he went so far, in expressing his affection for them, as to call them, "my sister": *My sister, my bride* (Song 5:1). Then he went so far, in expressing his affection for them, as to call them, "my mother": *Attend to me, O my people, and give ear to me, O my nation* (Is. 51:4). The letters that are read as "my nation" may also be read as "my mother."'

   D. "R. Simeon b. Yohai stood and kissed him on his head.

   E. "He said to him, 'Had I come only to hear this teaching, it would have been enough for me.'"

9. **A.** R. Joshua of Sikhnin in the name of R. Levi: "When the Holy One, blessed be He, said to Moses, 'Make me a tabernacle,' Moses might have brought four poles and spread over them [skins to make] the tabernacle. This teaches, therefore, that the Holy One, blessed be He, showed Moses on high red fire, green fire, black fire, and white fire.

B. "He said to him, 'Make me a tabernacle.'

C. "Moses said to the Holy One, blessed be He, 'Lord of the ages, where am I going to get red fire, green fire, black fire, white fire?'

D. *He said to him, "After the pattern which is shown to you on the mountain"* (Ex. 25:40).

10. **A.** R. Berekhiah in the name of R. Levi: "[The matter may be compared to the case of] a king who appeared to his household clothed in a garment [B&K, p. 11] covered entirely with precious stones.

B. "He said to him, 'Make me one like this.'

C. "He said to him, 'My lord, O king, where am I going to get myself a garment made entirely of precious stones?'

D. "He said to him, 'You in accord with your raw materials and I in accord with my glory.'

E. "So said the Holy One, blessed be He, to Moses, 'Moses, if you make what belongs above down below, I shall leave my council up here and go down and reduce my Presence so as to be among you down there.'

F. "Just as up there: *seraphim are standing* (Is. 6:2), so down below: *boards of shittim-cedars are standing* (Ex. 26:15).

G. "Just as up there are stars, so down below are the clasps."

H. Said R. Hiyya bar Abba, "This teaches that the golden clasps in the tabernacle looked like the fixed stars of the firmament."

11. **A.** *[Come out, daughters of Jerusalem, you daughters of Zion, come out and welcome King Solomon, wearing the crown with which his mother has crowned him,] on his wedding day, [on his day of joy]* (Song 3:11):

B. [B&K, p. 12:] the day he entered the tent of meeting.

C. *...on his day of joy:*

D. this refers to the tent of meeting.

E. Another interpretation of the phrase, *on his wedding day, on his day of joy* (Song 3:11):

F. *...on his wedding day,* refers to the tent of meeting.

G. *...on his day of joy* refers to the building of the eternal house.

H. Therefore it is said, *On the day that Moses completed the setting up of the Tabernacle, he anointed and consecrated it* (Num. 7:1).

The exegesis of Song 3:11 now receives attention in its own terms, our point of departure having been forgotten. No. 1 simply provides a play on one of the words of the verse under study. Nos. 2-6 proceed to work on the problem of the name of the king, Solomon. We have a striking and fresh approach at Nos. 2-3: the reference is now to God as King, and the name, Solomon, then is interpreted as God's function as bringing peace both among his holy creatures, the patriarchs and the angels, and also among the elements of natural creation. Both topics are introduced and then, at No. 4-6, the latter is worked out. God keeps water and fire working together and to do his bidding, they do not injure one another. The proof-text, Ex. 9:24, then leads us in its own direction, but at No. 6 discourse returns to the main point.

No. 7 moves us on to a fresh issue, namely, Solomon himself. And now we see the connection between the passage and our broader theme, the tabernacle. The Temple is now compared to a crown. No. 8 pursues the interpretation of the same clause. But the point of interest is the clause, not the theme under broader discussion, so what we have is simply a repertoire of exegeses of the cited verse. No. 9 carries forward the theme of making the tabernacle. It makes the point that Moses was to replicate the colors he had seen on high. I see no connection to the preceding. It is an essentially fresh initiative. No. 10 continues along that same line, now making yet another point, which is that the tabernacle on earth was comparable to the abode of God in heaven. No. 11 brings us back to our original verse. We take up a clause by clause interpretation of the matter. 11.H is an editorial subscript, with no connection to the foregoing except the rather general thematic one. But the original interest in working on the theme of the building of the tabernacle as Israel's wedding day to God is well expressed, beginning to end.

I:IV

1. A. *Who has ever gone up to heaven and come down again? Who has cupped the wind in the hollow of his hands? Who has bound up the waters in the fold of his garment? Who has fixed the boundaries of the earth? What is his name or his son's name, if you know it?* (Prov. 30:4):

   B. *...Who has ever gone up to heaven:* this refers to the Holy One, blessed be He, as it is written, *God has gone up to the sound of the trumpet* (Ps. 37:6).

   C. *...and come down again: The Lord came down onto Mount Sinai* (Ex. 19:20).

   D. *Who has cupped the wind in the hollow of his hands: In whose hand is the soul of all the living* (Job 12:10).

   E. *Who has bound up the waters in the fold of his garment: He keeps the waters penned in dense cloud-masses* (Job 26:8).

   F. *Who has fixed the boundaries of the earth: who kills and brings to life* (1 Sam. 2:6).

   G. *What is his name:* his name is the Rock, his name is The Almighty, his name is The Lord of Hosts.

   H. *...or his son's name, if you know it: My son, my first born is Israel* (Ex. 4:22).

2. A. Another interpretation of the verse, *Who has ever gone up to heaven:* Who is the one whose prayer goes up to heaven and brings down rain?

   B. This is one who sets aside the tithes that he owes with his hands, who brings dew and rain into the world.

   C. *Who has cupped the wind in the hollow of his hands? Who has bound up the waters in the fold of his garment? Who has fixed the boundaries of the earth?* Who is the one whose prayer does not go up to heaven and bring down rain?

   D. This is one who does not set aside the tithes that he owes with his hands, who does not bring dew and rain into the world.

3 . A. Another interpretation of the verse, *Who has ever gone up to heaven :*
   B. This refers to Elijah, concerning whom it is written, *And Elijah went up in a whirlwind to heaven* (2 Kgs. 2:11).
   C. *...and come down again:*
   D. *Go down with him, do not be afraid* (2 Kgs. 1:16).
   E. *Who has cupped the wind in the hollow of his hands:*
   F. *Lord, God of Israel, before whom I stand* (1 Kgs. 17:1).
   G. *Who has bound up the waters in the fold of his garment:*
   H. *And Elijah took his mantle and wrapped it together and smote the waters and they were divided* (1 Kgs. 2:8).
   I. *Who has fixed the boundaries of the earth:*
   J. *And Elijah said, See your son lives* (1 Kgs. 17:23).
4 . A. Another interpretation of the verse, *Who has ever gone up to heaven and come down again:*
   B. This refers to Moses, concerning whom it is written, *And Moses went up to God* (Ex. 19:3).
   C. *...and come down again:*
   D. *And Moses came down from the mountain* (Ex. 19:14).
   E. *Who has cupped the wind in the hollow of his hands:*
   F. *As soon as I have gone out of the city, I shall spread my hands out to the Lord* (Ex. 9:29).
   G. *Who has bound up the waters in the fold of his garment:*
   H. *The floods stood upright as a heap* (Ex. 15:8).
   I. *Who has fixed the boundaries of the earth:*
   J. This refers to the tent of meeting, as it is said, *On the day on which Moses completed setting up the tabernacle* (Num. 7:1) – for the entire world was set up with it.
5 . A. R. Joshua b. Levi in the name of R. Simeon b. Yohai: "What is stated is not 'setting up the tabernacle [without the accusative particle, *et*],' but 'setting up + *the accusative particle* + the tabernacle,' [and since the inclusion of the accusative particle is taken to mean that the object is duplicated, we understand the sense to be that he set up a second tabernacle along with the first].
   B. "What was set up with it? It was the world that was set up with [the tabernacle, that is, the tabernacle represented the cosmos].
   C. "For until the tabernacle was set up, the world trembled, but after the tabernacle was set up, the world rested on firm foundations."
   D. Therefore it is said, *On the day that Moses completed the setting up of the Tabernacle, he anointed and consecrated it* (Num. 7:1).

The fresh intersecting-verse, Prov. 30:4, is systematically applied to God, to tithing, then Elijah, finally Moses, at which point the exposition comes to a fine editorial conclusion. I cannot imagine a more representative example of the intersecting-verse/base-verse exposition. No. 5 is tacked on because it provides a valuable complement to the point of No. 4.

I:V

1 . A. Another interpretation of the verse: *On the day that Moses completed the setting up of the Tabernacle, he anointed and consecrated it* (Num. 7:1):

B. The letters translated as "completed" are so written that they be read "bridal," that is, on the day on which [Israel, the bride] entered the bridal canopy.

2. A. R. Eleazar and R. Samuel bar Nahmani:

B. R. Eleazar says, *"On the day that Moses completed* means on the day on which he left up setting up the tabernacle day by day."

C. It has been taught on Tannaite authority: Every day Moses would set up the tabernacle, and every morning he would make his offerings on it and then take it down. On the eighth day [to which reference is made in the verse, *On the day that Moses completed the setting up of the Tabernacle, he anointed and consecrated it]* he set it up but did not take it down again.

D. Said R. Zeira, "On the basis of this verse we learn the fact that an altar set up on the preceding night is inavlid for the offering of sacrifices on the next day."

E. R. Samuel bar Nahmani says, "Even on the eighth day he set it up and took it apart again."

F. And how do we know about these dismantlings?

G. It is in line with what R. Zeira said, *"On the day that Moses completed* means on the day on which he left up setting up the tabernacle day by day."

3. A. R. Eleazar and R. Yohanan:

B. R. Eleazar said, *"On the day that Moses completed* means on the day on which demons ended their spell in the world.

C. "What is the scriptural basis for that view?

D. *"No evil thing will befall you, nor will any demon come near you* [B&K p. 15] *by reason of your tent* (Ps. 91:10) – on the day on which demons ended their spell in the world."

E. Said R. Yohanan, "What need do I have to derive the lesson from another passage? Let us learn it from the very passage in which the matter occurs: *May the Lord bless you and keep you* (Num. 6:24) – keep you from demons."

4. A. R. Yohanan and R. Simeon b. Laqish:

B. R. Yohanan said, *"On the day that Moses completed* means on the day on which on the day on which hatred came to an end in the world. For before the tabernacle was set up, there was hatred and envy, competition, contention, and strife in the world. But once the tabernacle was sert up, love, affection, comradeship, righteousness, and peace came into the world.

C. "What is the verse of scripture that so indicates?

D. *"Let me hear the words of the Lord, are they not words of peace, peace to his people and his loyal servants and to all who turn and trust in him? Deliverance is near to those who worship him, so that glory may dwell in our land. Love and fidelity have come together, justice and peace join hands* (Ps. 85:8-10).

E. Said R. Simeon b. Laqish, "What need do I have to derive the lesson from another passage? Let us learn it from the very passage in which the matter occurs: *and give you peace.*

5. A. *[On the day that Moses completed] the setting up of the Tabernacle, [he anointed and consecrated it]:*

B. R. Joshua b. Levi in the name of R. Simeon b. Yohai: "What is stated is not 'setting up the tabernacle [without the accusative particle, *et*],' but 'setting up + *the accusative particle* + the tabernacle,' [and since the inclusion of the accusative particle is taken to mean that the object is duplicated, we understand the sense to be that he set up a second tabernacle along with the first].

C. "What was set up with it? It was the world that was set up with [the tabernacle, that is, the tabernacle represented the cosmos].

D. "For until the tabernacle was set up, the world trembled, but after the tabernacle was set up, the world rested on firm foundations."

We work our way through the clause, *on the day that Moses completed*. No. 1 goes over familiar ground. It is a valuable review of the point of stress, the meaning of the word *completed*. No. 2 refers to the claim that from day to day Moses would set up and take down the tent, until on the day at hand, he left it standing; so the "completed" bears the sense of ceasing to go through a former procedure. The word under study bears the further sense of "coming to an end," and therefore at Nos. 3, 4, we ask what came to an end when the tabernacle was set up. The matched units point to demons, on the one side, and hatred, on the other. No. 5 moves us along from the word KLT to the following set, *accusative + tabernacle*.

I:VI

1. A. *[On the day that Moses completed] the setting up of the Tabernacle, [he anointed and consecrated it]:*

B. Since it is written, *he anointed and consecrated it* , why does it also say, *he anointed them and consecrated them* (Num. 7:1)?

C. R. Aibu said, "R. Tahalipa of Caesarea, and R. Simeon:

D. "One of them said, 'After he had anointed each one, he then anointed all of them simultaneously.'

E. "The other of them said, *'And he anointed them* refers to an anointing in this world and another anointing in the world to come.'"

2. A. Along these same lines: *You shall couple the tent together* (Ex. 26:11), *You shall couple the curtains* (Ex. 26:6):

B. R. Judah and R. Levi, R. Tahalipa of Caesarea and R. Simeon b. Laqish:

C. One of them said, "Once he had coupled them all together, he went back and coupled them one by one."

D. The other said, *"You shall couple the curtains and it shall be one* meaning, one for measuring, one for anointing."

The exposition of the verse continues to occupy our attention, with the problem clear as stated.

I:VII

1. A. *The chief men of Israel, heads of families – that is, the chiefs of the tribes, [who had assisted in preparing the detailed lists –] came forward and brought their offering before the Lord* (Num. 7:2):

B. [(Following B&K, p. 16:) The word for *tribes* can mean *rods*, so we understand the meaning to be, they had exercised authority through rods] in Egypt.

C. *...who had assisted in preparing the detailed lists* – the standards.

The clause by clause interpretation of the base-verse does not vastly differ in intent from the interpretation generated by leading the intersecting-verse into the base-verse. That is to say, in both cases we have a highly allusive and wide-ranging reading of the matter, in which we construct meanings deriving from eternal categories, not one-time events but paradigms, as I said earlier. That trait of the exegetical-eisegetical mind of the later document emerges most strikingly in what follows.

2. A. *...came forward and brought their offering before the Lord, six covered wagons [and twelve oxen, one wagon from every two chiefs and from each one an ox]* (Num. 7:2):

B. The six corresponded to the six days of creation.

C. The six corresponded to the six divisions of the Mishnah.

D. The six corresponded to the six matriarchs: Sarah, Rebecca, Rachel, Leah, Bilhah, and Zilpah.

E. Said R. Yohanan, "The six corresponded to the six religious duties that pertain to a king: *He shall not have too many wives* (Deut. 17:17), *He shall not have too many horses* (Deut. 17:16), *He shall not have too much silver and gold* (Deut. 17:17), *He shall not pervert justice, show favor, or take bribes* (Deut. 16:9)."

3. A. The six corresponded to the six steps of the throne. How so?

B. When he goes up to take his seat on the first step, the herald goes forth and proclaims, *He shall not have too many wives* (Deut. 17:17).

C. When he goes up to take his seat on the second step, the herald goes forth and proclaims, *He shall not have too many horses* (Deut. 17:16).

D. When he goes up to take his seat on the third step, the herald goes forth and proclaims, *He shall not have too much silver and gold* (Deut. 17:17).

E. When he goes up to take his seat on the fourth step, the herald goes forth and proclaims, *He shall not pervert justice.*

F. When he goes up to take his seat on the fifth step, the herald goes forth and proclaims, *...show favor.*

G. When he goes up to take his seat on the sixth, step, the herald goes forth and proclaims, *...or take bribes* (Deut. 16:9).

H. When he comes to take his seat on the seventh step, he says, "Know before whom you take your seat."

4. A. *And the top of the throne was round behind* (1 Kgs. 10:19):

B. Said R. Aha, "It was like the throne of Moses."

C. *And there were arms on either side of the throne by the place of the seat* (1 Kgs. 10:19):

D. How so? There was a sceptre of gold suspended from behind, with a dove on the top, and a crown of gold in the dove's mouth, and he would sit under it on the Sabbath, and it would touch but not quite touch.

5. A. The six corresponded to the six firmaments.

B. But are they not seven?

    C.   Said R. Abia, "The one where the King dwells is royal property [not counted with what belongs to the world at large]."

We proceed with the detailed exposition of the verse at hand. The focus of interest, after No. 1, is on the reason for bringing six wagons. The explanations, Nos. 2 (+3-4), 5, relate to the creation of the world, the Torah, the life of Israel, the religious duties of the king, and the universe above. The underlying motif, the tabernacle as the point at which the supernatural world of Israel meets the supernatural world of creation, is carried forward.

I:VIII

1. A.   *[...came forward and brought their offering before the Lord , six] covered [wagons and twelve oxen, one wagon from every two chiefs and from each one an ox]* (Num. 7:2):

    B.   The word for covered wagons may be read to yield these meanings:

    C.   like a lizard-skin [B&K, p. 17: "it signifies that the outer surface of the wagons' frames was as delicately reticulated as the skin of a lizard"];

    D.   [and the same word may be read to indicate that the wagons were] decorated, or fully equipped.

    E.   It has been taught in the name of R. Nehemiah, "They were like a bent bow."

2. A.   *...twelve oxen, one wagon from every two chiefs ...:*

    B.   This indicates that two chiefs would together bring one wagon, while each tribe gave an ox.

3. A.   *These they brought forward before the tabernacle* (Num. 7:3):

    B.   This teaches that they turned them into their monetary value and sold them to the congregation at large [so that everyone had a share in the donation].

4. A.   *And the Lord spoke to Moses and said, [Accept these from them: they shall be used for the service of the tent of the presence"]:* (Num. 7:5):

    B.   What is the meaning of the word, *and said?*

    C.   R. Hoshaia taught, "The Holy One, blessed be He, said to Moses, 'Go and say to Israel words of praise and consolation.'

    D.   "Moses was afraid, saying, 'But is it not possible that the holy spirit and abandoned me and come to rest on the chiefs?'

    E.   "The Holy One, said to him, 'Moses, had I wanted them to bring their offering, I should have said to you to "say to them," [so instructing them to do so], but *Take – it is from them [at their own volition, not by my inspiration]* (Num. 7:5) is the language that meaning, they did it on their own volition [asnd have not received the holy spirit].'"

5. A.   And who gave them the good ideas [of making the gift]?

    B.   It was the tribe of sdimeon who gave them the good idea, in line with this verse: *And of the children of Issachar came men who had understanding of the times* (1 Chr. 12:33).

    C.   What is the sense of *the times?*

    D.   R. Tanhuma said, "The ripe hour [*kairos*]."

    E.   R. Yose bar Qisri said, "Intercalating the calendar."

    F.   *They had two hundred heads* (1 Chr. 12:33):

G. This refers to the two hundred heads of sanhedrins that were produced by the tribe of Issachar.

H. *And all of their brethren were subject to their orders* (1 Chr. 12:33):

I. This teaches that the law would accord with their rulings.

J. They said to the community, "Is this tent of meeting which you are making going to fly in the air? Make wagons for it, which will bear it."

6. A. Moses was concerned, saying, "Is it possible that one of the wagons might break, or one of the oxen die, so that the offering of the chiefs might be invalid?"

B. Said to Moses the Holy One, blessed be He, *They shall be used for the service of the tent of the presence* (Num. 7:5).

C. "To them has been given a long-term existence."

7. A. How long did they live?

B. R. Yudan in the name of R. Samuel bar Nahman, R. Honia in the name of Bar Qappara, *"In Gilgal they sacrificed the oxen* (Hos. 12:12)."

C. And where did they offer them up?

D. R. Abba bar Kahana said, "In Nob they offered them up."

E. R. Abbahu said, "In Gibeon they offered them up."

F. R. Hama bar Hanina said, "In the eternal house [of Jerusalem] they offered them up."

G. Said R. Levi, "A verse of Scripture supporting the view of R. Hama bar Hanina: *Solomon offered a sacrifice of peace-offerings, which he slaughtered for the Lord, twenty-two thousand oxen* (1 Kgs. 8:63)."

H. It was taught in the name of R. Meir, "They endure even to now, and they never produced a stink, got old, or produced an invalidating blemish."

I. Now that produces an argument a fortiori:

J. If the oxen, who cleaved to the work of the making of the tent of meeting, were given an eternal existence, Israel, who cleave to the Holy One, blessed be He, how much the more so!

K. *And you have cleave to the Lord your God are alive, all of you, this day* (Deut. 4:4).

The exegesis of the verse in its own terms leads us through the several phrases, No. 1, 2, 3. No. 4, continuing at No. 6, with an important complement at No. 5, goes on to its own interesting question. No. 7 serves No. 6 as No. 6 serves No. 5.

It seems superfluous at this point to observe that the one group of exegetes have virtually nothing in common with the other, even though, at some few points, the exegetes of Pesiqta deRab Kahana go over ground covered by those in Sifré Numbers. What one set of sages wishes to know in the verse of Scripture at hand scarcely coincides with the program of the other. The comparison of *midrashim* in this case yields a picture of differences so profound as to call into question the premise with which we started, which is that the authorships of the two documents derive from the same movement, share the same viewpoint, and therefore exhibit sufficient traits in common to justify our comparing the exegetical results of the one with those produced by the other. Once we undertake the comparison we find nothing in common: nothing.

IV

The Primacy of Documentary Discourse

We revert to the false proposition and now consider the correct one. The false proposition is that the verse, not the document, is the generative category. The correct proposition is that the document forms the primary framework of discourse. We have first to appeal to the concerns of the compilers and framers and editors of the document in which a given midrash-exegesis appears, asking about their context and interests and how these may or may not have shaped what they say about any given verse of Scripture. The primacy of documentary discourse, of course, in no way excludes other ranges of inquiry, whether philological or psychological, philosophical or theological, including the range of interest expressed in Kugel's definition(s) of midrash. But the entry into the interpretation of midrash-exegesis opens when we take up a midrash-compilation and open it. The present case by itself may form an exception, but it is noteworthy in itself. And, as I said, I can amass volumes of cases, which, all together, in my view demonstrate the facts of the matter. The premise of Kugel's reading of midrash-literature certainly appears to quake when the weight of these facts comes to bear.

For the upshot is that the two authorships go their respective ways, with little to say to one another. They may be characterized as *different people talking with reference to the same thing about different things to different people.* That is because the approach of each set of exegetes to the base-verse derives from a clearly-defined program of inquiry, one that imposes its issues on the base-verse but scarcely responds to the base-verse except in the verse's provision of exemplary detail for the main point already determined by the exegetes. Accordingly, neither of the documents merely assembles this and that, forming a hodgepodge of things people happen to have said. In the case of each document we can answer the question: Why this, not that? They are not compilations but compositions; seen as a group, therefore, (to state matters negatively) they are not essentially the same, lacking all viewpoint, serving a single undifferentiated task of collecting and arranging whatever was at hand.

Quite to the contrary, these documents of the Oral Torah's exegesis of the written Torah emerge as rich in differences from one another and sharply defined each through its distinctive viewpoints and particular polemics, on the one side, and formal and aesthetic qualities, on the other. We deal with a canon, yes, but with a canon made up of highly individual documents. But that, after all, is what a canon is: a mode of classification that takes a library and turns it into a cogent if composite statement. A canon comprises separate books that all together make a single statement. In terms of the Judaism of the dual Torah, the canon is what takes scriptures of various kinds and diverse points of origin and turns scriptures into Torah, and commentaries on those scriptures into Torah as well, making them all into the one whole Torah – of Moses, our rabbi. In starting, rather than ending, with the indicative character of the verse under discussion as the pricipitant of exegesis, Kugel has profoundly misunderstood the character of the Judaism of the dual Torah. That Judaism begins with the dual Torah, articulated through its diverse documentary components, realized in full and rich detail through their various statements: from whole to parts, from main proposition to illustrative detail. The primary framework of discourse finds definition in the document, which, in secular terms, stands for what, in theological ones, we call the Torah.

Chapter Three

Pattern and Proposition: Different People Saying Some of the Same Things in Different Ways

...midrash is an exegesis of biblical verses, not of books. The basic unit of the Bible for the midrashist is the verse: this is what he seeks to expound, and it might be said that there simply is no boundary encountered beyond that of the verse until one comes to the borders of the canon itself.[1]

Our midrashic compilations are in this sense potentially deceiving, since they seem to treat the whole text bit by bit; but with the exception of certain patterns, these "bits" are rather atomistic, and, as any student or rabbinic literature knows, interchangeable, modifiable, combinable – in short, not part of an overall exegesis at all.[2]

James Kugel

False Proposition II: Concerning Pattern and Proposition:
Modes of rhetoric transcend documentary lines because documents of midrash-compilations make no mark on midrash-exegesis

If the scriptural verse does not form the generative category for the study of the Judaic biblical interpretation called midrash, then we turn to a positive statement of the same implicit premise that documentary divisions make no difference in the interpretation of midrash-exegesis. It is that we may ignore documentary lines, because the rhetorical principles of midrash apply

---

[1]P. 93.

[2]P. 95.

indifferently to all documents that present midrash.[3] This is Kugel's explicit position, which he states in two different ways. Is it true?

In analyzing modes of expression, the forms of patterned speech, which predominate in the literature at hand and dictate to all authorships how they will give expression to their ideas – the premise of Kugel's definition(s) maintains – we may treat as null also the frontiers of documents, the limns and limits of their context and setting. Consequently, no context contributes its data to the interpretation of midrash, and everything may be read in the context of eternity, there alone. Because of that proposition, moreover, the actualities of the text, the "particular structure of meaning that the author intended to convey,"[4] and the realities of the situation of the authorship do not intersect. We note that Kugel's appreciation of the rhetorical character of midrash-documents exhibits certain flaws. He that accounts for his misrepresentation of the character of a passage he quotes concerning Gen. 21:1:

> Thus for example Genesis Rabbah assembles a host of opinions aimed at explaining away the apparent pleonasm of Gen. 21:1.
>
> And the Lord remembered Sarah as he had *said* [refers to the promises of God] introduced [in the text] by [the verb] say [as, e.g., God's promise in Gen. 17:19...]

Kugel proceeds to translate the passage, imposing a complete commentary through the device of adding language in square brackets. But his translation obscures the formal character of the passage, yielding this result:

> *Such countenancing of contradictory interpretations reflects on the essence of midrashic writings* per se, which are not compositions but compilations of comments that are usually focused on isolated, individual verses. *Consistency within individual sections of a midrash or even in larger units was apparently not an overriding consideration* [italics supplied].

Now what the passage in fact presents is a dispute between two sages, Nehemiah and Judah, who very commonly in Genesis Rabbah are given juxtaposted

---

[3]That is why, for example, another member of the *Prooftexts* coterie, David Stern, ignores the documentary variable in discussing the parable or mashal, treating all usages of that literary genre equally, without regard to the documents in which the data occur. As a result he cannot tell us whether the mashal in document A follows the same formal plan and carries through the same rhetorical or logical program as does the mashal in document B. Since the mashal forms a subdivision of the division, narrative, he further cannot explain differences exhibited by documents in their authorships' utilization of the genus, narrative. For a contrary reading of the genus, narrative, in accord with its species, among them, parable, see my *Judaism and Story: The Evidence of The Fathers According to Rabbi Nathan* (Chicago, anticipated for 1988: University of Chicago Press).

[4]Scott, p. 418.

positions. The dispute-form is standard in numerous rabbinic documents, from the Mishnah through the Talmud of Babylonia. It is followed with precision in the passage under discussion. Let me present the passage as Kugel does, then give it in its formal perfection:

> R. Nehemiah said, "As he had said" means what he had said to her by means of an angel; "as he had spoken" means he himself [Gen. 18:10 vs. 16:16]. R. Yehuda said, "And the Lord remembered Sarah" – to give her a son; "and the Lord did for Sarah" to bless her with milk...

But properly presenting the passage in line with what one might call its poetics requires the following:

> R. Nehemiah said, "As he had said" means what he had said to her by means of an angel; "as he had spoken" means he himself [Gen. 18:10 vs. 16:16]...
>
> R. Yehuda said, "And the Lord remembered Sarah" – to give her a son; "and the Lord did for Sarah" to bless her with milk...

What we have is a carefully balanced statement of opposing positions on a shared topic, the meaning of the verse(s) under discussion. The form is a commonplace, and it serves in legal and exegetical documents alike to collect and arrange conflicting opinion on a common problem. It is certainly not characteristic of midrash-compilations alone (to use Kugel's language) *as any student or rabbinic literature knows.*

Kugel ignores the ubiquity of the form because he does not understand it. The conclusions he draws therefore are awry. He thinks the presentation before us is distinctive to midrash-compilations: *Such countenancing of contradictory interpretations reflects on the essence of midrashic writings per se.* But then the essence of midrashic writings is the same as the essence of halakhic writings, in which the identical form is everywhere dominant. Kugel's definition of what is essential to midrash writings therefore rests upon a misrepresentation, unless Kugel regards the *halakhic* writings as *midrashic* – for "such countenancing of contradictory interpretations" in precisely the same form and for precisely the same rhetorical purpose is commonplace in the entirety of the documentary corpus of the Judaism of the dual Torah, and the Mishnah is only the beginning of the matter. What, then we are to make of Kugel's inference, "Consistency within individual sections of a midrash or even in larger units was apparently not an overriding consideration," I cannot say. Since "individual sections" of the halakhic literature assemble diverse opinions in precisely the same way, Kugel seems to think that the rabbinic documents simply threw things together without attention to proportion, cogency, and consistency. But the opposite is the fact, as I shall demonstrate on both rhetorical, logical and topical grounds, in the next five chapters. Documents exhibit rhetorical consistency. They follow a clearcut program of intelligible discourse. They make points and argue propositions and present syllogisms. Kugel's claim that Midrash-documents simply assemble this and that without regard for large-scale consistency and that the passage he has cited demonstrates that fact suggest a certain flawed grasp of the literature at hand. My sense is that he is simply saying things. Anyone who maintained that "Consistency within individual sections of a Mishnah" or "...of a halakhic discourse," in which the same formal arrangement of conflicting viewpoints is commonplace, would be judged uninformed. The considerable misrepresentation here (Kugel's dismissal of rhetorical formalization, at the small, medium, and large scale of composition,...*the exception of certain patterns*...in fact treats as "exceptional" nearly the whole of the compositions of which the documents are composed as well as the documents themselves, as I shall show) derives from Kugel's indifference to rhetorical data, a curious lapse in a literary critic writing in a volume on *Midrash and Literature.* But let us turn to the positive issue: is it true, as Kugel claims, that *these "bits" are rather atomistic, and, as any student or rabbinic literature knows, interchangeable,*[5] *modifiable, combinable?* If rhetorical forms float intact from document to document, then Kugel's judgment rests on the traits of the documents he claims to define. If rhetorical forms exhibit important variations as they move from document to document, then Kugel is wrong. To examine the matter, I take a form that received scholarship treats as interchangeable, modifiable, combinable (to use Kugel's catalogue of words), namely, the so-called *petihta*-form, in which a passage concerning a given verse opens with citation and exegesis of a verse deriving from a different book of Scripture. I shall define matters with greater precision in a moment.

I

Rhetorical Forms as Variables between Documents

Questions about the message of a document in its place and time of origin, the purpose of the authorship in selecting these materials and not others, in arranging them in this order and not in a different order (or in no perceptible order at all) – these may be set aside. They simply do not pertain. The proof derives from the character of the rhetorical program of the literature, midrash, as a

---

[5]Kugel seems to think that documents are made up mainly of floating sources, which can be used equally well everywhere and anywhere. That is not correct. Those documents which I have surveyed in detail are made up mainly of materials that are unique and not shared with other compilations, e.g., Leviticus Rabbah's parashiyyot probed by me prove 95% singular, less than 5% made up of materials that occur elsewhere. The issue is more complicated, of course, since the Talmud of Babylonia tends to draw heavily on prior literature. But Kugel is not talking about that Talmud (and is wrong about the other one). The "interchangeability" of pericopes is an exceedingly complicated question, and I imagine that, upon reflection, Kugel may wish to choose a different way of characterizing the established fact that some stories and sayings move from one document to another – and that a vast majority of the stories and sayings of the rabbinic canon of late antiquity do not and are unique to the document in which they occur.

whole. Since – this proposition has it – that rhetoric imparts its configuration on all documents equally, all documents are created equal, and none responds to a particular situation – let alone expressing the particular structure of meaning that its authorship intended to convey.

The refutation of this proposition consists in a detailed demonstration that what looks alike is not necessary alike at all, and that the authorships of two documents in using essentially the same form or rhetorical pattern in fact place the mark of their distinctive rhetorical programs, respectively, on the shared arrangement of words. Specifically, a rhetorical program effects a (prior) logical one, and the logical one is shaped in order to carry through the needs of syllogistic discourse of a cogent character. How an authorship wishes to define and present its syllogisms, therefore, will affect the rhetorical plans that dictate how ideas will reach expression not solely in words – propositional statements – but in arrangements of words – the pattern of language, e.g., the recurrent of syntactic forms.

If therefore I can show that the same people say in a different way pretty much the same thing, then I shall set aside the proposition that we may treat all documents equally and therefore as no variable at all. For if all documents share a single undifferentiated plane, because all share the same stylistic, rhetorical program, then the document does not define an arena for discourse at all, and we justifiably ignore documentary lines in interpreting what we find in the midrash-compilations, namely, exegesis-midrash. Since – it must follow within the present hypothesis – documents tell us nothing about their contents, being insufficiently differentiated on (mere) formal grounds, we may bypass all questions of a documentary character, e.g., the plan and program of a distinctive authorship, the context and circumstance and world-view of that authorship.

To test this hypothesis that the rhetoric transcends documentary lines, I take a subtle and therefore improbable case. It is the one of the composition of opening passages of a sustained chapter of a midrash-compilation through juxtaposing two verses of Scripture. One of these verses of Scripture will recur throughout the chapter, and I call it the base-verse, for it forms the basis for discourse of from three to twenty-five distinct paragraphs or completed units of thought. The other of these verses does not recur in the chapter at hand; it does not derive from the book of Scripture that is subject to discussion in that document. It emerges from some other book of Scripture. I call this other verse the intersecting-verse. Now in the opening segments of chapters of a number of midrash-compilations, we find a rhetorical pattern that cites an intersecting-verse and then a base-verse. The meeting of the two generates a syllogism, a proposition that can be stated in so many words and that (very commonly) emerges solely from the meeting of the two verses. That syllogism may be made explicit, though, more commonly, it is implicit and runs through the entire chapter or large stretches of it.

The rhetorical pattern of the intersecting-verse/base-verse characterizes a variety of midrash-compilations. Ordinarily, where it occurs, the same compilation will resort to a second rhetorical pattern, arranged, in sequence, after the intersecting-verse/base-verse one. This second pattern will focus upon the elements of the base-verse itself, and read each component of which it is made up in a systematic way, commonly, though not invariably, yielding from each a syllogism of some sort of another. That fact is important for what is to follow.

Now the experiment I have devised to test what I call False Proposition II is simple, and its requirements difficult to meet. What I want to know is whether when the same rhetorical pattern occurs in two documents, we can distinguish the utilization of that pattern in one document from its utilization in the other. If I can, it means that – in general – rhetorical patterns will undergo variation and accommodation to accord with the documentary plan of an authorship. And, once more, it must follow that the authorship intervenes and imposes its plan and program upon the materials of which it makes use. We therefore cannot ignore the lines of documentary boundaries when we propose to interpret midrash-exegesis, for, even on formal grounds, we realize, the document imposes its larger scheme – and therefore, the implicit facts of its context, as much as the implicit syllogism of its authorship, upon whatever the document in the end presents: the entirety of its contents of midrash-exegeses.

Of the twenty-eight *pisqaot* of Pesiqta deRab Kahana, five occur also in Leviticus Rabbah. If a chapter, or *pisqa,* occurs in two documents, does that mean that the documentary boundaries impose no variations on the shared materials? If I cannot distinguish the shared materials and demonstrate that the conform to the rhetorical plan of one document and violate that of the other, the upshot will be simple: documentary lines do not mark differences on the contents of shared materials. Then, as I said, our proposition that modes of rhetoric transcend documentary lines finds support, and the contrary proposition, that documents impose choices of a formal and rhetorical character, contradicts the facts.

But I shall now show that the *pisqaot* that occur in both Leviticus Rabbah and Pesiqta deRab Kahana in fact are distinctive, therefore primary, to Leviticus Rabbah and violate the rhetorical preferences characteristic of the twenty-three *pisqaot* that are unique to Pesiqta deRab Kahana and therefore taken over whole by that authorship. That fact will then close the possibility that materials produced we know not where were chosen at random and promiscuously by the framers of diverse documents and will demonstrate the opposite. The authorships of documents, illustrated here by that of Pesiqta deRab Kahana, followed a clearly-defined rhetorical plan. That plan, moreover, may be shown to be distinctive to the document that the authorship has created by comparison of pericopae of a document that are shared with other documents to those that are unique to the document at hand. Documents, therefore define the initial arena for discourse, and, it must follow, the circumstances of the authorships of documents demand heuristic consideration and the distinctive plan and program of the respective authorships requires hermeneutical attention in the reading of what is collected in the various documents.

In order to demonstrate these propositions, I have first to establish the traits of the rhetorical plan of Pesiqta deRab Kahana. This I do inductively, by dealing first with a single *pisqa,* then with two further *pisqaot,* so showing that rhetorically distinctive forms paramount in one *pisqa* in fact define the rhetorical plan of two others. (In a separate study I prove that the same rhetorical plan defines the entire document.) Then I compare the rhetorical forms of Pesiqta deRab Kahana with the forms of a *parashah* of Leviticus Rabbah that occurs also in Pesiqta deRab Kahana. I am able to demonstrate that the characteristic forms of the latter do not occur in the shared *pisqa/parashah* at all, and that other forms do. I am further able to explain the rhetorical differences between the two documents. We begin with our initial exercise, the proposal of a hypothesis on the definitive rhetorical program of the document. While the required demonstration requires detailed attention to a sizable sample of midrash-exegeses, I believe the effort necessary to show in detail the profound misrepresentation of the character of the midrash-compilation of midrash-exegeses, therefore also of the conditions for the definition of the midrash-process, presented by Kugel. The refutation of the position represented by Kugel on the differentiation of rhetoric by documents once more lays the weight of evidence against the larger definition(s) of midrash he purports to provide.

Let now me spell out what we are now to do, since the exercise is protracted. But I do not believe it will prove tedious. As we shall see, the intersecting-verse/base-verse characterizes Pesiqta deRab Kahana, as an inductive review of the intrinsic evidence demonstrates in the following protracted exercise. That same arrangement of verses and syllogistic expression through that arrangement characterizes Leviticus Rabbah, as I shall show presently. But the rhetorical programs in fact exhibit fundamental differences in the respective documents, so, when two authorships use what appears to be a single rhetorical form, they in fact impose important variations upon it, and these variations furthermore may be shown to express a deeper policy of syllogistic expression characteristic of one authorship and not the other.

There is a further issue, which is not solely to validate, but also to impose a test of falsification. That permits us to claim to know not only that we are right, but also whether or not we may be wrong. A test of falsification comes to hand specifically in the analysis of the traits of the rhetorical form involving the clause by clause exegesis of the base-verse.

For the second shared form, the systematic exegesis of the base-verse, involving citation of a clause, a brief explanation of that clause, then citation of the next clause of the same verse in sequence, involving explanation of that, also varies in its syllogistic character from the one document to the other. Just as readily as in the case of the intersecting-verse/base-verse form, we shall identify the rhetorical program of one document and differentiate that program, even in the case of what appears to be as form in common, from the rhetorical program of the other, so we can differentiate yet the second form shared by the two authorships. *And we can explain the differences.* Specifically, as we shall see, the basic mode of discourse chosen by one authorship requires that authorship to make use of a shared rhetorical form in a way congruent to its profound syllogistic purpose, whether cogent or diffuse.

It remains to explain that I use some analytical language that requires definition at the outset. Specifically, I refer, first, to contrastive-verse and base-verse, and these prove to be the prime building blocks of rhetorical analysis. The base-verse, as I noted just now, is the recurrent verse of Scripture that defines the point of recurrent reference for all *pisqaot* but two or three. I call it base-verse simply because it forms the basis of all discourse and imparts unity to each *pisqa*. The contrastive-verse is a verse that will be introduced to clarify the meaning of the base-verse. The contrast between the one and the other then yields a syllogism, and the purpose of the whole, as I shall show, is that syllogistic discourse. While in the body of the translation, I have used the language appropriate in earlier documents, hence intersecting-verse (explained above) and base-verse, here a more exact usage is required, because, as I have noted, the function of the intersecting-verse in Leviticus Rabbah, which is to permit extended discussion of everything but the base-verse, here shifts. Now the function of the outside verse (here: contrastive-verse) is to establish the main point of the syllogism, and it is in the intersecting of the contrastive-verse and the base-verse that that syllogism is brought to clear statement. We shall see, overall, that Pesiqta deRab Kahana presents its syllogisms in a far more powerful and direct medium of rhetoric than does Leviticus Rabbah.

Second, I have already referred to an *implicit syllogism.* By syllogism I mean a proposition that forms the recurrent principle a *pisqa* wishes to express and to prove in the way its authorship deems plausible and compelling. It is implicit because it is never stated in so many words, yet it is readily recognized and repeatedly imputed to one set of verses after another. The implicit syllogism, as we shall see, reaches expression in one of two ways, one through what I call propositional form, the other through exegetical form. Let me state with appropriate emphasis the rhetorical program represented by the two forms we shall now discern. *Both are ways of stating in the idiom our authorship has chosen, in the media of expression they have preferred, and through the modes of demonstration and evidentiary proof they deem probative, a truth they never spell out but always take for granted we shall recognize and adopt.*

II
Literary Structures of Pesiqta deRab Kahana *Pisqa* 6

VI:I

1. A. *If I were hungry, I would not tell you, for the world and all that is in it are mine. [Shall I eat the flesh of your bulls or drink the blood of he-goats? Offer to God the sacrifice of thanksgiving and pay your vows to the Most High. If you call upon me in time of trouble, I will come to your rescue and you shall honor me]* (Ps. 50:12-15):

B. Said R. Simon, "There are thirteen traits of a merciful character that are stated in writing concerning the Holy One, blessed be He.

C. "That is in line with this verse of Scripture: *The Lord passed by before him and proclaimed, The Lord, the Lord, God, merciful and gracious, long-suffering and abundant in goodness and truth; keeping mercy unto the thousandth generation, forgiving iniquity, transgression, and sin, who will be no means clear* (Ex. 34:6-7).

D. "Now is there a merciful person who would hand over his food to a cruel person [who would have to slaughter a beast so as to feed him]?

E. "One has to conclude: *If I were hungry, I would not tell you.*"

2. A. Said R. Judah bar Simon, "Said the Holy One, blessed be He, 'There are ten beasts that are clean that I have handed over to you [as valid for eating], three that are subject to your dominion, and seven that are not subject to your dominion.

B. "'Which are the ones that are subject to your dominion? *The ox, sheep, and he-goat* (Deut. 14:4).

C. "'Which are the ones not subject to your dominion? *The hart, gazelle, roebuck, wild goat, ibex, antelope, and mountain sheep* (Deut. 14:5).

D. "'Now [in connection with the sacrificial cult] have I imposed on you the trouble of going hunting in hills and mountains to bring before me an offering of one of those that are not in your dominion?

E. "'Have I not said to you only to bring what is in your dominion and what is nourished at your stall?'

F. "Thus: *If I were hungry, I would not tell you.*"

3. A. Said R. Isaac, "It is written, *[The Lord spoke to Moses and said, Give this command to the Israelites:] See that you present my offerings, the food for the food-offering of soothing odor, to me at the appointed time. [Tell them: This is the food-offering which you shall present to the Lord: the regular daily whole-offering of two yearling rams without blemish. One you shall sacrifice in the morning and the second between dusk and dark]* (Num. 28:1-4).

B. "Now is there any consideration of eating and drinking before Me?

C. "'Should you wish to take the position that indeed there is a consideration of eating and drinking before me, derive evidence to the contrary from my angels, derive evidence to the contrary from my ministers: *...who makes the winds your messengers, and flames of fire your servants* (Ps. 104:4).

D. "'Whence then do they draw sustenance? From the splendor of the Presence of God.

E. "'For it is written, *In the light of the presence of the King they live* (Prov. 16:15).'"

F. R. Haggai in the name of R. Isaac: *"You have made heaven, the heaven of heavens...the host...and you keep them alive* (Neh. 9:6, meaning, you provide them with livelihood [Leon Nemoy, cited by Braude and Kapstein, p. 125, n. 4]."

4. A. Said R. Simeon b. Laqish, "It is written, *This was the regular whole-offering made at Mount Sinai, a soothing odor, a food-offering to the Lord* (Num. 28:6).

    B. "[God says,] 'Now is there any consideration of eating and drinking before Me?

    C. "'Should you wish to take the position that indeed there is a consideration of eating and drinking before me, derive evidence to the contrary from Moses, concerning whom it is written, *And he was there with the Lord for forty days and forty nights. Bread he did not eat, and water he did not drink* (Ex. 34:28).

    D. "'Did he see me eating or drinking?

    E. "'Now that fact yields an argument *a fortiori*: now if Moses, who went forth as my agent, did not eat bread or drink water for forty days, is there going to be any consideration of eating and drinking before me?

    F. "Thus: *If I were hungry, I would not tell you."*

5. A. Said R. Hiyya bar Ba, "'Things that I have created do not need [to derive sustenance] from things that I have created, am I going to require sustenance from things that I have created?

    B. "'Have you ever in your life heard someone say, 'Give plenty of wine to this vine, for it produces a great deal of wine'?

    C. "'Have you ever in your life heard someone say, 'Give plenty of oil to this olive tree, for it produces a great deal of oil'?

    D. "'Things that I have created do not need [to derive sustenance] from things that I have created, am I going to require sustenance from things that I have created?'

    E. "Thus: *If I were hungry, I would not tell you."*

6. A. Said R. Yannai, "Under ordinary circumstances if someone passes though the flood of a river, is it possible for him to drink a mere two or three *logs* of water? [Surely not. He will have to drink much more to be satisfied.]

    B. "[God speaks:] 'But as for Me, I have written that a mere single *log* of your wine shall I drink, and from that I shall derive full pleasure and satisfaction.'"

    C. R. Hiyya taught on Tannaite authority, *"The wine for the proper drink-offering shall be a quarter of a hin for each ram; you are to pour out this strong drink in the holy place as an offering to the Lord* (Num. 28:7).

    D. "This statement bears the sense of drinking to full pleasure, satisfaction, and even inebriation."

7. A. Yose bar Menassia in the name of R. Simeon b. Laqish, "When the libation was poured out, the stoppers [of the altar's drains] had to be stopped up [Braude and Kapstein, p. 126: so that the wine overflowing the altar would make it appear that God could not swallow the wine fast enough]."

    B. Said R. Yose bar Bun, "The rule contained in the statement made by R. Simeon b. Laqish is essential to the proper conduct of the rite [and if the drains are not stopped up, the libation-offering is invalid and must be repeated]."

8. A. [God speaks:] "I assigned to you the provision of a single beast, and you could not carry out the order. [How then are you going to find the resources actually to feed me? It is beyond your capacity to do so.]'

   B. "And what is that? It is *the Behemoth on a thousand hills* (Ps. 50:10)."

   C. R. Yohanan, R. Simeon b. Laqish, and rabbis:

   D. R. Yohanan said, "It is a single beast, which crouches on a thousand hills, and the thousand hills produce fodder, which it eats. What verse of Scripture so indicates? *Now behold Behemoth which I made...Surely the mountains bring him forth food* (Job 40:15)."

   E. R. Simeon b. Laqish said, "It is a single beast, which crouches on a thousand hills, and the thousand hills produce all sorts of food for the meals of the righteous in the coming age.

   F. "What verse of Scripture so indicates? *Flocks shall range over Sharon and the Vale of Achor be a pasture for cattle; they shall belong to my people who seek me* (Is. 65:10)."

   G. Rabbis said, ""It is a single beast, which crouches on a thousand hills, and the thousand hills produce cattle, which it eats.

   H. "And what text of Scripture makes that point? *And all beasts of the field play there* (Job 40:20)."

   I. But can cattle eat other cattle?

   J. Said R. Tanhuma, *"Great are the works of our God* (Ps. 111:2), how curious are the works of the Holy One, blessed be He."

   K. And whence does it drink?

   L. It was taught on Tannaite authority: R. Joshua b. Levi said, "Whatever the Jordan river collects in six months it swallows up in a single gulp.

   M. "What verse of Scripture indicates it? *If the river is in spate, he is not scared, he sprawls at his ease as the Jordan flows to his mouth* (Job 40:23)."

   N. Rabbis say, "Whatever the Jordan river collects in twelve months it swallows up in a single gulp.

   O. "What verse of Scripture indicates it? *...he sprawls at his ease as the Jordan flows to his mouth* (Job 40:23).

   P. "And that suffices merely to wet his whistle."

   Q. R. Huna in the name of R. Yose: "It is not even enough to wet his whistle."

   R. Then whence does it drink?

   S. R. Simeon b. Yohai taught on Tannaite authority, *"And a river flowed out of Eden* (Gen. 2:10), and its name is Yubal, and from there it drinks, as it is said, *That spreads out its roots by Yubal* (Jer. 17:8)."

   T. It was taught on Tannaite authority in the name of R. Meir, *"But ask now the Behemoth* (Job 12:7) – this is *the Behemoth of the thousand hills* (Ps. 50:10), *and the fowl of the heaven will tell you* (Job 12:7), that is the *ziz*-bird (Ps. 50:10), *or speak to the earth that it tell you* (Job 12:8) – this refers to the Garden of Eden. Or *let the fish of the sea tell you* (Job 12:8) – this refers to Leviathan.

   U. *"Who does not know among all these that the hand of the Lord has done this* (Job 12:9)."

9. A. "I gave you a single king, and you could not provide for him. [How then are you going to find the resources actually to feed me? It is beyond your capacity to do so.] And who was that? It was Solomon, son of David."

B. *The bread required by Solomon in a single day was thirty kors of fine flower and sixty kors of meal* (1 Kgs. 5:2).

C. Said R. Samuel bar R. Isaac, "These were kinds of snacks. But as to his regular meal, no person could provide it: *Ten fat oxen* (1 Kgs 5:3), fattened with fodder, *and twenty oxen out of the pasture and a hundred sheep* (1 Kgs 5:3), also out of the pasture; *and harts, gazelles, roebucks, and fatted fowl* (1 Kgs. 5:3)."

D. What are these fatted fowl?

E. R. Berekhiah in the name of R. Judah said, "They were fowl raised in a vivarium."

F. And rabbis say, "It is a very large bird, of high quality, much praised, which would go up and be served on the table of Solomon every day."

G. Said R. Judah bar Zebida, "Solomon had a thousand wives, and every one of them made a meal of the same dimensions as this meal. Each thought that he might dine with her."

H. "Thus: *If I were hungry, I would not tell you.*"

10. A. "One mere captive I handed over to you, and you could barely sustain him too. [How then are you going to find the resources actually to feed me? It is beyond your capacity to do so.]"

B. And who was that? It was Nehemiah, the governor:

C. *Now that which was prepared for one day was one ox and six choice sheep, also fowls were prepared for me, and once in ten days store of all sorts of wine; yet for all this I demanded not the usual fare provided for the governor, because the service was heavy upon this people* (Neh. 5:18).

D. What is *the usual fare provided for the governor?*

E. Huna bar Yekko said, "[Braude and Kapstein, p. 114:] It means gourmet food carefully cooked in vessels standing upon tripods."

F. "Thus: *If I were hungry, I would not tell you.*"

11. A. It has been taught on Tannaite authority: **The incense is brought only after the meal** (M. Ber. 6:6).

B. Now is it not the case that the sole enjoyment that the guests derive from the incense is the scent?

C. Thus said the Holy One, blessed be He, "My children, among all the offerings that you offer before me, I derive pleasure from you only because of the scent: *the food for the food-offering of soothing odor, to me at the appointed time.*

The passage commences with what is clearly the contrastive-verse, Ps. 50:12, which stands in stark contrast to the base-verse, Num. 28:1ff., because what the latter requires, the former denigrates. No. 1 is open-ended, in that it does not draw us back to the base-verse at all. It simply underlines one meaning to be imputed to the contrastive-verse. No. 2 pursues the theme of the base-verse – the selection of beasts for the altar – and reverts to the intersecting one. Nos. 3, 4 and 5 then draw us back to the base-verse, but in a rather odd way. They treat it as simply another verse awaiting consideration, not as the climax of the exercise of explication of the many senses of the contrastive-verse. The purpose of the composition before us is not to explore the meanings of the contrastive-verse, bringing one of them to illuminate, also, the base-verse. The purpose of the composition before us is to make a single point, to argue a single proposition, through a single-minded repertoire of relevant materials, each of which makes the same point as all the others. We may say that if a principal interest of the components of Leviticus Rabbah is exegetical, another principal interest, syllogistic, the sole interest of our authorship in the type of form before us is to invoke a contrastive-verse to make the point that the base-verse must be shown to establish. Before explaining the implications of that simple fact, let me complete the review of the whole.

I see No. 5 as the conclusion of the main event, that is to say, the contrastive-verse has laid down its judgment on the sense of the base-verse and established the syllogism. No. 6 then underlines that single point by saying that the natural world presents cases in which considerable volumes of food or drink are necessary to meet this-worldly requirements. How then can we hope to meet the supernatural requirements of God? That point, made at No. 6, 8, 9, and 10, is essentially secondary to what has gone before. So we have a composition of two elements, Nos. 1-5, the systematic exposition of the base-verse in terms of the single proposition of the intersecting-verse, then No. 6-10, the secondary point that reinforces the main one. No. 11 resolves the enormous tension created by the contrast between the base-verse and the contrastive-verse. I do not need the food, but I get pleasure from the smell.

Let me now revert to the main formal point at hand. If, therefore, we were to draw a contrast between the contrastive-verse/base-verse construction as we know it in Leviticus Rabbah and the counterpart before us, we should have to see them as essentially different modes of organizing and expressing an idea. The difference may be stated very simply. Leviticus Rabbah's compositors draw on materials that systematically expound the intersecting-verse in a variety of ways, and only then draw back to the base-verse to impute to it a fresh and unusual sense, invited by one of the several possible interpretations laid out by the intersecting-verse. The framers of Pesiqta deRab Kahana, by contrast, draw upon an contrastive-verse in order to make a point – one point – which then is placed into relationship with the base-verse and which imposes its meaning on the base-verse. What this means is that our document aims at making a single point, and at doing so with a minimum of obfuscation through exploration of diverse possibilities. The function of the contrastive-verse is not to lay forth a galaxy of hermeneutical possibilities, one of which will be selected. It is, rather, to present a single point, and it is that point that we shall then impose upon our base-verse. What that fact means, overall, is that our document aims at a syllogism, expressed singly and forcefully, rather than at a diversity of explanation of a verse that, in the end, will yield a syllogism. The difference between Leviticus Rabbah's intersecting-verse and base-verse construction and Pesiqta deRab Kahana's contrastive-verse and base-verse construction is sharp and total. The form – one verse, then another verse – looks the same. But the deeper structure is utterly unrelated.

The foregoing anaysis has presented us with our first hypothetical rhetorical pattern, one formed out of the comparison and contrast of two verses of Scripture, with the result that a well-formed syllogism emerges. Let me now offer a clear description of the rhetorical pattern I believe underlies **VI:I**.

1. The Propositional Form: The implicit syllogism is stated through the intervention of an contrastive-verse into the basic proposition established by the base-verse.

This form cites the base-verse, then a contrastive-verse. Sometimes the base-verse is not cited at the outset, but it is always used to mark the conclusion of the *pisqa*. The sense of the latter is read into the former, and a syllogism is worked out, and reaches intelligible expression, through the contrast and comparison of the one and the other. There is no pretense at a systematic exegesis of the diverse meanings imputed to the contrastive-verse, only the comparison and contrast of two verses, the external or intersecting- and the base-verses, respectively. The base-verse, for its part, also is not subjected to systematic exegesis. This represents, therefore, a strikingly abstract and general syllogistic pattern, even though verses are cited to give the statement the formal character of an exegesis. But it is in no way an exegetical pattern. The purpose of this pattern is to impute to the base-verse the sense generated by the intersection of the base-verse and the contrastive-verse. Since the contrastive-verse dictates the sense to be imputed to the base-verse, therefore its fundamental proposition, we should further expect that the contrastive-verse/base-verse form will come first in the unfolding of a *pisqa,* as it does here. For any further exposition of a proposition will require a clear statement of what, in fact, is at stake in a given *pisqa,* and that, as I said, is the contribution of the contrastive-verse/base-verse form.

VI:II

1. A. *A righteous man eats his fill, [but the wicked go hungry]* (Prov. 13:25):
    B. This refers to Eliezer, our father Abraham's servant, as it is said, *Please let me have a little water to drink from your pitcher* (Gen. 24:17) – one sip.
    C. *...but the wicked go hungry:*
    D. This refers to the wicked Esau, who said to our father, Jacob, *Let me swallow some of that red pottage, for I am famished* (Gen. 28:30).
2. A. *[And Esau said to Jacob, Let me swallow some of that red pottage, for I am famished* (Gen. 25:30):]
    B. Said R. Isaac bar Zeira, "That wicked man opened up his mouth like a camel. He said to him, 'I'll open up my mouth, and you just toss in the food.'
    C. "That is in line with what we have learned in the Mishnah: **People may not stuff a camel or force food on it, but may toss food into its mouth** [M. Shab. 24:3]."
3. A. Another interpretation of the verse, *A righteous man eats his fill:*

B. This refers to Ruth the Moabite, in regard to whom it is written, *She ate, was satisfied, and left food over* (Ruth 2:14).

C. Said R. Isaac, "You have two possibilities: either a blessing comes to rest through a righteous man, or a blessing comes to rest through the womb of a righteous woman.

D. "On the basis of the verse of Scripture, *She ate, was satisfied, and left food over*, one must conclude that a blessing comes to rest through the womb of a righteous woman."

E. *...but the wicked go hungry:*

F. This refers to the nations of the world.

4. A. Said R. Meir, "Dosetai of Kokhba asked me, saying to me, "What is the meaning of the statement, *...but the wicked go hungry?*

B. "I said to him, 'There was a gentile in our town, who made a banquet for all the elders of the town, and invited me along with them. He set before us everything that the Holy One, blessed be He, had created on the six days of creation, and his table lacked only soft-shelled nuts alone.

C. "What did he do? He took the tray from before us, which was worth six talents of silver, and broke it.

D. "I said to him, 'On what account did you do this? [Why are you so angry?]'

E. "He said to me, 'My lord, you say that we own this world, and you own the world to come. If we don't do the eating now, when are we going to eat [of every good thing that has ever been created]?'

F. "I recited in his regard, *...but the wicked go hungry.*"

5. A. Another interpretation of the verse, *A righteous man eats his fill, [but the wicked go hungry]* (Prov. 13:25):

B. This refers to Hezekiah, King of Judah.

C. They say concerning Hezekiah, King of Judah, that [a mere] two bunches of vegetables and a *litra* of meat did they set before him every day.

D. And the Israelites ridiculed him, saying, "Is this a king? *And they rejoiced over Rezin and Remaliah's son* (Is. 8:6). But Rezin, son of Remaliah, is really worthy of dominion."

E. That is in line with this verse of Scripture: *Because this people has refused the waters of Shiloah that run slowly and rejoice with Rezin and Remaliah's son* (Is. 8:6).

F. What is the sense of *slowly?*

G. Bar Qappara said, "We have made the circuit of the whole of Scripture and have not found a place that bears the name spelled by the letters translated *slowly*.

H. "But this refers to Hezekiah, King of Judah, who would purify the Israelites through a purification-bath containing the correct volume of water, forty *seahs*, the number signified by the letters that spell the word for slowly."

I. Said the Holy One, blessed be He, "You praise eating? *Behold the Lord brings up the waters of the River, mighty and many, even the king of Assyria and all his glory, and he shall come up over all his channels and go over all his bands and devour you as would a glutton* (Is. 8:7)."

6. A. *...but the wicked go hungry:* this refers to Mesha.

B. *Mesha, king of Moab, was* a noked (2 Kgs. 3:4). What is the sense of *noked?* It is a shepherd.

    C.   *"He handed over to the king of Israel a hundred thousand fatted lambs and a hundred thousand wool-bearing rams (2 Kgs. 3:4)."*

    D.   What is the meaning of wool-bearing rams?

    E.   R. Abba bar Kahana said, "Unshorn."

7. A.   Another interpretation of the verse, *A righteous man eats his fill, [but the wicked go hungry]* (Prov. 13:25):

    B.   This refers to the kings of Israel and the kings of the House of David.

    C.   *...but the wicked go hungry* are the kings of the East:

    D.   R. Yudan and R. Hunah:

    E.   R. Yudan said, "A hundred sheep would be served to each one every day."

    F.   R. Hunah said, "A thousand sheep were served to each one every day."

8. A.   Another interpretation of the verse, *A righteous man eats his fill* (Prov. 13:25):

    B.   this refers to the Holy One, blessed be He.

    C.   Thus said the Holy One, blessed be He, "My children, among all the offerings that you offer before me, I derive pleasure from you only because of the scent: *the food for the food-offering of soothing odor, to me at the appointed time."*

Our contrastive-verse now makes the point that the righteous one gets what he needs, the wicked go hungry, with a series of contrasts at Nos. 1, 2, 3, 5, 6, 7, leading to No. 8: the Holy One gets pleasure from the scent of the offerings. I do not see exactly how the contrastive-verse has enriched the meaning imputed to the base-verse. What the compositors have done, rather, is to use the contrastive-verse to lead to their, now conventional, conclusion, so 8.C appears tacked on as a routine conclusion, but, as before, turns out to be the critical point of cogency for the whole. Then the main point is that God does not need the food of the offerings; at most he enjoys the scent. The same point is made as before at **VI:I.11**: what God gets out of the offering is not nourishment but merely the pleasure of the scent of the offerings. God does not eat; but he does smell. The exegesis of Prov. 13:25, however, proceeds along its own line, contrasting Eliezer and Esau, Ruth and the nations of the world, Hezekiah and Mesha, Israel's kings and the kings of the East, and then God – with no contrast at all.

VI:III

1. A.   *You have commanded your precepts to be kept diligently* (Ps. 119:4):

    B.   Where did he give this commandment? In the book of Numbers. [Braude and Kapstein, p. 132: "*In Numbers you did again ordain...* Where did God again ordain? In the Book of Numbers."]

    C.   What did he command?

    D.   *To be kept diligently* (Ps. 119:4): *The Lord spoke to Moses and said, Give this command to the Israelites: See that you present my offerings, the food for the food-offering of soothing odor, to me at the appointed time.*

    E.   That is the same passage that has already occurred [at Ex. 29:38-42] and now recurs, so why has it been stated a second time?

F.   R. Yudan, R. Nehemiah, and rabbis:

G.   R. Yudan said, "Since the Israelites thought, 'In the past there was the practice of making journeys, and there was the practice of offering daily whole offerings. Now that the journeying is over, the daily whole-offerings also are over.'

H.   "Said the Holy One, blessed be He, to Moses, 'Go, say to Israel that they should continue the practice of offering daily whole offerings.'"

I.   R. Nehemiah said, "Since the Israelites were treating the daily whole offering lightly, said the Holy One, blessed be He, to Moses, 'Go, tell Israel not to treat the daily whole offerings lightly.'"

J.   Rabbis said, "[The reason for the repetition is that] one statement serves for instruction, the other for actual practice."

2.   A.   R. Aha in the name of R. Hanina: "It was so that the Israelites should not say, 'In the past we offered sacrifices and so were engaged [in studying about] them, but now that we do not offer them any more, we also need not study about them any longer.'

B.   "Said the Holy One, blessed be He, to them, 'Since you engage in studying about them, it is as if you have actually carried them out.'"

3.   A.   R. Huna made two statements.

B.   R. Huna said, "All of the exiles will be gathered together only on account of the study of Mishnah-teachings.

C.   "What verse of Scripture makes that point? *Even when they recount [Mishnah-teachings] among the gentiles, then I shall gather them together* (Hos. 8:10)."

D.   R. Huna made a second statement.

E.   R. Huna said, "*From the rising of the sun even to the setting of the sun my name is great among the nations, and in every place offerings are presented to my name, even pure-offerings* (Malachi 1:11). Now is it the case that a pure-offering is made in Babylonia?

F.   "Said the Holy One, blessed be He, 'Since you engage in the study of the matter, it is as if you offered it up.'"

4.   A.   Samuel said, "*And if they are ashamed of all that they have done, show them the form of the house and the fashion of it, the goings out and the comings in that pertain to it, and all its forms, and write it in their sight, that they may keep the whole form of it* (Ez. 43:11).

B.   "Now is there such a thing as the form of the house at this time?

C.   "But said the Holy One, blessed be He, if you are engaged in the study of the matter, it is as if you were building it.'"

5.   A.   Said R. Yose, "On what account do they begin instruction of children with the Torah of the Priests [the book of Leviticus]?

B.   "Rather let them begin instruction them with the book of Genesis.

C.   "But the Holy One, blessed be He, said, 'Just as the offerings [described in the book of Leviticus] are pure, so children are pure. Let the pure come and engage in the study of matters that are pure.'"

6.   A.   R. Abba bar Kahana and R. Hanin, both of them in the name of R. Azariah of Kefar Hitayya: "[The matter may be compared to the case of] a king who had two cooks. The first of the two made a meal for him, and he ate it and liked it. The second made a meal for him, and he ate it and liked it.

B. "Now we should not know which of the two he liked more, except that, since he ordered the second, telling him to make a meal like the one he had prepared, we know that it was the second meal that he liked more.

C. "So too Noah made an offering and it pleased God: *And the Lord smelled the sweet savor* (Gen. 8:21).

D. "And Israel made an offering to him, and it pleased the Holy One, blessed be He.

E. "But we do not know which of the two he preferred.

F "On the basis of his orders to Israel, saying to them, *See that you present my offerings, the food for the food-offering of soothing odor, to me at the appointed time,* we know that he preferred the offering of Israel [to that of Noah, hence the offering of Israel is preferable to the offering of the nations of the world]."

7. A. R. Abin made two statements.

B. R. Abin said, "The matter may be compared to the case of a king who was reclining at his banquet, and they brought him the first dish, which he ate and found pleasing. They brought him the second, which he ate and found pleasing. He began to wipe the dish.

C. *"I will offer you burnt offerings which are to be wiped off* (Ps. 66:15), like offerings that are to be wiped off I shall offer you, like someone who wipes the plate clean."

D. R. Abin made a second statement:

E. "The matter may be compared to a king who was making a journey and came to the first stockade and ate and drank there. Then he came to the second stockade and ate and drank there and spent the night there.

F. "So it is here. Why does the Scripture repeat concerning the burnt-offering: *This is the Torah of the burnt-offering* (Lev. 3:5), *It is the burnt-offering* (Lev. 6:2)? It is to teach that the whole of the burnt-offering is burned up on the fires [yielding no parts to the priests]."

The rhetorical pattern now shifts. We have interest in the contrast between our base-verse and another one that goes over the same matter. That contrast, to be sure, is invited by Ps. 119:4. But that contrastive-verse does not function in such a way as to lead us to our base-verse, but rather, as is clear, to lead us to the complementary verse for our base-verse. That is, therefore, a different pattern from the one we have identified. The exegesis moves from text to context. We have two statements of the same matter, in Numbers and in Exodus, as indicated at No. 1. Why is the passage repeated? No. 1 presents a systematic composition on that question, No. 2 on another. No. 3 serves as an appendix to No. 2, on the importance of studying the sacrifices. But No. 3 obviously ignores our setting, since it is interested in the Mishnah-study in general, not the study of the laws of the sacrifices in particular. No. 4 goes on with the same point. No. 5 then provides yet another appendix, this one on the study of the book of Leviticus, with its substantial corpus of laws on sacrifice. No. 6 opens a new inquiry, this time into the larger theme of the comparison of offerings. It has no place here, but is attached to No. 7. That item is particular to Leviticus 6:2, but it concerns the same question we have here, namely, the repetition of statements about sacrifices, this timed Lev. 3:5, 6:2. So Nos. 6, 7 are tacked on because of the congruence of the question, not the pertinence of the proposition. In that case we look to No. 1 for guidance, and there we find at issue is the convergence of two verses on the same matter, and that is what stands behind our composition.

The rhetorical pattern is hardly clear. I see a problem – the convergence of verses – but not a pattern that would precipitate expectation of recurrent examples.

VI:IV

1. A. *...the regular daily whole-offering of two yearling rams without blemish:*
   B. [Explaining the selection of the lambs,] the House of Shammai and the House of Hillel [offered opinions as follows:]
   C. The House of Shammai say, "Lambs are chosen because the letters that spell the word for lamb can also be read to mean that 'they cover up the sins of Israel,' as you read in Scripture: *He will turn again and have compassion upon us, he will put our iniquities out of sight* (Micah 7:19)."
   D. And the House of Hillel say, "Lambs are selected because the letters of the word lamb can yield the sound for the word, *clean,* for they clean up the sins of Israel.
   E. "That is in line with this verse of Scripture: *If your sins are like scarlet, they will be washed clean like wool* (Is. 1:18)."
   F. Ben Azzai says, "*...the regular daily whole-offering of two yearling rams without blemish* are specified because they wash away the sins of Israel and turn them into an infant a year old."

2. A. *[...the regular daily whole-offering of]* two *[yearling rams without blemish. One you shall sacrifice in the morning and the second between dusk and dark]:*
   B. *Two a day* on account of [the sins of] the day.
   C. *Two a day* to serve as intercessor for that day: *They shall be mine, says the Lord of hosts, on the day that I do this, even my own treasure, and I will spare them, as a man spares his son who serves him* (Malachi 3:17).
   D. *Two a day* meaning that they should be slaughtered in correspondence to that day in particular.
   E. *Two a day* meaning that one should know in advance which has been designated to be slaughtered in the morning and which at dusk.

3. A. *...a daily whole-offering:*
   B. Said R. Yudan in the name of R. Simon, "No one ever spent the night in Jerusalem while still bearing sin. How so? The daily whole-offering of then morning would effect atonement for the sins that had been committed overnight, and the daily whole-offering of dusk would effect atonement for the transgressions that had been committed by day.
   C. "In consequence, no one ever spent the night in Jerusalem while still bearing sin.
   D. "And what verse of Scripture makes that point? *Righteousness will spend the night in it* (Is. 1:21)."

4. A. R. Judah bar Simon in the name of R. Yohanan: "There were three statements that Moses heard from the mouth of the Almighty, on account of which he was astounded and recoiled.

B. "When he said to him, *And they shall make me a sanctuary [and I shall dwell among them]* (Ex. 25:8), said Moses before the Holy One, blessed be He, 'Lord of the age, lo, the heavens and the heavens above the heavens cannot hold you, and yet you yourself have said, *And they shall make me a sanctuary [and I shall dwell among them]* .'

C. "Said to him the Holy One, blessed be He, 'Moses, it is not the way you are thinking. But there will be twenty boards' breadth at the north, twenty at the south, eight at the west, and I shall descend and shrink my Presence among you below.'

D. "That is in line with this verse of Scripture: *And I shall meet you there* (Ex. 25:20).

E. "When he said to him, *My food which is presented to me for offerings made by fire [you shall observe to offer to me]* (Num. 28:2), said Moses before the Holy One, blessed be He, 'Lord of the age, if I collect all of the wild beasts in the world, will they produce one offering [that would be adequate as a meal for you]?

F. "'If I collect all the wood in the world, will it prove sufficient for one offering,' as it is said, *Lebanon is not enough for altar fire, nor the beasts thereof sufficient for burnt-offerings* (Is. 40:16).

G. "Said to him the Holy One, blessed be He, "Moses, it is not the way you are thinking. But: *You shall say to them, This is the offering made by fire [he lambs of the first year without blemish, two day by day]* (Num. 28:3), and not two at a time but one in the morning and one at dusk, as it is said, *One lamb you will prepare in the morning, and the other you will prepare at dusk* (Num. 28:4).'

H. "And when he said to him, *When you give the contribution to the Lord to make expiation for your lives* (Ex. 30:15), said Moses before the Holy One, blessed be He, 'Lord of the age, who can give redemption-money for his soul?

I. "'*One brother cannot redeem another* (Ps. 49:8), *for too costly is the redemption of men's souls* (Ps. 49:9).'

J. "Said the Holy One, blessed be He, to Moses, 'It is not the way you are thinking. But: *This they shall give* – something like this [namely, the half-shekel coin] they shall give.'"

The rhetorical pattern is clear: the base-verse is analyzed, clause by clause. The point that is made is that the offerings achieve expiation and serve as intercessors. That is the same proposition that the contrastive-verse wishes to establish. The exegesis of the components of the base-verse accounts for the miscellany with which our *pisqa* draws to a close. But the point is cogent. The daily whole-offering effects atonement for sins of the preceding day. No. 1 makes that point in one way, No. 2 in another. Deriving from elsewhere, No. 3, bearing in its wake No. 4, says the same thing yet a third time. So the miscellany is a composite but makes a single point in a strong way.

The form in its purest exemplification would give us the base-verse clause by clause, with each of the clauses subjected to amplification and exposition. The rhetorical pattern then may be described as follows:

2. *The Exegetical Form: The implicit syllogism is stated through a systematic exegesis of the components of the base-verse on their own.*

That proposition is taken to be the message established by the base-verse. So the base-verse now serves as the structural foundation for the pericope. This form cites the base-verse alone. A syllogism is worked out, and reaches intelligible expression, through the systematic reading of the individual components of the base-verse. The formal traits: [1] citation of a base-verse, [2] a generalization or syllogistic proposition worked out through details of the base-verse. We should moreover anticipate that the exegetical form will follow in sequence upon the propositional form, since the propositional form through the interplay of contrastive-verse and base-verse establishes the theorem to be worked out, and only then does the exegetical form undertake the secondary amplification of that same message, now in terms of the base-verse alone. If this scheme is a sound one, then we should always find the sequence [1] propositional and [2] exegetical form.

Now we have to test the hypothesis framed here concerning the identification and definition of the recurrent rhetorical patterns of choice. At issue are two matters. First, we wish to know whether the formulations we have defined in fact dictate the mode of discourse at all, and this in regard to both the pattern of formulating ideas and also the sequence by which the two hypothetical forms or patterns occur, first one, then the other. Second, we want to find out whether these are not only necessary but also sufficient, or whether we shall have to define (not invent) yet other formal patterns to account for the recurrent modes by which intelligible propositions are framed.

III

Literary Structures of Pesiqta deRab Kahana *Pisqaot* 14 and 22

So far as I can see, the large units of *Pisqa* 6 all fall within the two patterns for formal compositions that we have now identified. Do these suffice or are other formal patterns to be defined? To answer these questions – at the risk of taxing the reader's patience – we proceed to two further *pisqaot*, selected at random. I shall then conduct a test by examining a *pisqa* that occurs also in another document, that is, *Pisqa* 27, which is shared with Leviticus Rabbah. This will allow us a negative test, since, if my claim is correct that Pesiqta deRab Kahana is the work of a distinctive authorship, which has made its singular choices as to rhetoric, then a *pisqa* not particular to that authorship should exhibit different traits altogether. Since my principal purpose is to test our hypothetical scheme of the rhetorical patterns of the document, the principal point of exposition addresses the question of whether we deal with propositional form, exegetical form, or some other.

XIV:I

1. A. *Therefore hear me you men of understanding, far be it from God that he should do wickedness, and from the almighty that he should do wrong. [For according to the work of a man he will requite him, and according to his ways he will make it befall him]* (Job 34:10-11):

   B. R. Azariah, R. Jonathan bar Haggai in the name of R. Samuel bar R. Isaac, "[With reference to the verse, *Then Jacob became angry and upbraided Laban. Jacob said to Laban, 'What is my offense? What is my sin, that you have hotly pursued me? Although you have felt through all my goods, what have you found of all your household goods? Set it here before my kinsmen and your kinsmen that they may decide between us two'* (Gen. 31:36-37),] Better the captiousness of the fathers than the irenic obsequiousness of the sons.

   C. "[We learn the former from this verse:] *Then Jacob became angry and upbraided Laban. Jacob said to Laban, 'What is my offense? What is my sin, that you have hotly pursued me?'* [Gen. R. 74:10 adds: You might imagine that, in consequence, there would be a brawl. But in fact there was nothing but an effort at reconciliation. Jacob made every effort to reconcile his father-in-law: *Although you have felt through all my goods, what have you found of all your household goods? Set it here before my kinsmen and your kinsmen that they may decide between us two.*]

   D. "[We learn about] the irenic obsequiousness of the sons from the case of David:

   E. *"And David fled from Naioth in Ramah and came and said before Jonathan, What have I done? What is my iniquity? and what is my sin before your father, that he seeks my life?* (1 Sam. 20:1).

   F. "Even while he is trying to reconcile with the other, he mentions bloodshed.

   G. Said R. Simon, "Under ordinary circumstances, when a son-in-law is living with his father in law and then proceeds to leave the household of his father-in-law, is it possible that the father-in-law will not find in his possession even the most minor item? But as to this [Jacob], even a shoelace, even a knife, was not found in his possession.

   H. "That is in line with this verse of Scripture: *Although you have felt through all my goods, what have you found of all your household goods? Set it here before my kinsmen and your kinsmen that they may decide between us two.*

   I. "Said the Holy One, blessed be He, 'By your life! In the very language by which you have rebuked your father-in-law, I shall rebuke your children: *What wrong did your fathers find in me that they went far from me and went after worthlessness and became worthless?*"

The issue before us is whether the contrastive-verse opens up any aspect of the base-verse. Clearly, the first point of interest is the use of the word "hear," shared by Job 34:10 and Jer. 2:4. But what is to be heard? It is that there is good reason for what God does (Job 34:10), and it must follow that God's complaint – there must be good reason for what man does – is justified. That seems to me a solid basis for classifying the composition as *the Propositional Form*. The implicit syllogism – there is a common bond of rationality that accounts for God's and man's deeds – is stated through the intervention of a contrastive-verse into the basic proposition established by the base-verse.

XIV:II

1. A. *[For the simple are killed by their turning away, and the complacence of fools destroys them;] but he who listens to me will dwell secure, and will be at ease, [without dread of evil]* (Prov. 1:33):
   B. There are four categories of hearing.
   C. There is one who listens and loses, there is one who listens and gains, one who does not listen and loses, one who does not listen and gains.
   D. There is one who listens and loses: this is the first Man: *And to Man he said, Because you listened to the voice of your wife* (Gen. 3:17).
   E. What did he lose? *For you are dust and to dust you will return* (Gen. 3:19).
   F. ...who listens and gains: this is our father, Abraham: *Whatever Sarah says to you, Listen to her voice* (Gen. 21:12).
   G. How did he gain? *For through Isaac will you have descendents* (Gen. 21:12)
   H. ...who does not listen and gains: this refers to Joseph: *And he did not listen to her, to lie with her* (Gen. 39:11).
   I. How did he gain? *And Joseph will place his hand over your eyes* (Gen. 46:4).
   J. ...who does not listen and loses: this refers to Israel: *They did not listen to me and did not pay attention* (Jer. 7:26).
   K. What did they lose? *Him to death, to death, and him to the sword, to the sword* (Jer. 15:2).
2. A. Said R. Levi, "The ear is to the body as the kiln to pottery. Just as in the case of a kiln, when it is full of pottery, if you kindle a flame under it, all of the pots feel it,
   B. "so: *Incline your ear and go to me and listen and let your souls live* (Is. 55:3)."

The choice of the contrastive-verse is accounted for by the reference at Prov. 1:33 to "he who listens will dwell secure." The proposition is that listening to God will produce a gain to a faithful people, in the model of Abraham. The category, once more, is *the Propositional Form.*

XIV:III

1. A. *If you are willing and listen, you shall eat the good of the land; but if you refuse and rebel, [you shall be devoured by the sword; for the mouth of the Lord has spoken]* (Is. 1:19-20):
   B. *[...you shall eat the good of the land:]* You shall eat carobs.
   C. Said R. Aha, "When an Israelite has to eat carobs, he will carry out repentance.
   D. Said R. Aqiba, "As becoming is poverty for a daughter of Jacob as a red ribbon on the breast of a white horse."
2. A. Said R. Samuel bar Nahman, "Even while a palace is falling, it is still called a palace, and even when a dung heap rises, it is still called a dung heap.

B. "Even while a palace is falling, it is still called a palace: *Hear the word of the Lord, O House of Jacob, and all the families of the House of Israel* (Jer. 2:4-6). When while they are declining, he still calls them *the House of Israel.*

C. "...and even when a dung heap rises, it is still called a dung heap: *Behold the land of the Chaldeans – this is the nation that was nothing* (Is. 23:13) – would that they were still nothing!"

3. A. Said R. Levi, "The matter may be compared to the case of a noble woman who had two family members at hand, one a villager, the other a city-dweller. The one who was a villager, [when he had occasion to correct her,] would speak in words of consolation: 'Are you not the daughter of good folk, are you not the daughter of a distinguished family.'

B. "But the one who was a city-dweller, [when he had occasion to correct her,] would speak in words of reprimand: 'Are you not the daughter of the lowest of the poor, are you not the daughter of impoverished folk?'

C. "So too in the case of Jeremiah, since he was a villager, from Anathoth, he would go to Jerusalem and speak to Israel in words of consolation [and pleading,] *Hear the word of the Lord, O House of Jacob, [and all the families of the House of Israel. Thus says the Lord: 'What wrong did your fathers find in me that they went far from me and went after worthlessness and became worthless?' They did not say, 'Where is the Lord who brought us up from the Land of Egypt, who led us in the wilderness, in a land of deserts and pits, in a land of drought and deep darkness, in a land that none passes through, where no man dwells?']* (Jer. 2:4-6).

D. "These are the improper deeds which your fathers did.'

E. "But Isaiah, because he was a city dweller, from Jerusalem, would speak to Israel in terms of reprimand: *Hear the word of the Lord, you rulers of Sodom, attend, you people of gomorrah, to the instruction of our God* (Is. 1:10).

F. "'Do you not come from the mold of the people of Sodom.'"

4. A. Said R. Levi, "Amoz and Amaziah were brothers, and because Isaiah was the son of the king's brother, he could speak to Israel in such terms of reprimand,

B. "in line with this verse: *A rich man answers impudently* (Prov. 18:23)."

The contrastive-verse once more focuses attention on listening, and that is the link to the base-verse. The implicit proposition is announced in that same verse: If you listen, you prosper, and if not, you lose out, so XIV:III.1. No. 2 leads us directly into our base-verse, commenting on the language that is used. No. 3, 4 then amplify that point by comparing Jeremiah and Isaiah. These form a secondary amplification of the theme; the proposition derives from No. 1. The category once more is *the Propositional Form.*

XIV:IV

1. A. Said R. Levi, "The matter may be compared to the case of a noble lady who [as her dowry] brought into the king two myrtles and lost one of them and was distressed on that account.

B. "The king said to her, 'Take good care of this other one as if you were taking care of the two of them.'

C. "So too, when the Israelites stood at Mount Sinai, they said, *Everything that the Lord has spoken we shall do and we shall hear* (Ex. 24:7). They lost the *we shall do* by making the golden calf.

D. "Said the Holy One, blessed be He, be sure to take care of the *we shall listen* as if you were taking care of both of them.'

E. "When they did not listen, the Holy One, blessed be He, said to them, *Hear the word of the Lord, O House of Jacob, [and all the families of the House of Israel. Thus says the Lord: 'What wrong did your fathers find in me that they went far from me and went after worthlessness and became worthless?' They did not say, 'Where is the Lord who brought us up from the Land of Egypt, who led us in the wilderness, in a land of deserts and pits, in a land of drought and deep darkness, in a land that none passes through, where no man dwells?']* (Jer. 2:4-6)."

2. A. [A further comment on the verse, *Hear the word of the Lord* (Jer. 2:4-6):] before you have to listen to the words of Jeremiah.

   B. Listen to the words of the Torah, before you have to listen to the words of the prophet.

   C. Listen to the words of prophecy before you have to listen to words of rebuke.

   D. Listen to words of rebuke before you have to listen to words of reprimand.

   E. Listen to words of reprimand before you have to listen to *the sound of the horn and the pipe* (Dan. 3:15).

   F. Listen in the land before you have to listen abroad.

   G. Listen while alive, before you have to listen when dead.

   H. Let your ears listen before your bodies have to listen.

   I. Let your bodies listen before your bones have to listen: *Dry bones, hear the word of the Lord* (Ez. 37:4).

3. A. R. Aha in the name of R. Joshua b. Levi, "Nearly eight times in Egypt the Israelites [Braude and Kapstein, p. 270:] stood shoulder to shoulder].

   B. "What is the scriptural verse that indicates it? *Come, let us take counsel against* him (Ex. 1:10).

   C. "On that account [God] took the initiative for them and redeemed them: *And I came down to save* him *from the hand of the Egyptians* (Ex. 3:8)."

4. A. R. Abin, R. Hiyya in the name of R. Yohanan: "It is written, *My mother's sons were displeased with me, they sent me to watch over the vineyards; so I did not watch over my own vineyard* (Song 1:6).

   B. "What brought it about that I watched over the vineyards? It is because *I did not watch over my own vineyard.*

   C. "What brought it about that in Syria I separate dough-offering from two loaves? It is because in the Land of Israel I did not properly separate dough-offering from one loaf.

   D. "I thought that I should receive a reward on account of both of them, but I receive a reward only on account of one of them.

   E. "What brought it about that in Syria I observe two days for the festivals? It is because in the Land of Israel I did not properly observe one day for the festivals.

   F. "I thought that I should receive a reward on account of both of them, but I receive a reward only on account of one of them."

G.   R. Yohanan would recitre the following verse of Scripture in this
connection: *And I also gave them ordinances that were not good* (Ez.
20:25).

This is a classic example of *the Exegetical Form.* The implicit syllogism
is stated through a systematic exegesis of the components of the base-verse on
their own. Formally, we know we are in fresh territory because No. 1 does not
begin with the citation of any verse at all, and it clearly does not carry forward
any prior discussion. So it stands at the head of a unit composed on a different
formal paradigm from the foregoing ones. No. 1 presents a powerful comment
on our base-verse. The proposition is that when Israel listens, they prosper, and
when they do not listen, they lose out, just as before. But God is bound by
reason and so expects man to be, hence, "What wrong...?" No. 2 moves in its
own direction, but its contrast between listening to A so that you will not have
to listen to B makes its point with great power as well. The relevance of Nos.
3, 4 is hardly self-evident. Speculation that these items illustrate entries on the
catalogue of No. 2 is certainly not groundless. And No. 4 is explicit that
obeying ("listening") yields rewards, and not obeying, penalties.

XIV:V

1.   A.   It is written, *Thus said the Lord, 'What wrong did your fathers find in me
that they went far from me and went after worthlessness and became
worthless?'* (Jer. 2:5)

B.   Said R. Isaac, "This refers to one who leaves the scroll of the Torah and
departs. Concerning him, Scripture says, *What wrong did your fathers
find in me that they went far from me.*

C.   "Said the Holy One, blessed be He, to the Israelites, 'My children, your
fathers found no wrong with me, but you have found wrong with me.

D.   "'The first Man found no wrong with me, but you have found wrong with
me.'

E.   "To what may the first Man be compared?

F.   "To a sick man, to whom the physician came. The physician said to
him, 'Eat this, don't eat that.'

G.   "When the man violated the instructions of the physician, he brought
about his own death.

H.   "[As he lay dying,] his relatives came to him and said to him, 'Is it
possible that the physician is imposing on you the divine attribute of
justice?'

I.   "He said to them, 'God forbid. I am the one who brought about my own
death. This is what he instructed me, saying to me, 'Eat this, don't eat
that,' but when I violated his instructions, I brought about my own death.

J.   "So too all the generations came to the first Man, saying to him, 'Is it
possible that the Holy One, blessed be He, is imposing the attribute of
justice on you?'

L.   "He said to them, 'God forbid. I am the one who has brought about my
own death. Thus did he command me, saying to me, *Of all the trees of
the garden you may eat, but of the tree of the knowledge of good and evil
you may not eat* (Gen. 2:17). When I violated his instructions, I brought

about my own death, for it is written, *On the day on which you eat it, you will surely die* (Gen. 2:17).'

M. "[God's speech now continues:] 'Pharaoh found no wrong with me, but you have found wrong with me.'

N. "To what may Pharaoh be likened?

O. "To the case of a king who went overseas and went and deposited all his possessions with a member of his household. After some time the king returned from overseas and said to the man, 'Return what I deposited with you.'

P. "He said to him, 'I did not such thing with you, and you left me nothing.'

Q. "What did he do to him? He took him and put him in prison.

R. "He said to him, 'I am your slave. Whatever you left with me I shall make up to you.'

S. "So, at the outset, said the Holy One, blessed be He, to Moses, *Now go and I shall send you to Pharaoh* (Ex. 3:10).

T. "That wicked man said to him, *Who is the Lord that I should listen to his voice? I do not know the Lord* (Ex. 2:5).

U. "But when he brought the ten plagues on him, *The Lord is righteous and I and my people are wicked* (Ex. 9:27).

V. "[God's speech now continues:] 'Moses found no wrong with me, but you have found wrong with me.'

W. "To what may Moses be compared?

X. "To a king who handed his son over to a teacher, saying to him, 'Do not call my son a moron."

Y. What is the meaning of the word moron?

Z. Said R. Reuben, "In the Greek language they call an idiot a moron."

AA. [Resuming the discourse:] "One time the teacher belittled the boy and called him a moron. Said the king to him, 'With all my authority I instructed you, saying to you, Do not call my son a fool,' and yet you have called my son a fool. It is not the calling of a smart fellow to go along with fools. [You're fired!]'

BB. "Thus it is written, *And the Lord spoke to Moses and to Aaron and commanded them concerning the children of Israel* (Ex. 6:13).

CC. "What did he command them? He said to them, 'Do not call my sons morons.' But when they rebelled them at the waters of rebellion, Moses said to them, *Listen, I ask, you morons* (Num. 20:10).

DD. "Said the Holy One, blessed be He, to them, 'With all my authority I instructed you, saying to you, Do not call my sons fools,' and yet you have called my sons fools. It is not the calling of a smart fellow to go along with fools. [You're fired!]'

EE. "What is written is not *You* [singular] *therefore shall not bring*, but *you* [plural] *therefore shall not bring* (Num. 20:12). [For God said,] 'Neither you nor your brother nor your sister will enter the Land of Israel.'

FF. "[God's speech now continues:] Said the Holy One, blessed be He, to Israel, 'Your fathers in the wilderness found no wrong with me, but you have found wrong with me.'

GG. "'I said to them, *One who makes an offering to other gods will be utterly destroyed* (Ex. 22:19), but they did not do so, but rather, *They prostrated themselves to it and worshipped it* (Ex. 32:8).

HH. "After all the wicked things that they did, what is written, *And the Lord regretted the evil that he had considered doing to his people* (Ex. 32:14)."

2. A. Said R. Judah bar Simon, "Said the Holy One, blessed be He, to Israel, 'Your fathers in the wilderness found no wrong with me, but you have found wrong with me.'

   B. "'I said to them, *For six days you will gather [the mana] and on the seventh day it is a Sabbath, on which there will be no collecting of mana* (Ex. 16:26).

   C. "'But they did not listen, but rather: *And it happened that on the seventh day some of the people went out to gather manna and did not find it* (Ex. 16:27).

   D. "'Had they found it, they would have gathered it [and violated his wishes, so he did not give manna on the seventh day, therefore avoiding the occasion of making them sin].'"

We have yet another perfect example of *the Exegetical Form.* The sustained and powerful story amplifies the statement, *What wrong did your fathers find in me.* The point is that the fathers found no fault with God, which makes the actions of Jeremiah's generation all the more inexplicable. The movement from the first Man to Pharaoh, then Moses and Aaron, leads then to Israel, and the complaint is remarkably apt: it has to do with the forty years in the wilderness, to which Jeremiah makes reference! So the story-teller has dealt with both parts of the complaint. First, the fathers found no fault with their punishment, that is, the forty years they were left to die in the wilderness, and, second, the forty years were a mark of grace. So complaining against God is without rhyme or reason. I cannot imagine a better example of a sustained amplification, through exegesis of intersecting-verses, parables, and syllogisms, of the basic proposition. While implicit, that proposition could not come to more explicit demonstration than it does in this exquisite composition.

XIV:VI

1. A. *...they went far from me and went after worthlessness and became worthless?* (Jer. 2:5)

   B. Said R. Phineas in the name of R. Hoshaiah, "For they would drive out those who did return to God.

   C. "That is in line with this verse of Scripture: *Therefore I chased him away from me* (Neh. 13:28), [Braude and Kapstein, p. 272, add: they chased away and made go far from me those who would have returned to me]."

The Exegetical Form characterizes this exposition of a further clause in the base-verse. The exegesis of a clause of the base-verse imparts to the message a still deeper dimension. The basic proposition seems to me the same as before.

XIV:VI

1. A. *...and went after worthlessness and became worthless?* (Jer. 2:5):

B. Said R. Isaac, "The matter may be compared to the case of a banker, against whom a debit was issued, and he was afraid, saying, 'Is it possible that the debit is for a hundred gold coins or two hundred gold coins.'

C. "Said the creditor to him, 'Do not fear, it covers only a kor of bran and barley, and in any event it's already been paid off.'

D. "So said the Holy One, blessed be He, to Israel, My children, as to the idolatry after which you lust, *it is nothing of substance, but they are nought, a work of delusion* (Jer. 10:15).

E. "But not like these is *the portion of Jacob, for he is the creator of all things, Israel are the tribes of his inheritance; the Lord of hosts is his name* (Jer. 10:16)."

The conclusion turns the final clause on its head. Since the Israelites went after what was worthless, it is easy for God to forgive them, and God does forgive them. This is fresh, but it does not change the formal pattern: the base-verse is systematically worked out.

Clearly, the entire *pisqa* works out its implicit proposition through first the intervention of a contrastive-verse, which imparts to the base-verse the fundamental proposition to be expounded, and then the systematic exposition of the base-verse, which reads the implicit proposition into – but also in terms of – that verse. We proceed to the second of the three text-*pisqaot*.

XXII:I

1. A. It is written, *Will you not revive us again [that your people may rejoice in you? Show us your steadfast love, O Lord, and grant us your salvation]* (Ps. 85:6-7):

   B. Said R. Aha, "May your people and your city rejoice in you."

2. A. *And Sarah said, God has made joy for me; everyone who hears will rejoice with me* (Gen. 21:6):

   B. R. Yudan, R. Simon, R. Hanin, R. Samuel bar R. Isaac: "If Reuben is happy, what difference does it make to Simeon? So too, if Sarah was remembered, what difference did it make to anyone else? For lo, our mother Sarah says, *everyone who hears will rejoice with me* (Gen. 21:6).

   C. "But this teaches that when our mother, Sarah, was remembered, with her many barren women were remembered, with her all the deaf had their ears opened, with her all the blind had their eyes opened, with her all those who had lost their senses regained their senses. So everyone was saying, 'Would that our mother, Sarah, might be visited a second time, so that we may be visited with her!'

   D. [Explaining the source common joy,] R. Berekhiah in the name of R. Levi said, "She added to the lights of the heavens. The word *making* ['God has made joy'] is used here and also in the following verse: *And God made the two lights* (Gen. 1:16). Just as the word making used elsewhere has the sense of giving light to the world, so the word making used here has the sense of giving light to the world."

   E. "The word 'making' ['God has made joy'] is used here and also in the following verse: *And he made a release to the provinces* (Est. 2:18).

F. "Just as the word 'making;' used there indicates that a gift had been given to the entire world, so the word 'making'; used there indicates that a gift had been given to the entire world."

3. A. R. Berekhiah in the name of R. Levi: "You find that when our mother, Sarah, gave birth to Isaac, all the nations of the world said, 'God forbid! It is not Sarah that has given birth to Isaac, but Hagar, handmaiden of Sarah, is the one who gave birth to him.'

B. "What did the Holy One, blessed be He, do? He dried up the breasts of the nations of the world, and their noble matrons came and kissed the dirt at the feet of Sarah saying to her, 'Do a religious duty and give suck to our children.'

C. "Our father, Abraham, said to her, 'This is not a time for modesty, but [now, go forth, and] sanctify the name of the Holy One, blessed be He, by sitting [in public] in the market place and there giving suck to children.'

D. "That is in line with the verse: *Will Sarah give suck to children* (Gen. 21:7).

E. "What is written is not, *to a child*, but, *to children*.

F. "And is it not an argument *a fortiori*: if in the case of a mortal, to whom rejoicing comes, the person rejoices and gives joy to everyone, when the Holy One, blessed be He, comes to give joy to Jerusalem, all the more so!

G. *"I will greatly rejoice in the Lord [my soul shall exult in my God; for he has clothed me with the garments of salvation, he has covered me with the robe of righteousness, as a bridegroom decks himself with a garland, and as a bride adorns herself with her jewels. For as the earth brings forth its shoots, and as a garden causes what is sown in it to spring up, so the Lord God will cause righteousness and praise to spring forth before all the nations]* (Isaiah 61:10-11)."

The implicit syllogism maintains that when Jerusalem rejoices, everyone will have reason to join in. That point links the clause, "praise to spring forth before all the nations" to the statement, I will greatly rejoice in the Lord. It is at No. 2 that the proposition emerges, even though the contrastive-verse, Ps. 85:6-7, comes first. I do not regard the pericope as a good example of the contrastive-verse/base-verse form, even though the implicit proposition is very powerfully expounded.

XXII:II

1. A. *This is the day which the Lord has made; let us rejoice and be glad in it* (Ps. 118:24):

B. Said R. Abin, "But do we not know in what to rejoice, whether in the day or in the Holy One, blessed be He? But Solomon came along and explained, We shall rejoice in you: in you, in your Torah, in you, in your salvation."

2. A. Said R. Isaac, "In you (BK) [the Hebrew letters of which bear the numerical value of twenty-two, hence:] – in the twenty-two letters which you have used in writing the Torah for us.

B. "The B has the value of two, and the K of twenty."

3. A. For we have learned in the Mishnah:

   B. If one has married a woman and lived with her for ten years and not produced a child, he is not allowed to remain sterile [but must marry someone else]. If he has divorced her, he is permitted to marry another. The second is permitted to remain wed with her for ten years. If she had a miscarried, one counts from the time of the miscarriage. The man bears the religious duty of engaging in procreation but the woman does not. R. Yohanan b. Beroqah says, "The religious duty pertains to them both, for it is said, *And God blessed them* (Gen. 1:28)" [M. Yeb. 15:6].

4. A. There was a case in Sidon of one who married a woman and remained with her for ten years while she did not give birth.

   B. They came to R. Simeon b. Yohai to arrange for the divorce. He said to her, "Any thing which I have in my house take and now go, return to your father's household."

   C. Said to them R. Simeon b. Yohai, "Just as when you got married, it was in eating and drinking, so you may not separate from one another without eating and drinking."

   D. What did the woman do? She made a splendid meal and gave the husband too much to drink and then gave a sign to her slave-girl and said to her, "Bring him to my father's house."

   E. At midnight the man woke up. He said to them, "Where am I?"

   F. She said to him, "Did you not say to me, 'Any thing which I have in my house, take and now go, return to your father's household.' And that is how it is: I have nothing more precious than you."

   G. When R. Simeon b. Yohai heard this, he said a prayer for them, and they were visited [with a pregnancy].

   H. The Holy One, blessed be He, visits barren women, and the righteous have the same power.

   I. "And is it not an argument *a fortiori:* if in the case of a mortal, to whom rejoicing comes, the person rejoices and gives joy to everyone, when the Holy One, blessed be He, comes to give joy to Jerusalem, all the more so! And when Israel looks forward to the salvation of the Holy One, blessed be He, all the more so!

   J. *"I will greatly rejoice in the Lord [my soul shall exult in my God; for he has clothed me with the garments of salvation, he has covered me with the robe of righteousness, as a bridegroom decks himself with a garland, and as a bride adorns herself with her jewels. For as the earth brings forth its shoots, and as a garden causes what is sown in it to spring up, so the Lord God will cause righteousness and praise to spring forth before all the nations]* (Isaiah 61:10-11)."

The contrastive-verse at No. 1 expresses a rather general interest in the theme of rejoicing. No. 2 carries forward the opening element. The implicit syllogism is that when one rejoices, so does the other, however, and that is the main point of Nos. 1, 2, and is made explicit. No. 3 leads us into No. 4, which is the goal of the framer of the whole, since 4.I states precisely what the syllogism wishes to maintain.

XXII:III

1. A. The matter may be compared to the case of a noble lady, whose husband, sons, and sons-in-law went overseas. They told her, "Your sons are coming."

   B. She said to them, "My daughters-in-law will rejoice."

   C. "Here come your sons-in-law!"

   D. "My daughters will rejoice."

   E. When they said to her, "Here comes your husband," she said to them, "Now there is occasion for complete rejoicing."

   F. So to, the former prophets say to Jerusalem, "*Your sons come from afar* (Is. 60:4)."

   G. And she says to them, "*Let Mount Zion be glad* (Ps. 48:12)."

   H. "*Your daughters are carried to you on uplifted arms* (Is. 60:4)."

   I. "*Let the daughters of Judah rejoice* (Ps. 48:12)."

   J. But when they say to her, "*Behold your king comes to you* (Zech. 9:9)," then she will say to him, "Now there is occasion for complete rejoicing."

   K. *I will greatly rejoice in the Lord [my soul shall exult in my God; for he has clothed me with the garments of salvation, he has covered me with the robe of righteousness, as a bridegroom decks himself with a garland, and as a bride adorns herself with her jewels. For as the earth brings forth its shoots, and as a garden causes what is sown in it to spring up, so the Lord God will cause righteousness and praise to spring forth before all the nations]* (Isaiah 61:10-11)

The rhetorical pattern shifts. There is no pretense at commencing with a contrastive-verse. The parable forces our attention on the base-verse, with its statement, *I in particular shall rejoice* . So we deal with an exegetical form, in which the parabolic medium is used for the delivery of the exegetical message. The next component of the *pisqa* follows suit.

XXII:IV

1. A. The matter may be compared to the case of an orphan-girl who was raised in a palace. When the time came for her to be married, they said to her, "Do you have [for a dowry] anything at all?"

   B. She said to them, "I do indeed: I have an inheritance from father and I have an inheritance from my grandfather."

   C. So Israel has the merit left to them by Abraham, and they have the inheritance of our father Jacob:

   D. *He has clothed me with garments of salvation* (Is. 61:10) on account of the merit left by our father, Jacob: *And the hides of the offspring of goats she wrapped on his hands* (Gen. 27:16).

   E. *He has covered me with the robe of righteousness* (Is. 61:10) refers to the merit left by our father, Abraham: *I have known him to the end that he may command his children...to do righteousness* (Gen. 16:19).

   F. *...as a bridegroom decks himself with a garland, and as a bride adorns herself with her jewels* (Isaiah 61:10-11):

   G. You find that when the Israelites stood at Mount Sinai, they bedecked themselves like a bride, opening one and closing another eye [as a sign of modesty (Mandelbaum), and that merit the Israelites bequeathed to their children as well].

The next stage in the unfolding of discourse, that is the exposition of the clauses of our base-verse leads to yet another parable. The parable now underlines the Israelites' merit in expecting God's renewed relationship with them, this time deriving from Abraham, Jacob, and the whole of Israel at Sinai. The formal character of the parable is familiar in our document: first the general statement of matters, then the specific restatement in terms of Israel in particular.

The final component of the *pisqa* – third in line in formal types – presents us with a different rhetorical pattern entirely. In what follows, the base-verse of our *pisqa* plays no important role at all. Rather, the pericope is built upon a syllogism proved through a set of examples, that is, an exercise in list-making science. The syllogism is explicit, not implicit, and it has no important relationship to the *pisqa* at hand. The pericope is tacked on at the end only because our base-verse occurs in it. And yet, it must be added, the syllogism of the list is in general entirely congruent with the implicit syllogism before us.

XXII:V

1. A. In ten passages the Israelites are referred to as a bride, six by Solomon, three by Isaiah, and one by Jeremiah:

   B. Six by Solomon: *Come with me from Lebanon, my bride* (Song 4:8), *you have ravished my heart, my sister, my bride* (Song 4:9), *how beautiful is your love, my sister, my bride* (Song 4:10), *your lips drip honey, my bride* (Song 4:11), *a locked garden is my sister, my bride* (Song 4:12), and *I am come into my garden, my sister my bride* (Song 5:1).

   C. Three by Isaiah: *You shall surely clothe you with them as with an ornament and gird yourself with them as a bride* (Is. 49:18), the present verse, *as a bridegroom decks himself with a garland, and as a bride adorns herself with her jewels* (Isaiah 61:10-11), and *As the bridegroom rejoices over the bride* (Is. 62:5).

   D. One by Jeremiah: *The voice of joy and the voice of gladness, the voice of the bridegroom and the voice of the bride* (Jer. 33:11).

   E. Corresponding to the ten passages in which Israel is spoken of as a bride, there are ten places in Scripture in which the Holy One, blessed be He, clothed himself in a garment appropriate to each occasion:

   F. On the day on which he created the world, the first garment which the Holy One, blessed be He, put on was one of glory and majesty: *You are clothed with glory and majesty* (Ps. 104:1).

   G. The second garment, one of power, which the Holy One, blessed be He, put on was to exact punishment for the generation of the flood: *the Lord reigns, he is clothed with power* (Ps. 93:1).

   H. The third garment, one of strength, which the Holy One, blessed be He, put on was to give the Torah to Israel: *the Lord is clothed, he has girded himself with strength* (Ps. 93:1).

I.   The fourth garment, a white one, which the Holy One, blessed be He, put on was to exact punishment from the kingdom of Babylonia: *his raiment was as white snow* (Dan. 7:9).

J.   The fifth garment, one of vengeance, which the Holy One, blessed be He, put on was to exact vengeance from the kingdom of Media: *He put on garments of vengeance for clothing and was clad with zeal as a cloak* (Is. 59:17). Lo, here we have two [vengeance, zeal].

K.   The seventh garment, one of righteousness and vindication, which the Holy One, blessed be He, put on was to exact vengeance from the kingdom of Greece: *He put on righteousness as a coat of mail and a helmet of deliverance upon his head* (Is. 59:17). Here we have two more [coat of mail, helmet].

L.   The ninth garment, one of red, which the Holy One, blessed be He, put on was to exact vengeance from the kingdom of Edom [playing on the letters that spell both Edom and red]: *Why is your apparel red* (Is. 63:2).

M.   The tenth garment, one of glory, which the Holy One, blessed be He, put on was to exact bengeance from Gog and Mag: *This one that is the most glorious of his apparel* (Is. 63:1).

N.   Said the community of Israel before the Holy One, blessed be He, "Of all the garments you have none more beautiful than this, as it is said, *the most glorious of his apparel* (Is. 63:1)."

The composition has been worked out in its own terms and is inserted here only because of the appearance of our base-verse as a proof-text.

IV

Literary Structures of Pesiqta deRab Kahana *Pisqa* 27 = Leviticus Rabbah *Parashah* 30

Now that we have worked out way through three *pisqaot* that are distinctive to Pesiqta deRab Kahana, we turn to one that is shared with Leviticus Rabbah. If my hypothesis concerning the rhetorical singularity of documents, typified by Pesiqta deRab Kahana, is sound, then we should find the formal patterns that serve our document out of phase with those that serve the other document.

What is particular to the rhetorical plan of Pesiqta deRab Kahana, specifically, is the the Propositional Form, in which the implicit syllogism is both defined and then stated through the intervention of an contrastive-verse into the basic proposition established by the base-verse. My analysis of the rhetorical plan of Leviticus Rabbah repeatedly produced the observation that *the intersecting-verse in that document was subjected to systematic and protracted exegesis* in its own terms *and not in terms of the proposition to be imputed, also, to the base-verse at the end.* By contrast, in Pesiqta deRab Kahana the contrastive-verse, which forms the counterpart to what I called the intersecting-verse in Leviticus Rabbah, is not subjected to sustained and systematic exegesis in its own terms. Quite to the contrary, as we have now seen many times, the contrastive-verse serves for the sole purpose of imposing upon the base-verse a very particular proposition, which then is repeated through a sequence of diverse contrastive-verses, on the one side, and also through a sustained reading of the successive components of the base-verse, on the other. We come then to a shared *pisqa* and pay close attention to how the contrastive-/intersecting-verse is treated.

XXVII:I

1. A. R. Abba bar Kahana commenced [discourse by citing the following verse]: *Take my instruction instead of silver, [and knowledge rather than choice gold]* (Prov. 8:10)."

   B. Said R. Abba bar Kahana, *"Take the instruction of the Torah instead of silver.*

   C. "Take the instruction of the Torah and not silver.

   D. *"Why do you weigh out money? Because there is no bread* (Is. 55:2).

   E. "'Why do you weigh out money to the sons of Esau [Rome]? [It is because] *there is no bread,* because you did not sate yourselves with the bread of the Torah.

   F. *"And [why] do you labor? Because there is no satisfaction* (Is. 55:2).

   G. *"Why do you labor* while the nations of the world enjoy plenty? *Because there is no satisfaction,* that is, because you have not sated yourselves with the bread of the Torah and with the wine of the Torah.

   H. "For it is written, *Come, eat of my bread, and drink of the wine I have mixed* (Prov. 9:5)."

2. A. R. Berekhiah and R. Hiyya, his father, in the name of R. Yose b. Nehorai: "It is written, *I shall punish all who oppress him* (Jer. 30:20), even those who collect funds for charity [and in doing so, treat people badly], except [for those who collect] the wages to be paid to teachers of Scripture and repeaters of Mishnah traditions.

   B. "For they receive [as a salary] only compensation for the loss of their time, [which they devote to teaching and learning rather than to earning a living].

   C. "But as to the wages [for carrying out] a single matter in the Torah, no creature can pay the [appropriate] fee in reward."

3. A. It has been taught on Tannaite authority: On the New Year, a person's sustenance is decreed [for the coming year],

   B. except for what a person pays out [for food in celebration] of the Sabbath, festivals, the celebration of the New Month,

   C. and for what children bring to the house of their master [as his tuition].

   D. If he adds [to what is originally decreed], [in Heaven] they add to his [resources], but if he deducts [from what he should give], [in Heaven] they deduct [from his wealth]. [Margulies, *Vayyiqra Rabbah*, p. 688, n. to 1. 5, links this statement to Prov. 8:10.]

4. A. R. Yohanan was going up from Tiberias to Sepphoris. R. Hiyya bar Abba was supporting him. They came to a field. He said, "This field once belonged to me, but I sold it in order to acquire merit in labor in the the Torah."

   B. They came to a vineyard, and he said, "This vineyard once belonged to me, but I sold it in order to acquire merit in labor in the the Torah."

   C. They came to an olive grove, and he said, "This olive grove once belonged to me, but but I sold it in order to acquire merit in labor in the the Torah."

D. R. Hiyya began to cry.

E. Said R. Yohanan, "Why are you crying?"

F. He said to him, "It is because you left nothing over to support you in your old age."

G. He said to him, "Hiyya, my disciple, is what I did such a light thing in your view? I sold something which was given in a spell of six days [of creation] and in exchange I acquired something which was given in a spell of forty days [of revelation].

H. "The entire world and everything in it was created in only six days, as it is written, *For in six days the Lord made heaven and earth* (Ex. 20:11)

I. "But the Torah was given over a period of forty days, as it was said, *And he was there with the Lord for forty days and forty nights* (Ex. 34:28). [Leviticus Rabbah adds: And it is written, *And I remained on the mountain for forty days and forty nights* (Deut. 9:9).]"

5. A. When R. Yohanan died, his generation recited concerning him [the following verse of Scripture]: *If a man should give all the wealth of his house for the love* (Song 8:7), with which R. Yohanan loved the Torah, *he would be utterly destitute* (Song 8:7).

B. When R. Abba bar Hoshaiah of Tiria died, they saw his bier flying in the air. His generation recited concerning him [the following verse of Scripture]: *If a man should give all the wealth of his house for the love* , with which the Holy One, blessed be He, loved Abba bar Hoshaiah of Tiria, *he would be utterly destitute* (Song 8:7).

C. When R. Eleazar b. R. Simeon died, his generation recited concerning him [the following verse of Scripture]: *Who is this who comes up out of the wilderness like pillars of smoke, perfumed with myrrh and frankincense, with all the powders of the merchant?* (Song 3:6).

D. What is the meaning of the clause, *With all the powders of the merchant?*

E. [Like a merchant who carries all sorts of desired powders,] he was a master of Scripture, a repeater of Mishnah traditions, a writer of liturgical supplications, and a poet.

6. A. Another interpretation of the verse, *Take my instruction instead of silver, [and knowledge rather than choice gold]* (Prov. 8:10): Said R. Abba bar Kahana, "On the basis of the reward paid for one act of *taking*, you may assess the reward for [taking] the palm branch [on the festival of Tabernacles].

B. "There was an act of taking in Egypt: *You will take a bunch of hyssop* (Ex. 12:22).

C. "And how much was it worth? Four *manehs.*, maybe five.

D. "Yet that act of taking is what stood up for Israel [and so made Israel inherit] the spoil of Egypt, the spoil at the sea, the spoil of Sihon and Og, and the spoil of the thirty-one kings.

E. "Now the palm-branch, which costs a person such a high price, and which involves so many religious duties – how much the more so [will a great reward be forthcoming on its account]!"

F. Therefore Moses admonished Israel, saying to them, *[On the fifteenth day of the seventh month, when you have gathered in the produce of the land, you shall keep the feast of the Lord seven days...] And you shall take on the first day [the fruit of goodly trees, branches of palm trees and boughs of leafy trees and willows of the brook; and you shall rejoice before the Lord your God seven days. You shall keep it as a feast to the*

Lord seven days in the year; it is a statute for ever throughout your generations; you shall keep it in the seventh month. You shall dwell in booths for seven days; all that are native in Israel shall dwell in booths, that your generations may know that I made the people of Israel dwell in booths when I brought them out of the land of Egypt: I am the Lord your God (Leviticus 23:39-43).

The notion of an implicit syllogism seems to me not to apply at all, since the point of interest of No. 1 is simply that study of the Torah is the source of Israel's sustenance. The theme of the intervening passages is established at 1.B, namely, Torah and the value and importance of study of Torah. Nos. 2, 3, 4, and 5 all present variations on amplifications of that theme. No. 2 makes that same point. No. 3 complements it, as do Nos. 3, 4, 5. Only at No. 6 do we revert to the intersecting-verse/contrastive-verse, which is now brought to bear upon our base-verse to make the point that the reward for "taking" is considerable, hence the taking of the fruit of goodly trees will produce a reward. That point is totally out of phase with the syllogism of Nos. 1-5, and therefore the rhetorical program at hand is not one in which the contrastive-verse is interpreted solely and finally to impute meaning to the base-verse and so to yield an implicit proposition. The rhetorical plan yields two points, one about the study of the Torah, which is irrelevant to our base-verse, the other about the reward for taking the species of the Festival, which is, then the main point. As I said above, it is only at No. 6 that Lev. 23:39 – with stress on the word "take" – recurs.

XXVII:II

1. A. *You show me the path of life, [in your presence] there is fulness of joy* (Ps. 16:11).
   B. Said David before the Holy One, blessed be He, "Lord of the ages, show me the open gateway to the life of the world to come."
   C. R.. Yudan and R. Azariah:
   D. R. Yudan said, "David said before the Holy One, blessed be He, 'Lord of the ages, Show me the path of life.'
   E. "Said the Holy One, blessed be He, to David, 'If you seek life, look for fear, as it is said, *The fear of the Lord prolongs life* (Prov. 10:27)."
   F. R. Azariah said, "[The Holy One, blessed be He], said to David, 'If you seek life, look for suffering (YYSWRYN), as it is said, *The reproofs of discipline (MWSR) are the way of life* (Prov. 6:23)." [Leviticus Rabbah adds: Rabbis say, "The Holy One, blessed be He, said to David, 'David, if you seek life, look for Torah,' as it is said, *It is a tree of life to those that hold fast to it* (Prov. 3:18)." R. Abba said, "David said before the Holy One, blessed be He, 'Lord of the ages, Show me the path of life.' Said to him the Holy One, blessed be He, 'Start fighting and exert yourself! Why are you puzzled? [Lieberman, in Margulies, *Vayyiqra Rabbah*, p. 880, to p. 692]. Work and eat: Keep my commandments and live (Prov. 4:4).'"]
2. A. *The fulness (SWB') of joy in your presence* (Ps. 16:11):

B. Satisfy (SB'NW) us with five joys in your presence: Scripture, Mishnah, Talmud, Supplements, and Lore.

3. A. Another matter: *In your presence is the fulness of joy* (Ps. 16:11):

B. Read not *fulness* (SWB') but *seven* (SB'). These are the seven groups of righteous men who are going to receive the face of the Presence of God.

C. And their face is like the sun, moon, firmament, stars, lightning, lilies, and the pure candelabrum that was in the house of the sanctuary.

D. How do we know that it is like the sun? As it is said, *Clear as the sun* (Song 6:10).

E. How do we know that it is like the moon? As it is said, *As lovely as the moon* (Song 6:10).

F. How do we know that it is like the firmament? As it is said, *And they that are wise shall shine as the brightness of the firmament* (Dan. 12:3).

G. How do we know that it is like the stars? As it is said, *And they that turn the many to righteousness as the stars forever and ever* (Dan. 12:3).

H. And how do we know that it is like the lightning? As it is said, *Their appearance is like torches, they run to and fro like lightning* (Nah. 2:5).

I. How do we know that it is like lilies? As it is said, *For the leader: upon the lilies* (Ps. 69:1).

J. How do we know that it will be like the pure candelabrum of the house of the sanctuary? As it is said, *And he said to me, What do you see? And I said, I looked and behold [there was] a candelabrum all of gold* (Zech. 4:2).

4. A. *At your right hand is bliss for evermore* (Ps. 16:11).

B. Said David before the Holy One, blessed be He, "Lord of the ages, now who will tell me which group [among those listed above] is the most beloved and blissful of them all?"

C. There were two Amoras [who differed on this matter]. One of them said, "It is the group that comes as representative of the Torah and commandments, as it is said, *With a flaming fire at his right hand* (Deut. 33:2)."

D. And the other said, "This refers to the scribes, the Mishnah repeaters, and those who teach children in their fear, who are going to sit at the right hand of the Holy One, blessed be He.

E. "That is in line with the following verse of Scripture: *I keep the Lord always before me, because he is at my right hand, I shall not be moved* (Ps. 16:8)."

5. A. Another matter concerning the verse *You show me the path of life, in your presence there is fulness of joy, in your right hand are pleasures for evermore* (Ps. 16:11): *In your presence there is fulness (SWB') of joy* (Ps. 16:11):

B. [Leviticus Rabbah adds: Read only "seven (SB') joys."] These are the seven religious duties associated with the Festival [Tabernacles].

C. These are they: the four species that are joined in the palm branch, [the building of] the Tabernacle, [the offering of] the festal sacrifice, [the offering of] the sacrifice of rejoicing.

6. A. If there is the offering of the sacrifice of rejoicing, then why is there also the offering of the festal sacrifice? And if there is [the offering of] the festal sacrifice, then why also is there [the offering of] the sacrifice of rejoicing?

B. Said R. Abin, "The matter may be compared to two who came before a judge. Now we do not know which one of them is the victor. But it is the one who takes the palm branch in his hand who we know to be the victor.

C. "So is the case of Israel and the nations of the world. The [latter] come and draw an indictment before the Holy One, blessed be He, on the New Year, and we do not know which party is victor.

E. "But when Israel goes forth from before the Holy One, blessed be He, with their palm branches and their citrons in their hands, we know that it is Israel that are the victors."

F. Therefore Moses admonishes Israel, saying to them, *[On the fifteenth day of the seventh month, when you have gathered in the produce of the land, you shall keep the feast of the Lord seven days...] And you shall take on the first day [the fruit of goodly trees, branches of palm trees and boughs of leafy trees and willows of the brook; and you shall rejoice before the Lord your God seven days. You shall keep it as a feast to the Lord seven days in the year; it is a statute for ever throughout your generations; you shall keep it in the seventh month. You shall dwell in booths for seven days; all that are native in Israel shall dwell in booths, that your generations may know that I made the people of Israel dwell in booths when I brought them out of the land of Egypt: I am the Lord your God* (Leviticus 23:39-43).

The intersecting-verse – Ps. 16:11 – leads us to the base-verse, after a long and majestic sequence of exegeses of the three elements of the intersecting-verse. But the implicit syllogism associated with the base-verse does not form the sole and principal interest of the exegesis of the intersecting-verse/contrastive-verse. When we do reach the base-verse, the connection turns out to be tight and persuasive. The original repertoire of key words – Torah, commandments, and the like – is reviewed. Nos. 5-6 go over the same verse with respect to Israel, introducing the matter of the New Year, Day of Atonement, and Festival. Then each clause suitably links to the several themes at hand. 6 of course is tacked on, since the composition concludes properly with No. 5, at which point the intersecting-verse has reached the base-verse.

XXVII:III

1. A. *He will regard the prayer of the destitute [and will not despise their supplication]* (Ps. 102:17):

   B. Said R. Reuben, "We are unable to make sense of David's character. Sometimes he calls himself king, and sometimes he calls himself destitute.

   C. "How so? When he foresaw that righteous men were going to come from him, such as Asa, Jehoshaphat, Hezekiah, and Josiah, he would call himself king as it is said, *Give the king your judgments, O God* (Ps. 72:1).

   D. "When he foresaw that wicked men would come forth from him, for example, Ahaz, Manasseh, and Amon, he would call himself destitute, as it is said, *A prayer of one afflicted, when he is faint [and pours out his complaint before the Lord]* (Ps. 102:1)."

2. A. R. Alexandri interpreted the cited verse *He will regard the prayer of the destitute [and will not despise their supplication]* (Ps. 102:17) to speak of a worker: "[Margulies, *ad loc.*, explains: The one afflicted is the worker. The word for faint, 'TP, bears the meaning, *cloak oneself,* hence in prayer. The worker then has delayed his prayer, waiting for the overseer to leave, at which point he can stop and say his prayer. So he postpones his prayer.] [So Alexandri says], "Just as a worker sits and watches all day long for when the overseer will leave for a bit, so he is late when he says [his prayer], [so David speaks at Ps. 102:1: *Hear my prayer, O Lord; let my cry come to you]."*

   B. "That [interpretation of the word 'TP] is in line with the use in the following verse: *And those that were born late belonged to Laban* (Gen. 30:42)."

   C. What is the meaning of *those that were born late*?

   D. R. Isaac bar Haqolah said, *"The ones that tarried."*

3. A. [Another interpretation: *He will regard the prayer of the destitute [and will not despise their supplication]* (Ps. 102:17):] Said R. Simeon b. Laqish, "As to this verse, the first half of it is not consistent with the second half, and vice versa.

   B. "If it is to be, 'He will regard the prayer of the destitute [individual],' he should then have said, 'And will not despise *his* supplication.'

   C. "But if it is to be, 'He will not despise *their* supplication,' then he should have said, 'He will regard the prayer of *those* who are destitute.'

   D. "But [when David wrote,] *He will regard the prayer of the individual destitute,* this [referred to] the prayer of Manasseh, king of Judah.

   F. "And [when David wrote,] *He will not despise* their *supplication,* this [referred to] his prayer and the prayer of his fathers.

   G. "That is in line with the following verse of Scripture: *And he prayed to him, and he was entreated (Y'TR) of him* (2 Chron. 33:13)."

   H. What is the meaning of the phrase, *He was entreated of him*?

   I. Said R. Eleazar b. R. Simeon, "In Arabia they call a breach an *athirta* [so an opening was made for his prayer to penetrate to the Throne of God]" (Slotki, p. 385, n. 3).

   J. *And he brought him back to Jerusalem, his kingdom* (2 Chron. 33:13).

   K. How did he bring him back?

   L. R. Samuel b. R. Jonah said in the name of R. Aha, "He brought him back with a wind.

   M. "That is in line with the phrase [in The Prayer], *He causes the wind to blow."*

   N. At that moment: *And Manasseh knew that the Lord is God* (2 Chron. 33:13). Then Manasseh said, "There is justice and there is a judge."

4. A. R. Isaac interpreted the verse *He will regard the prayer of the destitute [and will not despise their supplication]* (Ps. 102:17) to speak of these generations which have neither king nor prophet, neither priest nor Urim and Thummim, but who have only this prayer alone.

   B. "Said David before the Holy One, blessed be He, 'Lord of the ages, do not despise their prayer. *Let this be recorded for a generation to come'* (Ps. 102:18).

   C. "On the basis of that statement, [we know that] the Holy One, blessed be He, accepts penitents.

   D. *"So that a people yet unborn may praise the Lord* (Ps. 102:18).

E. "For the Holy One, blessed be He, will create them as a new act of creation."

5. A. Another interpretation: *Let this be recorded for a generation to come* (Ps. 102:18):

B. This refers to the generation of Hezekiah, [Leviticus Rabbah adds: which was tottering toward death].

C. *So that a people yet unborn may praise the Lord* (Ps. 102:18): for the Holy One, blessed be He, created them in a new act of creation.

6. A. Another interpretation: *Let this be recorded for a generation to come* (Ps. 102:18):

B. This refers to the generation of Mordecai and Esther, which was tottering toward death.

C. *So that a people yet unborn may praise the Lord* (Ps. 102:18): for the Holy One, blessed be He, created them in a new act of creation.

7. A. Another interpretation: *Let this be recorded for a generation to come* (Ps. 102:18):

B. This refers to these very generations [in our own day], which are tottering to death.

C. *So that a people yet unborn may praise the Lord* (Ps. 102:18):

D. For the Holy One, blessed be He, is going to create them anew, in a new act of creation.

8. A. What do we have to take [in order to reach that end]? Take up the palm branch and citron and praise the Holy One, blessed be He.

B. Therefore Moses admonishes Israel, saying, *[On the fifteenth day of the seventh month, when you have gathered in the produce of the land, you shall keep the feast of the Lord seven days...] And you shall take on the first day [the fruit of goodly trees, branches of palm trees and boughs of leafy trees and willows of the brook; and you shall rejoice before the Lord your God seven days. You shall keep it as a feast to the Lord seven days in the year; it is a statute for ever throughout your generations; you shall keep it in the seventh month. You shall dwell in booths for seven days; all that are native in Israel shall dwell in booths, that your generations may know that I made the people of Israel dwell in booths when I brought them out of the land of Egypt: I am the Lord your God* (Leviticus 23:39-43).

This is a fine example of how the framers of a perciope of the intersecting-verse/base-verse classification dwell on the intersecting-verse and provide an ample picture of its diverse meanings. The difference between this rhetorical pattern and the one dominant in Pesiqta deRab Kahana proves blatant, since the implicit syllogism to be imputed to the base-verse is simply not to be found in any aspect of the intersecting-verse/contrastive-verse – not at any point! The established pattern – the tripartite exegesis of Ps. 102:17, 18 – is worked out at No. 1 (supplemented by Nos. 2 and 3), then Nos. 4-7. Until the very final lines, No. 8, we have no reason at all to associate the exegesis of Ps. 102:17-18 with the theme of the Festival. On the contrary, all of the materials stand autonomous of the present "base-verse," and none of them hints at what is to come at the end.

XXVII:IV

1. A. *Let the field exult and everything in it. [Then shall all the trees of the wood sing for joy before the Lord, for he comes, for he comes to judge the earth]* (Ps. 96:12-13):

    B. *Let the field exult* refers to the world, as it is said, *And it came to pass, when they were in the field*   (Gen. 4:8) [and determined to divide up the world between them].

    C. *And everything in it* refers to creatures.

    D. That is in line with the following verse of Scripture: *The earth is the Lord's, and all that is in it* (Ps. 24:1).

    E. *Then shall all the trees of the wood sing for joy* (Ps. 96:12).

    F. Said R. Aha, "The forest and all the trees of the forest.

    G. *"The forest* refers to fruit-bearing trees.

    H. *"And all the trees of the forest* encompasses those trees that do not bear fruit."

    I. Before whom? *Before the Lord* (Ps. 96:14).

    J. Why? *For he comes* on New Year and on the Day of Atonement.

    K. To do what? *To judge the earth. He will judge the world with righteousness, and the peoples with his truth* (Ps. 96:13).

Ps. 96:12-14 supplies direct connections to the theme of Tabernacles, with its reference to trees of the wood, exultation and rejoicing, judgment, and the like. These topics are explicitly read into the intersecting-verse at the end, but I am inclined to see the whole as a single and unified construction, with 1.F-H as an interpolated comment. But the base-verse makes no appearance at all, on the one side, and among the holy days mentioned, The Festival is not one. So the passage is included for less than self-evident reasons.

XXVII:V

1. A. *I wash my hands in innocence [and go about your altar, O Lord, singing aloud a song of thanksgiving, and telling all your wondrous deeds]* (Ps. 26:6-7):

    B. [What I require I acquire] through purchase, not theft.

    C. [Leviticus Rabbah adds:] **For we have learned there: A stolen or dried up palm branch is invalid. And one deriving from an *asherah* or an apostate town is invalid** (M. Suk. 3:1A-B).

    D. *And go about your altar, O Lord* (Ps. 26:7).

    E. That is in line with what we have learned there: **Every day they circumambulate the altar one time and say, "We beseech you, O Lord, save now. We beseech you, O Lord, make us prosper now** [Ps. 118:25]. **R. Judah says, "I and him, save now." On that day they circumambulate the altar seven times** (M. Suk. 4:5).

2. A. *Singing aloud a song of thanksgiving* (Ps. 26:7) – this refers to the offerings.

    B. *And telling all your wondrous deeds* (Ps. 26:7):

    C. Said R. Abun, "This refers to the *Hallel* Psalms [Ps. 113-118], which contain [praise for what God has done] in the past, also [what he has

done] during these generations, as well as what will apply to the days of
the Messiah, to the time of Gog and Magog, and to the age to come.

D.   *When Israel went forth from Egypt* (Ps. 114:1) refers to the past.

E.   *Not for us, O Lord, not for us* (Ps. 115:1) refers to the present
generations.

F.   *I love for the Lord to hear* (Ps. 116:1) refers to the days of the Messiah.

G.   *All the nations have encompassed me* (Ps. 118:10) speaks of the time of
Gog and Magog.

H.   *You are my God and I shall exalt you* (Ps. 118:28) speaks of the age to
come."

I see no formal counterpart in Pesiqta deRab Kahana's other *pisqaot* – those
not shared with Leviticus Rabbah – to this rather odd composition.   The
elements are quite discrete and in no way convey demonstrations of a single
syllogism, quite the opposite.   No. 1 makes a point distinct from No. 2.   "The
innocence" of Ps. 26:6 refers to the fact that one must not steal the objects used
to carry out the religious duty of the waving of the palm branch at Tabernacles.
I assume that the allusion to Tabernacles in Ps. 26:6-7 is found in the referring
to circumambulating the altar, such as is done in the rite on that day, as 1.C
makes explicit.   No. 2 then expands on the cited verse in a different way.   To be
sure, the *Hallel* Psalms are recited on Tabernacles, but they serve all other
festivals as well.   Only No. 1 therefore relates to the established context of Lev.
23:40.   It follows that the exegeses of Ps. 26:6-7 were assembled and only then
utilized – both the relevant and also the irrelevant parts – for the present purpose.
The syllogisms are worked out in terms that are otherwise alien to our
document.

Now we reach the more familiar territory of the clause by clause exegesis of
the base-verse, with the syllogism imputed through the reading of each of those
discrete components.   But the intersecting-verse/contrastive-verse exercises have
not yielded a single and paramount syllogism.   If my thesis is correct, that the
rhetorical preferences of Leviticus Rabbah dominate here and those of Pesiqta
deRab Kahana make no impact, then we should uncover no cogent syllogism
read consistently into one component after another of the base-verse.   Rather, we
should anticipate quite the opposite, namely, a diverse program of syllogisms,
all of them relevant to the established theme, but none of them deeply engaged
with any other of them in the set.

For the effect of the contrastive-verse/base-verse construction is to produce a
single syllogism, which then serves to impart to the base-verse the meaning that
will be discovered everywhere, in each of its details.   If we have not been given a
syllogism on the foundation of the contrast between the external verse and the
base-verse, then we also should have no syllogism to emerge from each of the
components of the base-verse, and a diversity of (thematically appropriate, but
syllogistically diverse) propositions should emerge.   We shall now see that that
is the case.   Let me state with emphasis the operative criterion together with the

reason for it: *We have been given no implicit syllogism stated through the intervention of an contrastive-verse into the basic proposition established by the base-verse. We therefore shall discover no implicit syllogism stated through a systematic exegesis of the components of the base-verse on their own.*

XXVII:VI

1. A. *And you will take for yourselves* (Lev. 23:40):
   B. R. Hiyya taught, "The act of taking must be accomplished by each and every one of you."
   C. "For yourselves" – for every one of you. They must be yours and not stolen.
2. A. Said R. Levi, "One who takes a stolen palm branch – to what is he comparable? To a thief who sat at the cross roads and mugged passersby.
   B. "One time a legate came by, to collect the taxes for that town. [The thug] rose before him and mugged him and took everything he had. After some time the thug was caught and put in prison. The legate heard and came to him. He said to him, 'Give back what you grabbed from me, and I'll argue in your behalf before the king.'
   C. "He said to him, 'Of everything that I robbed and of everything that I took, I have nothing except for this rug that is under me, and it belongs to you.'
   D. "He said to him, 'Give it to me, and I'll argue in your behalf before the king.'
   E. "He said to him, 'Take it.'
   F. "He said to him, 'You should know that tomorrow you are going before the king for judgment, and he will ask you and say to you, "Is there anyone who can argue in your behalf," and you may say to him, "I have the legate, Mr. So-and-so, to speak in my behalf," and he will send and call me, and I shall come and argue in your behalf before him.'
   G. "The next day they set him up for judgment before the king. The king asked him, saying to him, 'Do you have anyone to argue in your behalf?'
   H. "He said to him, 'I have a legate, Mr. So-and-so, to speak in my behalf.'
   I. "The king sent for him. He said to him, 'Do you know anything to say in behalf of this man?'
   J. "He said to him, 'I do indeed have knowledge. When you sent me to collect the taxes of that town, he rose up before me and mugged me and took everything that I had. That rug that belongs to me gives testimony against him.'
   K. "Everyone began to cry out, saying, 'Woe for this one, whose defense attorney has turned into his prosecutor.'
   L. "So a person acquires a palm branch to attain merit through it. But if it was a stolen one, [the branch] cries out before the Holy One, blessed be He, 'I am stolen! I am taken by violence.'
   M. "And the ministering angels say, 'Woe for this one, whose defense attorney has turned into his prosecutor!'"

The theme of the preceding, the prohibition against using a stolen palm branch, is given two further treatments. Except in a formal way none of this pretends to relate to the specific verses of Lev. 23:40ff., nor do we find an intersecting-verse.

XXVII:VII

1. A. *On the fifteenth day of the seventh month, when you have gathered the produce of the land, you shall keep the feast of the Lord seven days;] on the first day [shall be a solemn rest]* (Lev. 23:40).

   B. This in fact is the fifteenth day, yet you speak of the first day!

   C. R. Mana of Sheab and R. Joshua of Sikhnin in the name of R. Levi said, "The matter may be compared to the case of a town which owed arrears to the king, so the king went to collect [what was owing]. [When he had reached] ten *mils* [from the town], the great men of the town came forth and praised him. He remitted a third of their [unpaid] tax. When he came within five *mils* of the town, the middle-rank people came out and acclaimed him, so he remitted yet another third [of what was owing to him]. When he entered the town, men, women, and children, came forth and praised him. He remitted the whole [of the tax].

   D. "Said the king, 'What happened happened. From now on we shall begin keeping books [afresh].'

   E. "So on the eve of the New Year, the Israelites repent, and the Holy One, blessed be He, remits a third of their [that is, Israel's] sins. On the ten days of repentance from the New Year to the Day of Atonement outstanding individuals fast, and the Holy One, blessed be He, remits most of their [that is, Israel's] sins. On the Day of Atonement all Israel fasts, so the Holy One, blessed be He, forgives them for all their sins [Leviticus Rabbah: says to Israel, 'What happened happened. From now on we shall begin keeping books afresh].'"

2. A. Said R. Aha, *"For with you there is forgiveness* (Ps. 80:4). From the New Year forgiveness awaits you.

   B. "Why so long? *So that you may be feared* (Ps. 80:4). To put your fear into creatures.

   C. "From the Day of Atonement to the Festival, all the Israelites are kept busy with doing religious duties. This one takes up the task of building his tabernacle, that one preparing his palm branches. On the first day of the Festival, all Israel they take their palm branches and citrons in their hand and praise the Holy One, blessed be He. The Holy One, blessed be He, says to them, 'What happened happened. From now on we shall begin keeping books [afresh].'"

   D. Therefore Scripture says, *On the first day.* What is the sense of the first day? It is first in the task of reckoning sins [done in the future], that is, from the first day of the festival.

Nos. 1 and 2 go over the same matter. It seems to me that Aha's version puts into concrete terms the basic point of Levi's. 2.D is out of place, since it ignores the antecedent materials and takes as its proof text a formula in no way important in the preceding. There can be no doubt that we have an implicit syllogism, which is that the Festival is an occasion for forgiveness, and that that fact derives from the wording of the base-verse. If we were in a composition particular to Pesiqta deRab Kahana, we should now expect further expositions of other clauses of the base-verse to demonstrate this same proposition – an important and powerful one. But that is not what we shall now find.

XXVII:VIII

1. A. *On the first day* (Lev. 23:40):
   B. By day and not by night.
   C. *On the...day* – even on the Sabbath.
   D. *On the* first *day* – only the first day [of the Festival] overrides the restrictions [of Sabbath rest. When the Sabbath coincides with other than the first day of the Festival, one does not carry the palm branch.]

2. A. *[And you shall take...] the fruit of a goodly tree [branches of palm trees and boughs of leafy trees and willows of the brook]* (Lev. 23:40).
   B. R. Hiyya taught, "A tree: the taste of the wood and fruit of which is the same. This is the citron."
   C. *Goodly (HDR)*: Ben Azzai said, "[Fruit] that remains [HDR] on its tree from year to year."
   D. Aqilas the proselyte translated [HDR] as, "That which dwells by water (Greek: *hudor*)."
   E. *Branches of a palm tree* (Lev. 23:40): R. Tarfon says, "[As to branch of palm tree (KPWT)], it must be bound. If it was separated, one has to bind it up."
   F. *Boughs of leafy trees*: The branches of which cover over the wood. One has to say, "This is the myrtle."
   G. *Willows of the brook*: I know only that they must come from a brook. How do I know that those that come from a valley or a hill [also are valid]? Scripture says, "*And* willows of a brook."
   H. Abba Saul says, "'*And* willows of the brook' refers to the requirement that there be two, one willow for the palm branch, and a willow for the sanctuary."
   I. R. Ishmael says, "'The fruit of goodly trees' indicates one; 'branches of palm tree' also one; 'boughs of leafy trees,' three; 'willows of the brook,' two. Two [of the myrtles] may have the twigs trimmed at the top, and one may not."
   J. R. Tarfon says, "Even all three of them may be trimmed."

We have a mass of exegetical materials, linking laws of the Festival to the verses of Scripture at hand. There is no pretense of interest an any implicit syllogism. Quite to the contrary, we might as well be in the deepest heart of Sifra or Sifré to Numbers, with their rather discrete exposition of verses, clause by clause. No. 1 conducts an inquiry into law, and No. 2 provides a word-for-word exegesis of the cited verse. Pages such as the present one in Pesiqta deRab Kahana are few and far between.

XXVII:IX

1. A. R. Aqiba says, *"The fruit of goodly (HDR) trees* refers to the Holy One, blessed be He, concerning whom it is written, *You are clothed with glory and majesty (HDR)* (Ps. 104:1).

B. *"Branches of palm trees* refers to the Holy One, blessed be He, concerning whom it is written, *The Righteous One shall flourish like a palm tree* (Ps. 92:13).

C. *"Boughs of leafy trees* refers to the Holy One, blessed be He, concerning whom it is written, *And he stands among the leafy trees* (Zech. 1:8).

D. *"And willows of the brook* refers to the Holy One, blessed be He, concerning whom it is written, *Extol him who rides upon the willows, whose name is the Lord* (Ps. 68:5)."

2. A. Another interpretation: *The fruit of goodly (HDR) trees* (Lev. 23:40):

B. This refers to Abraham, whom the Holy One, blessed be He, honored (HDR) with a goodly old age,

C. as it is said, *And Abraham was an old man, coming along in years* (Gen. 24:1).

D. [Leviticus Rabbah adds:] And it is written, *And you will honor (HDR) the face of an old man* (Lev. 19:32).

E. *Branches (KPWT) of palm trees* (Lev. 23:40):

F. This refers to Isaac, who was tied (KPWT) and bound upon the altar.

G. *And boughs of leafy trees* (Lev. 23:40):

H. This refers to Jacob. Just as a myrtle is rich in leaves, so Jacob was rich in children.

I. *Willows of the brook* (Lev. 23:40):

J. This refers to Joseph. Just as the willow wilts before the other three species do, so Joseph died before his brothers did.

3. A. Another interpretation: *The fruit of goodly tree* (Lev. 23:40):

B. This refers to Sarah, whom the Holy One, blessed be He, honored with a goodly old age, as it is said, *And Abraham and Sarah were old* (Gen. 18:11).

C. *Branches of palm trees* (Lev. 23:40): this refers to Rebecca. Just as a palm tree contains both edible fruit and thorns, so Rebecca produced a righteous and a wicked son [Jacob and Esau].

D. *Boughs of leafy trees* (Lev. 23:40): this refers to Leah. Just as a myrtle is rich in leaves, so Leah was rich in children.

E. *And willows of the brook* (Lev. 23:40): this refers to Rachel. Just as the willow wilts before the other three species do, so Rachel died before her sister.

4. A. Another interpretation: *The fruit of goodly trees* (Lev. 23:40) refers to the great Sanhedrin of Israel, which the Holy One, blessed be He, honored (HDR) with old age, as it is said, *You will rise up before old age* (Lev. 19:32).

B. *Branches (KPWT) of palm trees* (Lev. 23:40): this refers to disciples of sages, who compel (KWPYN) themselves to study Torah from one another.

C. *Boughs of leafy trees* refers to the three rows of disciples who sit before them.

D. *And willows of the brook* (Lev. 23:40): this refers to the court scribes, who stand before them, one on the right side, the other on the left, [and write down the opinions of those who vote to acquit and those who vote to convict].

5. A. Another interpretation: *The fruit of goodly trees* refers to Israel.

B. Just as a citron has both taste and fragrance, so in Israel are people who have [the merit of both] Torah and good deeds.

C. *Branches of palm trees* (Lev. 23:30): refers to Israel. Just as a palm has a taste but no fragrance, so in Israel are people who have [the merit of] Torah but not of good deeds.

D. *Boughs of leafy tree* refers to Israel. Just as a myrtle has a fragrance but no taste, so in Israel are people who have the merit of good deeds but not of Torah.

E. *Willows of the brook* refers to Israel. Just as a willow has neither taste nor fragrance, so in Israel are those who have the [merit] neither of Torah nor of good deeds.

F. Said the Holy One, blessed be He, "Utterly to destroy them is not possible.

G. "Rather, let them all be joined together in a single bond, and they will effect atonement for one another.

H. "And if you have done so, at that moment I shall be exalted."

I. Therefore Moses admonishes Israel: *[On the fifteenth day of the seventh month, when you have gathered in the produce of the land, you shall keep the feast of the Lord seven days...] And you shall take on the first day [the fruit of goodly trees, branches of palm trees and boughs of leafy trees and willows of the brook; and you shall rejoice before the Lord your God seven days. You shall keep it as a feast to the Lord seven days in the year; it is a statute for ever throughout your generations; you shall keep it in the seventh month. You shall dwell in booths for seven days; all that are native in Israel shall dwell in booths, that your generations may know that I made the people of Israel dwell in booths when I brought them out of the land of Egypt: I am the Lord your God* (Leviticus 23:39-43).

The base-text is systematically read in line with intersecting-verses referring to God. The species are read as symbolizing, in sequence, God, the patriarchs and matriarchs, Torah institutions, and Israel. The powerful result of the exegesis at Nos. 2, 3, is to link the species of the Festival to the patriarchs and matriarchs of Israel. It is continuous with the foregoing, linking the species to God, and with what is to follow, as the species will be compared to Israel's leadership, on the one side, as well, finally, to ordinary people, on the other. The reading of the symbols of the Festival at No. 4 as a parable of Israel's life continues, as noted above, now with reference to the (imaginary) national government. The final exegesis reaches its climax here, concluding, then, with the redactional subscript. The composition follows a single program, beginning to end, as it rehearses the several intersecting realms of Judaic symbol systems. Always at the climax come Torah and good deeds. The base-verse in the present composition yields diverse propositions and the notion of an implicit syllogism stated through a systematic exegesis of the components of the base-verse on their own has no bearing upon this interesting composition.

XXVII:X

1. A. R. Berekhiah in the name of R. Levi: "[God speaks], 'Through the merit [attained in fulfilling the commandment], *And you will take for yourself on the first day* ... (Lev. 23:40), lo, I shall be revealed to you first; I shall exact punishment for you from the first one; I shall build for you first; and bring to you the first one.'"

   B. "I shall be revealed for you first, as it is said, *I the Lord am first* (Is. 41:4).

   C. "I shall exact punishment for you from the first one refers to the wicked Esau, as it is written, *And the red one came forth first* (Gen. 24:24).

   D. "And I shall build for you first refers to the house of the sanctuary, concerning which it is written, *You throne of glory, on high from the first* (Jer. 17:12).

   E. "And I shall bring to you the first one, namely, the king messiah, concerning whom it is written, *The first to Zion I shall give* (Is. 41:27)."

The eschatological-salvific character of the Festival is now spelled out in specific detail. Esau, that is, Rome, will be punished, the Temple will be rebuilt, and the Messiah will come, all by virtue of the merit attained in observing the Festival. That all this is fresh and without preparation in the prior components of the *pisqa* requires no demonstration.

V
The Primacy of Documentary Discourse

The upshot may be stated very simply. The formal analysis of the characteristic rhetorical plan of Pesiqta deRab Kahana shows definitive traits: a *pisqa* aims at arguing a single, cogent syllogism, and this is in two rhetorical forms. A *pisqa* in Pesiqta deRab Kahana systematically presents a single syllogism, which is expressed through, first the contrast of an external verse with the base-verse – hence, the Propositional Form, in which the implicit syllogism is stated through the intervention of an contrastive-verse into the basic proposition established by the base-verse, and then through the a systematic exegesis of the components of the base-verse on their own, hence through the Exegetical Form.

In Leviticus Rabbah's *parashah* 30 which is also Pesiqta deRab Kahana's *pisqa*, we find neither of these forms. Since these forms otherwise characterize our document, that is, Pesiqta deRab Kahana, it follows that *Pisqa* 27 does not fit well with the rhetorical program of Pesiqta deRab Kahana, so far as the materials distinctive to our document, viewed whole, define that program. What is striking is that both components that prove relevant, *the intersecting-verse/base-verse construction* of Leviticus Rabbah = *the Propositional Form* made up of the contrastive-verse/base-verse construction of Pesiqta deRab Kahana, and also the Exegetical Form shared between both documents, with its clause by clause exegesis of the base-verse, prove remarkably disparate.

Since we have travelled a considerable distance from our point of departure, let me now briefly state the results of this exercise.

A. Pesiqta deRab Kahana's authorship resorted to three rhetorical patterns:

1. *The Propositional Form:* The implicit syllogism is stated through the intervention of an contrastive-verse into the basic proposition established by the base-verse.

2. *The Exegetical Form:* The implicit syllogism is stated through a systematic exegesis of the components of the base-verse on their own.

3. *The Syllogistic List:* The syllogism is explicit, not implicit, and is proven by a list of probative examples.

B. The nature of these rhetorical preferences also suggests that the order in which these types of forms occur will be as just now given, first the syllogism generated by the intersection of the contrasting and base-verses, then the syllogism repeated through a systematic reading of the base-verse on its own, finally, whatever miscellanies the framers have in hand (or later copyists insert).

C. When we compare our document with another by examining a *pisqa* of Pesiqta deRab Kahana that is not unique to that composition but is shared with Leviticus Rabbah, we see that the definitive rhetorical traits of our document also prove distinctive – and differ from the rhetorical plan elsewhere shown to characterize that other document.

The results are to be stated with appropriate emphasis.

Rhetorical analysis has yielded the proposition that Pesiqta deRab Kahana consists of twenty-eight syllogisms, each presented in a cogent and systematic way by the twenty-eight pisqaot, respectively. Each pisqa contains an implicit proposition, and that proposition may be stated in a simple way. It emerges from the intersection of an external verse with the base-verse that recurs through the pisqa, and then is restated by the systematic dissection of the components of the base-verse, each of which is shown to say the same thing as all the others.

The pisqa shared with Leviticus Rabbah violates the rhetorical plan characteristic of the twenty-three pisqaot that are unique to Pesiqta deRab Kahana but (as I have shown elsewhere) it conforms with great precision to the rhetorical plan characteristic of all of the parashiyyot of Leviticus Rabbah.

Pisqaot of Pesiqta deRab Kahana that are shared with Leviticus Rabbah conform to the rhetorical plan of that document and therefore are primary to Leviticus Rabbah and secondary to Pesiqta deRab Kahana. The reason that the authorship of the latter document has made use of these materials requires explanation as part of the larger syllogistic program of Pesiqta deRab Kahana.

These results show us that, when we read two documents that share what appear to be a single rhetorical program, we find that we have different people saying some of the same things in quite different ways. In this rather difficult and subtle case, modes of rhetoric not only do not transcend documentary lines, they express in subtle ways the deeper mode of syllogistic discourse that the authorships of the respective documents have chosen for themselves. The differences in rhetoric therefore may be explained in accord with the requirements of documentary discourse. Ignoring the boundaries of documents and treating all midrash-exegeses as interchangeable among documents violates the rhetorical character of the midrash-compilations that preserve those midrash-exegeses. Here too it would appear that Kugel has misrepresented the character of the literary genre he proposes to define. Having shown that fact as to the rhetorical and topical program of the midrash-compilations under discussion, we now proceed to the still more consequential issue, that of the logical cogency of documents. We shall now ask whether the documents constitute nothing more than scrapbooks, indifferent containers to whatever people wish to preserve, or whether they constitute cogent statements, made within a clearly-defined and precisely executed theory of discourse: syllogisms that rest upon a proportioned and sustained inner logic that produces intelligible and persuasive propositions.

Part Three

THE LOGIC OF INTELLIGIBLE DISCOURSE
THE INTEGRITY OF THE MIDRASH-DOCUMENT
FIVE CASES

Prologue

The Logic of Intelligible Discourse

*Forever after, one cannot think of the verse or hear it recited without
also recalling the solution to its problematic irritant—indeed,
remembering it in the study-house or synagogue, one would certainly
pass it along to others present, and together appreciate its cleverness and
erudition. And so midrashic explications of individual verses no doubt
circulated on their own, independent of any larger exegetical context.
Perhaps in this sense it would not be inappropriate to compare their
manner of circulating to that of jokes in modern society; indeed, they
were a king of joking, a learned and sophisticated play about the biblical
text, and like jokes they were passed on, modified, and improved as they
went, until a great many of them eventually entered into the common
inheritance of every Jew, passed on in learning with the text of the Bible
itself.[1]*

James Kugel

Kugel maintains that the principal mode of formulating and transmitting
midrash-exegeses was not documentary but discrete. So he states, *And so
midrashic explications of individual verses no doubt circulated on their own,
independent of any larger exegetical context.* He does not tell us for how long
these "explications of individual verses" circulated on their own, independent of
any larger exegetical context, or how, or why, they then formed into aggregates.
He does not indicate whether or not he thinks that the (later) conglomeration of
exegeses of verses into larger composites, then into still larger ones, and finally
into complete documents, persisted even after (some) documents took shape.
Indeed, the position he wishes to maintain does not intersect with analysis of
any document as a whole or even as to its larger parts, so we cannot be certain
we have understood precisely what, if anything, Kugel has in mind. Let me
turn, therefore, to the contrary proposition, to be stated with precision and then
demonstrated thoroughly and in detail.

While the data of rhetoric prove suggestive, the principle that documents
define the initial limits of discourse stands or falls upon a single claim. It is
that a given document establishes through a *cogent* program of rhetoric, topic,
and logic the point that, through all detailed discourse within the document, the
authorship of the document wishes to make. The proportions of the whole, the

---

[1]P. 95.

cogency of the parts, the integrity of detail and proposition, of rhetoric, topic, and logic – all form a whole and distinctive entity, speaking metaphorically, a book with beginning, middle, and end. If that principle does not hold in the description of midrash-literature, then a hermeneutic that ignores documentary limits and treats as primary not the document but components – the atoms, not the molecules, so to speak – proves congruent to the character of the literature's program, if not to its rhetorical plan. If I cannot demonstrate documents' fundamental cogency, in rhetoric, logical principle of intelligible discourse, and program and proposition, then Kugel is right that *midrashic explications of individual verses no doubt circulated on their own, independent of any larger exegetical context*. But a principle of interpretation that imposes on the literature premises contradictory of the character of the literature cannot stand and must be set aside.

When we uncover what holds a document together, we may state what we conceive to be the logic of intelligible discourse of that document. And others may devise tests of verification and falsification as well. That is, we may explain what turns discrete sentences into paragraphs, paragraphs into chapters, chapters into a book: a whole and complete statement, one cogent within itself and exhibiting integrity, one also congruent to those patterns of judgment and argument that govern discourse beyond the pages of the book and so allow us to read that book among other books: the deep syntax and structure of intellect of one kind rather than some other. Under discussion therefore is the mode of shared intelligibility leading to the possibility of making sense of, and accepting, the propositions at hand. The matter of logic proves central, for it is through the logic of intelligible and cogent discourse that an authorship proposes to communicate – and succeeds in doing so. When we grasp the distinctive principles of intelligibility, we also uncover what is common between the authorship of the document and its readership beyond. Then the context becomes clear, the original setting known, and the power of the literature to transcend the limits of context and setting affects even us, so long afterward.

The criteria for analyzing midrash as literature – rhetoric, topic, and logic – therefore draw us onward to the issue of logic, as is now clear, the logic of shared intelligibility that – to repeat – lends proportion and position to the parts and a proposition of cogency and integrity to the whole The questions we therefore bring to our documents are these:

1.   Structure: how, overall, does the document organize its materials? do the framers follow a clearly discernible principle or organization, through which they wish to establish a proposition? or are matters haphazard?

2.   Plan: does the document at hand follow a fixed and limited plan, a repertoire of rhetorical forms? or do the framers simply use whatever comes to hand, without attention to the rhetorical traits of their materials?

3.   Program: do these forms yield cogent and intelligible proposition(s), one(s) that, in some recurrent interest(s) or point(s) of emphasis, may make of

the whole if not more than, then at least, the sum of the parts? or does the authorship simply assemble this and that on whatever subject comes to mind?

Affirmative answers to these questions yield the hermeneutic that the document defines the lines of structure, therefore dictates the opening questions of analysis and interpretation. Negative answers justify ignoring documentary lines and attending solely to the smallest whole units of discourse, the completed units of thought, inclusive of proposition, that we may discern one by one.

How shall we identify what I claim to be evidences of a well-composed plan for the rhetoric, logic, and topic of a document? It is by uncovering, on the basis of systematic inquiry, the fundamental literary structures inherent in a document. A literary structure is a set of rules that dictate recurrent conventions of expression, organization, proportion, as well as modes of cogent and intelligible discourse even encompassing an implicit syllogism, that are *extrinsic* to the message of the author. The conventions at hand bear none of the particular burden of the author's message, which is delivered only or mainly in the details, so they are not idiosyncratic. They convey in their context the larger world-view expressed within the writing in which they are used, so prove systemic and public. That is because a literary structure conforms to rules that impose upon the individual writer a limited set of choices about how he will convey whatever message he has in mind. Or the formal convention will limit an editor or redactor to an equally circumscribed set of alternatives about how to arrange received materials. These conventions then form a substrate of the literary culture that preserves and expresses the world view and way of life of the system at hand.

On the basis of what merely appears to us to be patterned or extrinsic to particular meaning and so entirely formal, we cannot allege that we have in hand a fixed, literary structure. Such a judgment would prove subjective. Nor shall we benefit from bringing to the text at hand recurrent syntactic or grammatical patterns shown in other texts even of the same canon of literature to define conventions for communicating ideas in those other texts. Quite to the contrary, we find guidance in a simple principle: *A text has to define its own structures for us*. This its authors do by repeatedly resorting to a given set of linguistic patterns and literary conventions and no others. On the basis of inductive evidence alone we testify the thesis that the authors at hand adhere to a fixed canon of literary forms. If demonstrably present, we may conclude that these forms will present an author or editor with a few choices on how ideas are to be organized and expressed in intelligible – again, therefore, public – compositions.

So internal evidence and that alone testifies to the literary structures of a given text. When, as in the present exercise, we draw together and compare five distinct documents, each one to begin with has to supply us with evidence on its own literary structures. It follows that the adjective "recurrent" constitutes a redundancy when joined to the noun "structure." For we cannot know that we have a structure if the text under analysis does not repeatedly resort to the presentation of its message through that disciplined structure external to its message on any given point. And, it follows self-evidently, we do know that we have a structure when the text in hand repeatedly follows recurrent conventions of expression, organization, or proportion *extrinsic* to the message of the author. How shall we proceed to identify the structures of the documents before us? It seems to me that, as we did in Chapter Three, we had best move first to the analysis of a single whole and large unit of a document, e.g., a *pisqa* or *parashah*. We seek, within that *parashah*, to identify what holds the whole together. The second step then is to see whether we have identified something exemplary, or what is not an example of a fixed and formal pattern, but a phenomenon that occurs in fact only once or at random.

In the survey that follows we therefore pursue the issues of rhetorical plan and topical and logical program. The purpose is to demonstrate that, for the five documents of our sample, the documents do impart to the materials contained within them distinctive and recurrent characteristics of intellect. In my studies of other documents of the canon of the dual Torah of late antiquity, the Mishnah, Tosefta, tractate Abot, The Fathers According to Rabbi Nathan, the Talmud of the Land of Israel, the Talmud of Babylonia, and so forth, I have pursued the same analyses of rhetoric, logic, and topic, and in each case have shown that a document exhibits distingive, even singular traits in all of the three dimensions of literary analysis. But since Kugel proposes to define in particular the literature of midrash in particular,[2] I restrict my sample to documents that fall within that category of the larger literature of the ancient rabbis.

It must follow that viewed within their larger documentary contexts, discrete thought units that we find within the documents belong within them (if *not* only within them) because each of these discrete thought units, in some detail, and all of them in the aggregate, carry out the overall plan and program of the authorship of the documents. Then the declared and manifest policy of reading the contents of the documents without any reference whatsoever to the definitive power of those documents violates the character of the literature, midrash, that the critics claim to interpret.

---

[2] I remain puzzled by his making statements about what is essential to the definition of midrash that apply equally accurately (or inaccurately) to what is essential to the definition of halakhic writings as well. But his position, that *at heart midrash is nothing less than the foundation stone of rabbinic Judaism and it is as diverse as Jewish creativity itself* presumably finds its corollary in the homogenizing of all literature within the category, midrash. Had he used the word Torah, he would have chosen a term more appropriate to his theological position.

Chapter Four

Sifra

I

Structure

A clear picture of the overall mode of organization derives from a sample of Sifra, as follows:[1]

PARASHAT NEGAIM PEREQ 1

A. *And the Lord spoke to Moses and to Aaron saying, A man (Adam) when there will be on the skin of his body* (Lev. 13:1-2) –

B. Why does Scripture say so [speaking of Adam + will be]?

C. Because it is said, *And a man or a woman, when there will be on the skin of his flesh bright spots [the priest shall make an examination, and if the spots on the skin of his body are of a dull white, it is tetter that has broken out in the skin; he is clean]* (Lev. 13:38-9) –

D. [This refers to] clean bright spots.

E. It is hardly necessary to speak [in Lev. 13:2] of [GRA: I know only about] bright spots which do not exhibit the colors of plagues and which have not come into the category [of uncleanness, for Lev. 13:38-9 includes them].

F. But [there are, in accord with Lev. 13:2, clean] bright spots which do [nonetheless] exhibit the colors of plagues [namely]:

G. Which were on him and he converted –
on the infant and he was born –
on the crease [of the flesh] and it was unfolded –
on the head and on the beard –
on the festering boil and burning and blister –

H. Their [those items in G] colors changed, whether to produce a lenient or a stringent ruling –
R. Eleazar b. Azarah declares clean.
R. Eleazar b. Hisma says, "To produce a lenient ruling – it is clean, and to produce a stringent ruling – let it be examined afresh."
R. Aqiva says, "Whether to produce a lenient or a stringent ruling, it is examined afresh" [M. Neg. 7:1].

---

[1]See my *Sifra. The Judaic Commentary on Leviticus. A New Translation. The Leper. Leviticus 13:1-14:57.* Chico, 1985: Scholars Press for Brown Judaic Studies. Based on the translation of *Sifra Parashiyyot Negaim* and *Mesora* in *A History of the Mishnaic Law of Purities. VI. Negaim. Sifra.* [With a section by Roger Brooks.]

I.   Therefore it is said, *A man (Adam) – when there will be* (Lev. 13:1).

N1:1

A.   *When there will be* (Lev. 12:2) –
B.   From the [time at which this law is] proclaimed [namely, Sinai] onward.
C.   And is it not logical?
D.   It [Scripture] has declared unclean with reference to Zabim and has declared unclean with reference to plagues.
E.   Just as in the case of Zabim, it declared clear [such appearances of uncleanness as occurred] before the pronouncement [of the Torah], so in reference to plagues, it declared clear [such appearances of uncleanness as occurred] on them before the pronouncement.

N1:2

F.   It [moreover] is an argument *a fortiori*:
     If in the case of Zabim, whose uncleanness and uncleanness may be determined by anyone, it [Scripture] has declared free before the declaration, plagues, the uncleanness or cleanness of which may be declared only by a priest, is it not logical that it should declare them clear before the declaration?
G.   No. If you have so stated concerning Zabim, whom it [Scripture] did not declare unclean when [the flux is] accidental, will you say so concerning plague, which is declared unclean [even when the uncleanness is] accidental?
H.   Since is declared unclean [even when the uncleanness is] accidental, will it declare them clear before the pronouncement [of the Scriptural law]?
I.   Therefore Scripture says, When it well be, meaning, from the pronouncement [at Sinai] and onward.

N1:3

A.   *On the skin of his flesh* (Lev. 13:2).
B.   What does Scripture mean to say?
C.   Because it is said, *And hair in the diseased spot has turned white,* (Lev. 13:3), might one say I have reference only to a place which is suitable to grow white hair? But a place which is not suitable to grow white hair – how do we know [that it is susceptible]?
D.   Scripture says, *On the skin of his flesh* – as an inclusionary clause.
[E.   *A swelling or an eruption or a spot* (Lev. 13:2).]
F.   *A swelling* – this is a swelling.
G.   *A spot* – this is a spot.
H.   *An eruption (SPHT)* – this is secondary [in color] to the bright spot.
I.   *And its shade is deep [Lev. 13:3: And the shade of the plague is deep]* – [the color of the SPHT is] secondary to that of the swelling.
J.   What is the meaning of the word eruption (ST)? Prominent (MWBHQT) (GRA: MWGBHT).
K.   **Like the shades of the shadow, which are higher than the appearance of the sun.**
L.   What is the meaning of the word deep (MWQ)?
M.   **Deep as the shades of the sun, which are deeper than the shadow.**
N.   What is the meaning of the work eruption (SPHT)? Secondary (TPYLH).

O. As it is said, *Put me (SPHYNY), I pray you, in one of the priest's places...* (I Sam. 2:36).

P. *And it will be* (Lev. 13:2) – teaches that they [the colors] join together with one another to declare clear and to certify and to shut up.

Q. *On the skin of his flesh* (Lev. 13:2) – on the skin of that flesh which can be seen [or: in accord with its appearance].

R. On this basis have they said:

A bright spot appears dim on a German and the dim one on the Ethiopian appears bright.

N1:4

S. R. Ishmael says, "The house of Israel – lo, I am atonement for them – lo, they are like boxwood, not black and not white but intermediate."

T. R. Aqiva says, "The artists have pigments with which they color skin black, white, and intermediate. One brings the intermediate pigment and surrounds it [the bright spot] on the outer perimeter, and it will appear like the intermediate."

U. R. Yose says, "One Scripture says, *On the skin of the flesh* (Lev. 13:2), and another Scripture says, *On the skin of the flesh* (Lev. 13:2)."

V. We therefore find that

the specification of colors of plagues are meant to produce a lenient ruling, but not to produce a strict ruling. One therefore examines the German in accord with his skin-tone to produce a lenient ruling.

W. It comes out that [thereby] one carries out, On the skin of his flesh.

X. And the Ethiopian is adjudged in accord with the intermediate pigment to produce a lenient ruling.

Y. It comes out that [thereby] one carries out, On the skin of the flesh.

Z. And sages say, "This [and this are adjudged in accord with] the intermediate [M. Neg. 2:1]."

N1:5

A. *And it will be on the skin of his flesh [for a plague]* (Lev. 13:2).

B. This teaches that he is pained by it.

C. And how do we know that also others are pained by it?

D. They see him, that he is pained by it.

E. Scripture says, *For a plague* (Lev. 13:2).

F. *A leprosy [sign]* (Lev. 13:2) – the size of a split bean.

G. And is it not logical?

H. It has declared unclean here [where there is white hair], and it has declared unclean in reference to quick flesh.

I. Just as quick flesh is the size of a split bean, so also here [we require] a sign the size of a split bean.

N1:6

J. No. If you have said so concerning quick flesh, which must be the size of a lentil, will you say so concerning [a leprosy sign, marked as unclean by] white hair, for the space of white hair requires nothing [no specific area].

K. Scripture says, *Leprosy* (Lev. 13:2) – a sign the size of a split bean.

N1:7

A. *And he will be brought to Aaron [the priest or to one of his sons the priests]* (Lev. 13:2).
B. I know only about Aaron himself.
C. How do we know to include another priest?
D. Scripture says, *The priest* (Lev. 13:2).
E. How do we know to include [as suitable examining priests] those [priests who are] injured?
F. Scripture says, *Among his sons* (Lev. 13:2).
G. Then perhaps should I also include profaned [disqualified priests, HLLYM]?
H. Scripture says, *The priests* (Lev. 13:2) – the disqualified priests are excluded.
I. And how do we know to include any Israelite [qualified to examine the plague]?
J. Scripture says, *Or to one.*

N1:8

K. If our end is to include every Israelite, why does Scripture say, Or to one of his sons the priests?
L. But to teach that the actual declaration of uncleanness or cleanness is only by a priest.
M. How so?
N. A sage who is an Israelite examines the plagues **and says to the priest, even though he is an idiot, "Say, Unclean," and he says, "Unclean." "Say, Clean," and he says, "Clean"** [M. Neg. 3:1].
O. Another matter:
P. Why does Scripture say, *Or to one of his sons the priests* (Lev. 13:2)
Q. Since it is said, *In accord with their instructions will be every dispute and every plague* (Deut. 21:5), controversies are linked to plagues. Just as plagues must be decided by day, so controversies must be judged by day.

N1:9

R. **Just as controversies may not be settled by relatives, so plagues may not be examined relatives** [M. Neg. 2:5].
S. If [we should now attempt to continue]: Just as controversies must be with three [judges] so plagues must be examined by three [priests] – it is an argument a fortiori.
T. If his property [dispute] is settled by a decision of three judges, should his body not be examined by three?
U. Scripture says, *Or to one of his sons the priests* (Lev. 13:2).
V. This teaches that a single priest examines the plagues.

N1:10

The structure of Sifra is readily described. The document is organized as a sequence of exegeses of verses of the book of Leviticus. A further important trait stands out. The document further introduces into the amplification of the chosen verses of Scripture citations of the Mishnah or the Tosefta. A substantive trait is a strong interest in showing that the rules of the Mishnah or the Tosefta in fact derive from Scripture, not from the working of processes of reason.

II

Plan

The rhetorical plan of the Sifra, as the sample indicates, involves two fundamental rhetorical patterns, first, a citation of a verse followed by a few words that state the sense or meaning of that verse; second, the verbatim citation of a passage of the Mishnah in association with a verse of Scripture. We may call the former plan exegetical, the latter polemical, in that the latter rhetoric always serves to demonstrate the proposition stated just now, the priority of Scripture within the dual Torah of written and oral media.

We may distinguish the two rhetorical forms by reference to the use of attributions. The former tends not to attribute its materials, the latter does. That is to say, in the main Sifra tends not to attribute its materials to specific authorities, and most of the pericopae containing attributions are shared with Mishnah and Tosefta. Of 354 items in my surveyed population, a total of 76 contain attributions, 21% of the whole. But of these, all but 20 are shared with Mishnah and Tosefta, 5% of the whole. We may say that it is highly uncommon for Sifra to attribute to named authorities materials peculiar to itself.[2]

The polemical form requires differentiation in yet another way. Sifra contains a fair sample of pericopae which do not make use of the forms common in the exegesis of specific Scriptural verses and, mostly do not pretend to explain the meaning of verses, but rather resort to forms typical of Mishnah and Tosefta. When Sifra uses forms other than those in which its exegeses are routinely phrased, it commonly, though not always, draws upon materials also found in Mishnah and Tosefta. Of 87 pericopae which are non-exegetical but follow forms typical of Mishnah and Tosefta, all but 16, 18%, are in fact common to Sifra and Mishnah and Tosefta. Of these 16, moreover, Nos. 40, 48, 54, and 62 are exegetical in substance, that is, dispute-forms are applied to exegetical materials. That leaves not more than 12 items, 14% of the whole sample of non-exegetical pericopae, unique to Sifra and not concerning exegetical problems in a substantive manner. Accordingly, we may conclude that it is uncommon

---

[2]All factual statements in this chapter derive from my *History of the Mishnaic Law of Purities*. VII. *Negaim. Sifra* (Leiden, 1976: E. J. Brill). The sample is 13% of the whole of Sifra.

for Sifra to make use of non-exegetical forms for materials peculiar to its compilation.

We may further differentiate within the exegetical pericope between the simplest exegetical form and somewhat more elaborate renditions of it. We now turn to those pericopae, predominant in Sifra, in which the center of interest is the exegesis of Scripture. These may be categorized as follows. First is the simple, in which a verse, or an element of a verse, is cited, and then a very few words explain the meaning of that verse. Second is the complex, in which a simple exegesis is augmented in some important way, commonly by questions and answers, so that we have more than simply a verse and a brief exposition of its elements or of its meaning as a whole. Second is the complex form, commonly involving a dialectical exegesis. Every example of a complex form, that is, a pericope in which we have more than a cited verse and a brief exposition of its meaning, may be called "dialectical," that is, moving or developing an idea through questions and answers, sometimes implicit, but commonly explicit. What "moves" is the argument, the flow of thought, from problem to problem. The movement is generated by the raising of contrary questions and theses. There are several subdivisions of the dialectical exegesis, so distinctive as to be treated by themselves. Let us begin with the largest catalogue. All of the items which follow are marked by the presence of more than a single unit of thought or the exposition of a range of questions, and all exhibit a flow of logical argument, unfolding in questions and answers, characteristic, in the later literature, of *gemara*.

One important subdivision of the complex form consists of those items, somewhat few in number but all rather large in size and articulation, intended to prove that logic alone is insufficient, and that only through revealed law will a reliable view of what is required be attained. The polemic in these items is pointed and obvious; logic (DYN) never wins the argument, though at a few points flaws in the text seem to suggest disjunctures in the flow of logic. A further, unimportant subdivision of the stated form consists of those items whose primary purpose is to show that Scripture has good reasons for whatever it tells us. Each of the following begins, "Why does Scripture say so?" When Sifra makes use of materials common to Sifra and Mishnah and Tosefta, it commonly relies upon a fairly limited, and normally quite clear-cut, set of phrases which join an antecedent exegesis to a pericopae found also in Mishnah and Tosefta.

The rhetorical plan of the document may be stated very simply. First, the authorship of the Sifra does not commonly attribute its traditions to named authorities, and when it does, it is in the context of materials common to Sifra and Mishnah and Tosefta. Second, Sifra contains a predominance of exegetical pericopae, of 356 counted above, only 85 (23%) are non-exegetical in formal character and intent. Of these 85, fully 69 are shared by Sifra and Mishnah and Tosefta, and of the remainder, four are exegetical in substance, not in form (they are disputes). Accordingly, a negligible proportion of the whole – evidently approximately 12 items or 3% of the estimated total number of pericopae – in fact are both non-exegetical and also distinctive to Sifra. Where Sifra does not draw upon materials common to Mishnah and Tosefta, it is nearly wholly exegetical in character. In a fair number of items – 73 (20% of 356) – Sifra makes use of a very simple exegetical form, consisting of the citation of a verse followed by the provision of a few words explaining the meaning of the verse or of a word or phrase in the verse. All of the remaining exegetical items – 186 (as much as 60-65% of the whole) – are characterized as dialectical. They present an argument which moves from point to point through a series of questions and answers.

The literary analysis strikingly distinguishes the literary traits of those shared pericopae from those of pericopae distinctive to Sifra. Pericopae found in both Sifra and Mishnah and Tosefta accord with the literary preferences and forms common to Mishnah and Tosefta and conflict with those peculiar to Sifra. The materials common to Sifra and Mishnah and Tosefta nearly always take the forms and formulaic patterns characteristic of Mishnah and Tosefta and found in Sifra, with remarkably few exceptions, primarily in those shared materials. Sifra commonly makes not the slightest effort to link each element of the shared materials to the exegesis of Scriptures, which is its primary interest. Or if there is a connection between exegesis and the law stated in the materials common to both compilations, then that exegesis touches only one aspect, not always an important one, of the stated law.

III

Program

Sifra's authorship clearly has undertaken a well-considered program, which guides them in their reading of the verses of Scripture they have selected for exegesis. We may define that program solely in its relationship to the Mishnah and Tosefta, because, as the formal plan has already indicated, a principal and recurrent point of interest is the relationship of Scripture's law to that in the Mishnah. The first problem is, at what points do Sifra and Mishnah and Tosefta share a common agenda of interests, and at what points does one compilation introduce problems, themes, or questions unknown to the other? The answer to these questions will show that Sifra and Mishnah and Tosefta form two large concentric circles, sharing a considerable area in common. Sifra, however, exhibits interests peculiar to itself.

While as much as one third of the corpus of Sifra covers rules not known to Mishnah and Tosefta, when we eliminate refinements of laws known, explicitly or implicitly, to Mishnah and Tosefta, as well as narrowly exegetical statements, we reduce the number to 56. Seventy-five percent of all items peculiar to Sifra cover matters in which Mishnah and Tosefta cannot be said to be much interested. Sifra and Mishnah and Tosefta, where they do have common interests to begin with, are nearly wholly concentric. That is to say, with Sifra as the base and Mishnah and Tosefta as the variable, the two corpora seem to have in common 94% of all important items; a minimum of 81% of all pertinent items, important and unimportant, are shared in substance and even in exact language. The former figure will become still more important when we use Mishnah as the base and Sifra as the variable, for, as we shall see in a moment, the same procedure will yield nearly the same percentage of shared themes, interests, and pericopae using the same language. It would seem that, on the criterion of common themes and interests, with the sole omission of purification rites, in which Sifra clearly has a unique and predominant concern, Mishnah and Tosefta and Sifra exhibit a remarkable unity. This underlines the conclusion reached in the examination of forms and the obvious implication of shared pericopae, which is that Mishnah and Tosefta and Sifra draw upon pretty much the same common stratum of materials and reflect a single set of conceptions and issues.

Remarkably few pericopae in Mishnah will have surprised the pericopae unique to Mishnah go over ground. We may with some confidence say that, with Mishnah as the base and Sifra as the variable, Sifra covers nearly the whole 96% of Mishnah's themes and problems. On the surface, this would argue that Mishnah follows Sifra. But this is hardly a decisive consideration. Our earlier results make it far more likely that both compilations derive in their main conceptual traits from the last quarter of the second century and the first quarter of the third. Both documents make use of discrete pericopae completed in Ushan times and in the period of Rabbi – and cite them in pretty much identical language. As we now see, both documents also cover the same ground, sharing something like 90-95% of the same themes and ideas, not to mention laws. The major compilations – Sifra, the Mishnah and Tosefta – share a common agenda of legal interests. Both evidently draw upon materials which reached their state before the redaction of either – as a whole or in large constitutive elements – commenced. Neither can be treated in isolation from the other.

IV

Document

In a few words we may revert to our opening issue and settle the questions raised there.

1.   Structure: how, overall, does the document organize its materials? The framers follow a clearly discernible principle or organization, citing verses one by one to amplify their sense or to join the verse to a passage of Scripture. The document is exegetical in a strict sense: it systematically explains the meaning of verses of Scripture and it organizes its materials in line with the order of those verses.

2. Plan: does the document at hand follow a fixed and limited plan, a repertoire of rhetorical forms? There are two rhetorical patterns, and these govern throughout.

3. Program: do these forms yield cogent and intelligible proposition(s), one(s) that, in some recurrent interest(s) or point(s) of emphasis, may make of the whole if not more than, then at least, the sum of, the parts? We can discern at least one important polemic, and, beyond that, we see a systematic picture of the sense and meaning of the cited passage. There is nothing random or casual about the propositional program of the document.

It follows that the overall plan and program of the authorship of our document do impart to the parts a cogency of rhetoric, syllogistic logic of cogent discourse, and even proposition or topic, making of the parts something that joins and therefore transcends them all. Ignoring the plan and program of the authorship of Sifra renders incomprehensible what is in fact an intelligible and cogent statement. I look in vain for evidence in support of Kugel's allegation that *Our midrashic compilations are in this sense potentially deceiving, since they seem to treat the whole text bit by bit; but with the exception of certain patterns, these "bits" are rather atomistic, and, as any student or rabbinic literature knows, interchangeable, modifiable, combinable – in short, not part of an overall exegesis at all.* I do not see a single passage in the brief sample of Sifra we have reviewed, which is interchangeable with any other, let alone "modifiable" or "combinable" with any other, outside of its concrete context. The "certain patterns" of our sample of Sifra govern the whole. They are two, and they dictate the character of the details – if not, in the nature of things, the content. And yet a severe and recurrent polemic operates even in the details, as we shall now see, once more, in our encounter with the companion document, Sifré to Numbers.

Chapter Five

Sifré to Numbers

I

Structure

Sifré to Numbers falls into the classification of Sifra, as a document formed around another document, hence, a commentary to a text. The order of the completed units of thought follows that of the base-document, and the program as we shall see is worked out in response to the statements of that base-document, the book of Numbers. That fact by itself cannot demonstrate that the book of Numbers has defined the program of Sifré to Numbers, because, as a matter of fact, Sifré to Numbers as we know it reveals a fair amount of picking and choosing on the part of the compilers of its materials. The results of Chapter Two, moreover, underline the simple fact that compilers of a document make choices in terms of their broader program of syllogisms, and the results of Chapter Three demonstrate that the principle of logical discourse affects the way in which syllogisms are expressed. In Chapter Four we have seen how an important polemic of the authorship of Sifra imparts its imprint upon both the plan and the program of that document, specifically, the concern to demonstrate the priority of Scripture over logical inquiry. It follows that the rhetorical plan expresses the logic and the topic of a document, that is to say, in our case, the document's syllogistic method and the substantive program, respectively.

Sifré to Numbers is laid out as a commentary to blocks of verses of the book of Numbers, though not as a systematic commentary to everything in that book. It follows that the authorship at hand wishes to amplify passages in its base-text and finds in that base-text a sufficient topical program, rhetorical structure and logical principle of cogency. But the document's authorship has then contributed its composition, with a clearly identifiable rhetoric, logic, and topic of its own. So, it follows that authorship had in mind a method and a message to amplify or extend or otherwise augment those of the base-document. Part of what that authorship contributed becomes clear when we realize that even the structure provided by the base-document represents a choice and a rejection of other possibilities. For other (I think, later) framers of midrash-comilations made other choices entirely. What the authorships of Sifra, Sifré to Numbers, not to mention Sifré to Deuteronomy, chose to do, therefore, should not be taken for granted. Those authorships form one circle of redaction and formulation. The fact that a document finds its organizing principle in the plan and program of some other – midrash-compilation in Scripture, Sifré to Numbers in the Book of Numbers – will prove suggestive when we see how other documents approach their task in different ways, ignoring the primacy of a book or passage of Scripture when laying out the sequence of ideas and issues at hand.

II

Plan

As in the case of Pesiqta deRab Kahana, presented in Chapter Two, we shall work inductively, by taking up a sample *pisqa* of Sifré to Numbers and forming a thesis on the character of its rhetorical plan, then testing that thesis on the strength of two other *pisqaot*. What we shall see is that the same rhetorical plan characteristic of Sifra applies to Sifré to Numbers, exegesis of a base-verse, linking of a base-verse to a Mishnah- or Tosefta-passage with the repeated allegation that reason alone will not have yielded a firm foundation for the rule stated in the Mishnah or the Tosefta.

VI:I

1. A.   *...every man's holy thing shall be his; whatever any man gives to the priest shall be his* (Num. 5:10).
   B.   All manner of consecrated produce originally was covered by the general principle stated here: "...every man's holy thing shall be his; whatever any man gives to the priest shall be his."
   C.   Scripture thus drew all Holy Things and assigned them to the priest, among them omitting reference only to the thanksgiving-offering, peace-offering, Passover-offering, tithe of cattle, produce in the status of Second Tithe, and fruits of an orchard in the fourth year after its planting, all of which are to belong to the farmer [not to the priest].

The form consists of the citation of an opening verse, followed by an issue stated in terms extrinsic to the cited verse. That is to say, no word or phrase of the base-verse (that is, the cited verse at the beginning) attracts comment. Rather a general rule of exegesis is invoked. C then introduces a broad range of items not at all subject to attention in the verse at hand. The formal traits: [1] citation of a base-verse from Numbers, [2] a generalization ignoring clauses or words in the base-verse, [3] a further observation without clear interest in the verse at hand. But the whole is linked to the theme of the base-verse – and to that alone.   So an extrinsic exegetical program comes to bear. We shall provisionally call this the extrinsic exegetical form. In due course the extrinsic patterns will undergo their own differentiation, as will the corresponding internal ones.

VI:II

1. A.   *...every man's holy thing shall be his; whatever any man gives to the priest shall be his* (Num. 5:10).

B. On the basis of this statement you draw the following rule:

C. If a priest on his own account makes a sacrificial offering, even though it falls into the week [during which] another priestly watch than his own [is in charge of the actual cult, making the offerings and receiving the dues], lo, that priest owns the priestly portions of the offering, and the right of offering it up belongs to him [and not to the priest ordinarily on duty at that time, who otherwise would retain the rights to certain portions of the animal] [T. Men. 13:17].

What we have is simply a citation of the verse plus a law in prior writing (Mishnah, Tosefta) which the verse is supposed to sustain. The formal traits require [1] citation of a verse, with or without comment, followed by [2] verbatim citation of a passage of the Mishnah or the Tosefta. What we have is a formal construction in which we simply juxtapose a verse, without or with intervening words of explanation, with a passage of the Mishnah or the Tosefta.

VI:III

1. A. ...*every man's holy thing shall be his; whatever any man gives to the priest shall be his* (Num. 5:10).

B. "Why does Scripture make this statement?

C. "Because, with reference to the fruit of an orchard in the fourth year after its planting, it is said, *And in the fourth year all their fruit shall be holy, an offering of praise to the Lord* (Lev. 19:24), [I do not know whether the sense is that] it is holy for the farmer or holy for the priesthood. Accordingly, Scripture says, '...every man's holy thing shall be his; whatever any man gives to the priest shall be his,' Scripture thereby speaks of produce of an orchard in the fourth year after its planting, indicating that it should belong to the farmer," the words of R. Meir.

D. R. Ishmael says, "It is holy to the farmer.

E. "You maintain that it is holy for the farmer. Or is it holy for the priesthood? Lo, this is how you may logically [rather than by reference to the exegesis, B-C, based on Scripture] deal with the problem:

F. "Produce in the status of second tithe is called holy, and the fruit of an orchard in the fourth year after its planting is called holy. If I draw the analogy to produce in the status of second tithe, which belongs only to the farmer, then likewise produce of an orchard in the fourth year after its planting should belong only to the farmer."

G. No, produce separated as heave-offering [for priestly use] proves to the contrary, for it too is called Holy, but it belongs only to the priest. And that furthermore demonstrates for produce of an orchard in the fourth year after its planting that even though it is called holy, it should belong only to the priesthood.

H. "You may then offer the following argument to the contrary [showing the correct analogy is to be drawn not to heave-offering but to produce in the status of second tithe, as follows:] the correct separation of produce in the status of second tithe involves bringing the produce to the holy place [of Jerusalem, where it is to be eaten], and, along these same lines, produce of an orchard in the fourth year after its planning likewise involves bringing that produce to the holy place. If, therefore, I draw the rule for produce in the status of second tithe, maintaining that it belongs to the owner, so produce of an orchard in the fourth year after its planting likewise should belong only to the owner."

I.   [No, that argument can be disproved from another variety of produce entirely:] lo, produce designated as first fruits will prove to the contrary, for such produce likewise has to be brought to the holy place, but it belongs only to the priest. So produce in that classification will prove for produce of an orchard in the fourth year after its planting, showing that even though it has to be brought to the holy place, it also should belong only to the priests. [So the labor of classification continues.]

J.   "You may compose [the following argument to reply to the foregoing:] The [result of the] separation of produce in the status of second tithe falls into the classification of holy and has to be brought to the holy place, but further is subject to redemption [in that one can redeem the actual fruit and replace it with ready cash, and one may then bring that cash to Jerusalem and buy for it produce to be eaten in Jerusalem under the rules governing second tithe]. Produce of an orchard in the fourth year after its planting likewise is called holy, has to be brought to the holy place, and is subject to the rules of redemption. But let the matter of heave offering not come into the picture, for even though it is called holy, it does not have to be brought to the holy place [but is eaten wherever it is located], and let the matter of first fruit likewise not enter the picture, for even though it is produce that has to be brought to the holy place, it is not called holy."

K.   Lo, there is the case of the firstling, which *is* called holy, and which has to be brought to the holy place, but which belongs only to the priesthood. [So we can now provide an appropriate analogy.] And that case will prove [the rule for other sorts of produce subject to the same traits, specifically] produce of an orchard in the fourth year after its planting, for, even though it is called holy, and even though it has to be brought to the holy place, it should belong only to the priesthood.

L.   "You may invoke the consideration of separating [the produce into one of its several classifications]. Let me call to account three distinct considerations in a single exercise:

M.   "[1] Food in the status of second tithe is called holy, requires delivery to the holy place, and is subject to the rules of redemption,

N.   "[2] Produce of an orchard in the fourth year after its planting is called holy, requires delivery to the holy place, and is subject to the rules of redemption.

O.   "[1] But let not food that has been designated as heave-offering enter into consideration. For even though it is called holy, it does not require delivery to the holy place,

P.   "And [2] let not first fruits enter into consideration. For even though it requires delivery to the holy place, it is not called holy.

Q.   "Nor should [3] the firstling enter into consideration. For even though it is called holy and requires delivery to the holy place, it is not subject to the rules of redemption.

R.   "Let me then draw the appropriate analogy from the correct source, and let me then compose a logical argument on the basis of the correct traits of definition.

S. "I shall draw an analogy on the basis of three shared traits from one matter to another, but I shall not drawn an analogy from something which exhibits three traits to something which does not share these same traits, but only one or two of them.

T. "If then I draw an analogy to produce in the status of second tithe, which belongs only to the owner, so too in the case of produce of an orchard in the fourth year after its planting, it should belong only to the owner."

VI:IV

2. A. R. Joshua says, "What is called holy belongs to the owner.

B. "You maintain that what is called holy belongs to the owner. But perhaps it belongs only to the priesthood?

C. "Scripture states, 'But in the fifth year you may eat of their fruit that they may yield more richly for you' (Lev. 19:25). To whom does the increase go? To him to whom the produce already has been assigned [that is to say, the farmer, not the priesthood]."

We have a debate on whether reason unaided by Scripture can prevail. A-C prove essential to what is to follow, since Ishmael's purpose is not merely to make his point, D, but to demonstrate that logic, without Scripture, can sustain that same point, E-T. The form of argument is fairly standard through our document, with a series of arguments by analogy. We prove that the item at hand is like another item and therefore follows its rule, or is unlike that item and therefore follows the opposite of its rule. The argument is formalized to an extreme, and there are very few variations among exempla of this form, though one – the matter of length – should not be missed. The exegesis of the verse at hand plays no substantial role, beyond its initial introduction. What is critical is the issue of the reliability of logic. The base-verse before us contributes virtually nothing and in no way serves as the foundation for the composition at hand, which is sustained and handsomely executed. The fundamental issue, of course, transcends the subject-matter: can we on the basis of unaided reason reach the correct conclusions (which, as a matter of fact, we already know)? Ishmael shows we can, Meir first, then Joshua offer a narrowly-exegetical proof for the same proposition.

VI:IV

1. A. *...every man's holy thing shall be his; whatever any man gives to the priest shall be his* (Num. 5:10).

B. Why is this verse articulated? Because it is said, *All the holy offerings which the people of Israel present to the Lord I give to you [priests]* (Num. 18:19), might I infer that the priests may seize these gifts by force?

C. Scripture says, *...every man's holy thing shall be his; whatever any man gives to the priest shall be his* (Num. 5:10).

D. This indicates that the gratitude for the benefit of holy things belongs to the farmer [and the priest cannot seize the things by force but must accept them as gifts and give gratitude to the farmer for assigning those gifts to him in particular].

The verse itself is clarified in contrast with another verse that makes the same point. Now the focus is on the base-verse and not a broader issue. We may call this an intrinsic exegetical form, in that the focus of exegesis is on the verse, which is cited and carefully spelled out.

VI:V

1. A. ...*every man's holy thing shall be his; whatever any man gives to the priest shall be his* (Num. 5:10).

   B. Lo, if one has taken the measure of the produce on the ground, and further produce is added to them pile, is it possible that I may invoke in connection with the pile as a whole the verse, ...*every man's holy thing shall be his* (Num. 5:10) [so that the farmer now owns all of the produce]?

   C. Scripture states, "...whatever any man gives to the priest shall be his." [The priest retains the right to the produce originally designated but cannot stake a claim on the priestly share of the additional produce.]

   D. Or is it possible that even if one has measured out the designated produce in a basket, and further produce is added to what has been designated, I may invoke in that regard, "...every man's holy thing shall be his"?

   E. Scripture states, "...whatever any man gives to the priest shall be his." [The priest retains the right to the produce originally designated.]

VI:V

2. A. R. Yose says, "Lo, if one has paid the priest the redemption money for his first born son within the thirty days after birth, but the infant has died, might I invoke in that case, '...whatever any man gives to the priest shall be his [the priest's]? [Then the priest would not have to return the money.] [No, for] Scripture further states, '...every man's holy thing shall be his.' [The priest does have to return the money.]

   B. "If the child dies after thirty days, the money may not be recovered from the priest's possession, and I recite in that connection, '...whatever any man gives to the priest shall be his [the priest's].'"

Once again the apparent contradiction between the two clauses of the verse is smoothed out, by assigning each statement to a different circumstance. The exegesis of the verse then forms the center of interest. Thus the classification is the intrinsic exegetical form. We may now define the formal conventions of *Pisqa* 6:

i. Extrinsic Exegetical Form

The form consists of the citation of an opening verse, followed by an issue stated in terms extrinsic to the cited verse. That is to say, no word or phrase of the base-verse (that is, the cited verse at the beginning) attracts comment. Rather a general rule of exegesis is invoked. C then introduces a broad range of items not at all subject to attention in the verse at hand. The formal traits: [1] citation of a base-verse from Numbers, [2] a generalization ignoring clauses or words in the base-verse, [3] a further observation without clear interest in the verse at hand. But the whole is linked to the theme of the base-verse – and to that alone. So an extrinsic exegetical program comes to bear. We shall call this the extrinsic exegetical form. But in our final catalogue, we shall find reason to differentiate among a number of extrinsic-exegetical forms.

ii. Intrinsic Exegetical Form

The verse itself is clarified. In the first instance, the exegesis derives from the contrast with another verse that makes the same point. But the formal trait should not be missed. It is that the the focus is on the base-verse and not on a broader issue. We may call this an intrinsic exegetical form, in that the focus of exegesis is on the verse, which is cited and carefully spelled out. We shall know that we have it when the base-verse is cited, clause by clause or in other ways, and then given an ample dose of attention.

The distinction between extrinsic and intrinsic exegesis emerges from a simple formal trait: do verses other than the base-verse, that is, the verse of the book of Numbers under discussion, play a considerable part? Are there many such verses besides the base one, or only a few? Do those many verses deal with the topic of the base-verse or other topics? If the former, then they may serve to illuminate the verse under discussion, if the latter, then all the verses together, including the one chosen from the book of Numbers, may serve to demonstrate a given proposition external to all of the proof-texts. These questions find answers not in impressions but in simple facts: number of verses other than the base-verse, origins of those other verses. No one can answer those questions merely on the basis of subjective impressions. But we have now to move quickly to the promised differentiation within the two gross categories, extrinsic and intrinsic.

iii. Dialectical Exegesis: Intrinsic

While this form does not occur above, it is so important that we should introduce it in our initial catalogue. It consists of a sequence of arguments about the meaning of a passage, in which the focus is upon the base-verse, and a sequence of possibilities is introduced to spell out the meaning of that verse. At issue is not the power of logic but the meaning of the base-verse, but that issue is pursued through an argument of many stages.

iv. Dialectical Exegesis: The Fallacy of Logic Uncorrected by Exegesis of Scripture

Whether or not this is an intrinsic or an extrinsic exegesis is beside the point, because the pattern at hand is not interested in the exegesis of a verse, though exegesis plays a role in the pattern. Rather, the focus is upon an issue that applies to all exegeses: is exegesis necessary at all, or can logic, independent of the evidence of scriptural verses, reach firm and reliable conclusions?

Formally, we deal with another moving, or dialectical, exegetical form, but while the basic trait is familiar – a sequence of shifts and turns in the possibility of interpretation, all of them subjected to close logical scrutiny, the purpose is different. And the purpose comes to expression not in content, particular to diverse passages, but in form. The formal indicator is the presence of the question, in one of several versions: is it not a matter of logic? That is the never-failing formal indicator. From that clause we invariably move on to a set of arguments of a highly formalized character on taxonomic classification: what is like, or unlike? What is like follows a given rule, what is unlike follows the opposite rule, and it is for us to see whether the likenesses or unlikenesses prevail. (When Ishmael's name occurs, they prevail, and when Aqiba's occurs, they do not. But these seem rather conventional.) The argument is formalized to an extreme, and there are very few variations among our document's exempla of this form, though one – the matter of length – should not be missed. The exegesis of the verse at hand plays no substantial role, beyond its initial introduction. What is critical is the issue of the reliability of logic. The base-verse before us contributes virtually nothing and in no way serves as the foundation for the composition at hand. An important example is given at **CVII:III.3**, but there are many others. Let us quickly review a fine example of the form.

CVII:III

3 . A. Issi b. Aqabia says, "'...to the Lord from the herd or from the flock...to make a pleasing odor to the Lord' means, from this species by itself or from that species by itself.

B. "You say that it means, from this species by itself or from that species by itself.

C. "But perhaps one may bring both simultaneously?

D. "For there is an argument *a fortiori:* Now if the lambs brought for the Pentecost offering, which are brought in pairs, are valid if they come from a single species, a burnt-offering, which is not brought in a pair [but is brought all by itself], surely should be valid if it is of the same species as [the species of the other beast which accompanies it]!

E. "No, if you have stated that rule in the case of the two lambs brought for Pentecost, concerning which Scripture imposed fewer requirements in connection with bringing them, and so validated them even if they come from a single species, will you say the same of the burnt-offering, in which case Scripture has imposed more requirements in connection with the offering. Therefore it should not be valid unless it [and the beast accompanying it] derive from two different species.

F. "Now the goats brought on the Day of Atonement and those brought on the New Month should prove the contrary. For Scripture has imposed on those offerings multiple requirements and yet they are valid if they all come of a single species. So they should provide a valid analogy for the burnt-offering, so that, even though it comes along with numerous requirements, it too should be valid if it [and the beasts accompanying it] come from a single species.

G. "No, if you have stated that rule concerning the goats brought on the Day of Atonement and those brought on the New Month, for even though Scripture has imposed on those offerings multiple requirements, they are not brought on every day of the year [but only on specified occasions], and therefore they all may derive from a single species. But will you say the same of the burnt-offering, for, even though it comes along with numerous requirements, it may be offered on every day of the year. Therefore it should be valid only if it is accompanied by beasts of other species.

H.   "Lo, a sin-offering will prove to the contrary. For in its regard Scripture has imposed numerous requirements, and it may be offered on every day of the year, and it may come only if it is from a single species. So that should prove the rule for the burnt-offering, in which case, even though Scripture has imposed numerous requirements, and even though it is brought every day of the year, it should be valid only if it derives from a single species.

I.   "No, if you have stated that rule concerning the sin-offering, on which Scripture has imposed limitations, since it may not be brought by reason of a vow or a freewill offering, and therefore it is valid only if it derives from a single species, will you say the same of the burnt-offering, which is available for a variety of purposes, since it may be brought in fulfilment of a vow or as a freewill offering? Therefore it should be valid only if it derives from a single species.

J.   "Why then is it necessary for Scripture to specify, '...to the Lord from the herd or from the flock...to make a pleasing odor to the Lord,' meaning, from this species by itself or from that species by itself."

Issi's proof, No. 3, is that only Scripture can give reliable guidance as to the law. The issue again is whether the beasts for the specified offerings encompass both sheep and goats, or whether one may bring two sheep or two goats. The exercise presents the usual frustrations, since each analogy is shown to be inadequate. In consequence, argument by analogy by itself does not suffice, and only a clear exegesis of Scripture settles the question. As we see, there is no interest only in the explanation of the cited verses or even of their topic. The real issue – the generative and precipitating intellectual program of the pericope – lies elsewhere. It is whether or not logic alone suffices. That issue is extrinsic to the passage at hand. But it occurs throughout our document and forms one of its recurrent formal choices.

v.   Scriptural Basis for a Passage of the Mishnah

What we have is simply a citation of the verse plus a law in prior writing (Mishnah, Tosefta) which the verse is supposed to sustain. The formal traits require [1] citation of a verse, with or without comment, followed by [2] verbatim citation of a passage of the Mishnah or the Tosefta. So far as I can see, then five large units of Pisqa 6 all fall within these formal compositions. Do these suffice? Are other formal patterns to be defined? To answer these questions we proceed to two further *pisqaot*, selected at random.

Sifré to Numbers 59

LIX:I.

1. A. *Now the Lord said to Moses, Say to Aaron and tell him, When you set up the lamps, [the seven lamps shall give light in front of the lampstand. And Aaron did so. He set up its lamps to give light in front of the lampstand, as the Lord commanded Moses. And this was the workmanship of the lampstand, hammered work of gold; from its base to its flowers, it was hammered work; according to the pattern which the Lord had shown Moses, so he made the lampstand]* (Num. 8:1-4):

   B. Why is this passage spelled out?

   C. Because Scripture says, *Make seven lamps for this and mount them to shed light over the space in front of it* (Ex. 25:37).

   D. On this basis should I infer that all of the lights should illumine the entire face of the candelabrum?

   E. Scripture says, "...shall give light in front of the lampstand."

   F. It is so that the lamps will converge on the candelabrum and the candelabrum on the lamps. How so? Three will go toward the east, three to the west, one in the middle, so that all of them converge on the middle one.

   G. On this basis R. Nathan says, "The one in the middle is the most honored of them all."

   Form II: Intrinsic-Exegetical

XLIX:I

2. A. "...Say to Aaron":

   B. Because the entire matter depends on the action of Aaron, Aaron is included in the statement to begin with.

   Form II: Intrinsic-Exegetical

XLIX:I

3. A. "... and tell him":

   B. Lo, in this way Aaron is admonished.

   Form II: Intrinsic-Exegetical

XLIX:I

4. A. "...When you set up the lamps":

   B. [Since the word for "set up" and the word for "steps" make use of the same root, the sense is:] make steps [for the candelabrum].

   Form II: Intrinsic-Exegetical

XLIX:I

5. A. "... in front of the lampstand":

   B. Make for the candelabrum a front and an inner part.

   Form II: Intrinsic-Exegetical

XLIX:I

6. A. "...the seven lamps shall give light [in front of the lampstand]":

   B. May I infer that they should give light at all times?

   C. Scripture says, *...from dusk to dawn before the Lord* (Lev. 24:3).

D. May I infer that then the priest should put out the lamp?

E. Scripture says, *...from dusk to dawn before the Lord   continually* (Lev. 24:3).

F. How so?   The seven lamps will give light from evening to morning, "before the Lord continually."

G. The sense is that the westernmost lamp should be kept burning continually, and from that the lamp is to be kindled at dusk.

Form II: Intrinsic-Exegetical

XLIX:I

7. A. "...the seven lamps shall give light [in front of the lampstand]":

B. May I infer that they should give light at all times?

C. Scripture says, *...from dusk to dawn before the Lord* (Lev. 24:3).

D. May I infer that then the priest should put out the lamp?

Form II: Intrinsic-Exegetical

Sifré to Numbers 106

CVII:I

1. A. *The Lord said to Moses, "Say to the people of Israel, When you come into the land you are to inhabit"* (Num. 15:1-16):

B. R. Ishmael says, "Scripture's purpose is to indicate that the Israelites were obligated to bring drink-offerings [to accompany animal-offerings] only after they had entered the land."

Form II: Intrinsic-Exegetical

CVII:I

2. A. [Continuing the thesis of Ishmael:] Scripture addresses the period after the division and inheritance [settlement] of the Land.

B. You say that Scripture addresses the period after the division and settlement of the Land.   But perhaps it speaks of the time immediately upon their entry into the Land [and before the division and settlement]?

C. Scripture says, *When you come into the land which the Lord your God is giving to you and have inherited it and settled in it* (Deut. 17:14).

D. Since the word "coming" is mentioned without further specification, and, further, Scripture has given you details of the meaning of the word in one of the cases in which it occurs, namely, that "coming" speaks only after actual inheritance and settlement, so here too, in all places in which the word "coming" occurs in the Torah, it speaks only of the case after the inheritance and settlement.

Form II: Intrinsic-Exegetical

CVII:I

3. A. And the further fact is that every such passage refers to your dwelling *in* the land [and not outside of it].

B. Said to him R. Aqiba, "Since Scripture says, *It is a Sabbath to the Lord in all your dwellings* (Lev. 23:3), may I draw the inference that that is both in the land and outside of the land?"

C. Said to him R. Ishmael, "It is not a necessary inference at all.   Just as the most minor of religious duties pertain both outside of the land and in the land, the Sabbath, a principal religious duty, all the more so should apply in the land as well as outside of the land."

Form I: Extrinsic Exegetical
[No special interest in the terms of the cited verse at all, but this is continuous with the foregoing]

CVII:I

4. A. Said one of the disciples of R. Ishmael, "The verse of Scripture comes to tell you that an individual was obligated to bring drink-offerings only after the entry into the land."

   B. R. Simeon b. Yohai says, "Scripture comes to tell you in regard to drink-offerings that they are to be offered on a high place [before the building of the Temple]."

   C. Abba Hanin says in the name of R. Eliezer, "Why is this statement made? It is because one might have reasoned thus: since we find that the number of garments used for the cult in the eternal house [the Temple in Jerusalem] is greater than the number of garments to be worn in the tent of meeting, so we should require more drink-offerings in the eternal house than the number of drink-offerings required in the tent of meeting.

   D "Scripture therefore states, '...and you offer to the Lord from the herd or from the flock an offering by fire or a burnt-offering or a sacrifice,' to indicate that even though the number of garments used for the cult in the eternal house [the Temple in Jerusalem] is greater than the number of garments to be worn in the tent of meeting, we not should require more drink-offerings in the eternal house than drink-offerings in the tent of meeting."

Form I: Extrinsic Exegetical
[No special interest in the terms of the cited verse at all]

CVII:II

1. A. "...and you offer to the Lord from the herd or from the flock an offering by fire [or a *burnt-offering* or a *sacrifice*, to fulfil a vow or as a freewill offering, or at your appointed feasts]":

   B. May I infer that whatever is offered as an offering by fire requires a drink-offering?

   C. Scripture refers specifically to a burnt-offering.

   D. I know only that that is the case of a *burnt-offering*.

   E. How do I know that the same rule applies to peace-offerings?

   F. Scripture alludes to a *sacrifice*.

   G. How about a thank-offering?

   H. Scripture refers to a sacrifice.

   I. Is the implication that one bring drink-offerings with these and likewise with a sin-offering or a guilt-offering?

   J. Scripture states, "...to fulfil a vow or as a freewill offering:" I have therefore encompassed within the rule [that drink-offerings are required] only Holy Things that are brought on account of a vow or a freewill-offering.

   K. Then the inference is that I exclude these [a sin-offering or a guilt-offering, which do not require drink-offerings], but then I should further exclude a burnt-offering brought in fulfilment of an obligation on the pilgrim festivals [since that would be excluded by the rule that what is brought on one's own option requires the drink-offerings].

L. When Scripture makes explicit reference to "at your appointed feasts," Scripture encompasses the obligatory burnt-offering brought on festivals. [That sort of offering requires drink-offerings as well.]

M. Then the inference is that one encompasses in the requirement of bringing drink-offerings a burnt-offering brought as a matter of obligation on pilgrim festivals and likewise a sin-offering that also is brought as a matter of obligations on festivals.

N. Scripture says, "... you offer to the Lord from the herd or from the flock." An animal "from the herd" was encompassed by the general rule but singled out from the general rule to teach you a trait of the encompassing rule itself.

O. That is, specifically, just as an animal of the herd is brought on account of a vow or as a freewill-offering and requires drink-offerings, so whatever is brought on account of a vow or as a freewill-offering requires drink-offerings.

P. Then a sin-offering and a guilt-offering are excluded, for these do not come on account of keeping a vow or as a thank-offering [but only when the obligation is imposed on account of an inadvertent violation of the law], and so these do not require drink-offerings.

Form III: Dialectical Exegesis: Intrinsic

This is a masterpiece of dialectical exegesis, in which a single line of thought is spun out through a variety of possibilities. The exegesis is moving, as it progresses from point to point, but remarkably cogent. I cannot imagine how a more uniform composition can have been written. At every point each issue is addressed to the base-verse, and every conceivable problem of analogical logic has been worked out. And the base-verse is always in focus.

CVII:III

1. A. "'...from the herd or from the flock an offering by fire or a burnt-offering or a sacrifice, to fulfil a vow or as a freewill-offering, or at your appointed feasts, to make a pleasing odor to the Lord:'

   B. "Why is this stated?

   C. "Since it is said, '... and you offer to the Lord from the herd or from the flock an offering by fire or a burnt-offering or a sacrifice,' I might infer that the same rule applies to a burnt-offering brought of fowl, namely, that drink-offerings should be required.

   D. "Scripture specifies, '...from the herd or from the flock,' to indicate that burnt-offerings of fowl do not require drink-offerings," the words of R. Josiah.

   E. R. Jonathan says, "Such an argument is not required. For in any case it is said, '...or a sacrifice.' Just as a sacrifice always derives from a beast, so a burnt-offering under discussion here involves a beast [and not fowl, so drink-offerings are not required for fowl].

   F. "Why then does Scripture say, "...from the herd or from the flock an offering by fire or a burnt-offering or a sacrifice, to fulfil a vow or as a freewill-offering, or at your appointed feasts, to make a pleasing odor to the Lord'?

G. "Because Scripture says, 'and you offer to the Lord from the herd or from the flock an offering by fire.'

H. "The point is, if someone has said, 'Lo, incumbent on me is a burnt-offering and peace-offerings,' should I infer that he should bring the two of them simultaneously [of the same species]?

I. "Scripture says, '...from the herd or from the flock,' to indicate that one brings a beast of this species by itself and one of that species by itself."

Form II: Intrinsic Exegetical

CVII:III

2. A. On the basis of the present passage, furthermore, you may derive the rule governing the animal to be designated as a Passover-offering.

B. Since Scripture says, *Your lamb shall be without blemish, a male a year old; you shall take it from the sheep or from the goats* (Ex. 12:5), the meaning is, from this species by itself or from that species by itself.

C. You say that one should take a beast from this species by itself or from that species by itself.

D. Or perhaps one may bring from both species simultaneously?

E. Scripture says, *If his gift for a burnt-offering is from the flock, from the sheep or goats, he shall offer a male without blemish* (Lev. 1:10).

F. Now that statement produces an argument *a fortiori*: if a burnt-offering, which is a weighty matter, is suitable if it derives from a single species, a Passover, which is a lighter-weight offering, all the more so that it should be valid if it come from one species. Then why does Scripture say, "...you shall take it from the sheep or from the goats"? To indicate, from this species by itself or from that species by itself.

Form I: Extrinsic Exegetical

CVII:III

3. A. [Given above.]

Form IV: Dialectical Exegesis: Fallacy of Logic

No. 3, proves that only Scripture can give reliable guidance as to the law. Each analogy is shown to be inadequate. In consequence, argument by analogy by itself does not suffice, and only a clear exegesis of Scripture settles the question.

CVII:IV

1. A. ...*then [the one who brings the offering] shall offer:* (Num. 15:1-16):

B. I know only that a man is subject to the rule. How do I know that the woman also is required [to bring drink-offerings]?

C. Scripture says, *"The one who brings* the offering" – encompassing all cases.

Form II: Intrinsic Exegetical

CVII:IV

2. A. *...then [the one who brings the offering] shall offer:* (Num. 15:1-16):

   B. R. Nathan says, "This passage forms the generative analogy for all cases in which one voluntarily brings a meal-offering, that he should bring no less than a tenth ephah of fine flour and a log of oil."

   Form II: Intrinsic Exegetical

CVII:IV

3. A. "...then he who brings his offering shall offer to the Lord a cereal offering of a tenth of an ephah of fine flour, mixed with a fourth of a hin of oil, and wine for the drink-offering, a fourth of a hin:"

   B. The oil is for stirring and the wine for a drink-offering.

   Form II: Intrinsic Exegetical

CVII:V

1. A. *...[then he who brings his offering shall offer to the Lord a cereal-offering of a tenth of an ephah of fine flour, mixed with a fourth of a hin of oil, and wine for the drink-offering, a fourth of a hin,] you shall prepare with the burnt-offering, or for the sacrifice, for each lamb* (Num. 15:1-16):

   B. Why is the statement made, [that is, "...you shall prepare with the burnt-offering, or for the sacrifice, for each lamb"]?

   C. Since Scripture says, "...you offer to the Lord from the herd or from the flock an offering by fire or a burnt-offering or a sacrifice," if then someone has said, "Lo, incumbent on me is a burnt-offering, lo, incumbent on me are peace-offerings," might I infer that one may bring a single drink-offering to cover both pledges?

   D. Scripture states, "...you shall prepare with the burnt-offering, or for the sacrifice, for each lamb" so as to indicate that one brings drink-offerings for this beast by itself and for that beast by itself. [The partitive language of Scripture is explicit that a burnt-offering or a sacrifice requires individual drink-offerings.]

   Form II: Intrinsic Exegetical

CVII:V

   E. Abba Hanin says in the name of R. Eliezer, "The contrary rule might have appeared logical: if in a case in which the rites required for an offering are the same, namely, the rites for offering an ox as a burnt-offering and the rites required for a lamb as a burnt-offering [since both are subject to the same rule, that is, the rule governing the burnt-offering], the two offerings are not equivalent as to the requirement of drink-offerings, in a case in which the rites required for the one are *not* the same as the rites required for the other, namely, the rites of a lamb offered as a burnt-offering as compared to the rites required of the lamb as peace-offerings [the burnt-offering is wholly consumed by the altar fire, the peace-offering yields meat for the priest and the sacrifier and his family], is it not reasonable to suppose that the rule regarding drink-offerings should not be the same? [In fact, the rule *is* the same, so logic would have misled us.]

   F. "On that account Scripture says, '...you shall prepare with the burnt-offering, or for the sacrifice,' to indicate that even though the rites required for the lamb offered as a burnt-offerings are not the same as the rites required for a lamb when offered as peace-offerings, nonetheless they are equivalent as to the requirement of drink-offerings."

Form IV: Dialectical Exegesis: Fallacy of Logic

CVII:V

2. A. R. Nathan says, "'...you shall prepare with the burnt-offering,' refers to the burnt-offering brought by the leper. '...for the sacrifice,' refers to the sin-offering brought by him. '...or for the sacrifice' then encompasses his guilt-offering."
   B. R. Jonathan says, "'...for each lamb,' encompasses the burnt-offering brought by a woman after childbirth, who has to bring drink-offerings, a rule which we have not derived anywhere else in the entire Torah.
   C. "Or perhaps it speaks only of the ram?
   D. "When Scripture says, '... for a ram you shall prepare for a cereal-offering two tenths of an ephah of fine flour mixed with a third of a hin of oil; *and for the drink-offering* you shall offer a third of a hin of wine,' lo, reference is made to the ram. So how shall I interpret the statement, "...for each lamb'? It is to encompass the burnt-offering brought by a woman after childbirth, who has to bring drink-offerings, a rule which we have not derived anywhere else in the entire Torah."
   E. Another matter: "...for each lamb" encompasses the eleventh lamb produced in the tithing of the flock.

Form II: Intrinsic Exegetical

CVII:VI

1. A. "...for a ram you shall prepare for a cereal-offering":
   B. The purpose of Scripture is to distinguish the drink-offerings of a lamb from the drink-offerings of a ram. [There is a different rule for each classification of animal.]
   C. For one might have reasoned to the contrary: an animal taken from the herd requires drink-offerings, and an animal taken from the flock requires drink-offerings. If therefore I draw an analogy to the animal taken from the herd, in which case the Torah has not distinguished the drink-offerings brought for a calf from those brought for a full-grown ox, so the law should not distinguish the drink-offerings brought for a lamb from the drink-offerings brought for a ram. [They should be the same in all cases.]
   D. So Scripture states, "...for a ram you shall prepare for a cereal-offering:"
   E. The purpose of Scripture is to distinguish the drink-offerings of a lamb from the drink-offerings of a ram. [Even though such a distinction does not cover the calf and the ox, it does cover the lamb and the ram.]

Form IV: Dialectical Exegesis: Fallacy of Logic

CVII:VI

2. A. Abba Hanin says in the name of R. Eliezer, "Why is this statement made? It is because reason would have led me to a different conclusion.
   B. "Specifically: if in a case in which Scripture required many drink-offerings, Scripture did not distinguish among the drink-offerings required

for a calf from those required for an ox, in a case in which Scripture did not demand many drink-offerings, is it not reasonable that we should not require more for a ram than a lamb?

C. "Scripture says, '....for a ram you shall prepare for a cereal-offering.' Scripture thus makes the point that even though Scripture has diminished the number of drink-offerings that are required, it has made an increase whether for a lamb or for a ram."

D. Another matter: "....for a ram you shall prepare for a cereal-offering:" Scripture thereby encompasses a ram brought as a burnt-offering, etc. [sic!].

Form IV: Dialectical Exegesis: Fallacy of Logic

The point in both cases is the same. Scripture makes the points that is does because reason unguided by Scripture will have led us to false conclusions. Reason would have led us astray.

CVII:VII

1. A. "...[for a ram] you shall prepare for a cereal-offering two tenths of an ephah of fine flour [mixed with a third of a hin of oil; and for the drink-offering you shall offer a third of a hin of wine, a pleasing odor to the Lord]:

   B. Why is this statement made?

   C. Since logic would have led to the contrary conclusion: since the lamb brought with the sheaf of first grain requires two tenths of fine flour, and the ram that is brought as a burnt-offering requires two tenths of fine flour, if I draw an analogy to the lamb that is brought with the sheaf of first grain, in which case even though the number of tenths is doubled, the number of drink-offerings is not doubled, so in the case of the ram brought as a burnt-offering, even though the law has required double the number of tenths, we should not double the number of drink-offerings.

   D. Scripture thus says, "...for a ram you shall prepare for a cereal-offering two tenths of an ephah of fine flour mixed with a third of a hin of oil; and for the drink-offering you shall offer a third of a hin of wine," so informing us that just as the Torah has doubled the number of tenths to be brought with it, so it has doubled the volume of drink-offerings.

   Form IV: Dialectical Exegesis: Fallacy of Logic

CVII:VII

2. A. "...and for the drink-offering you shall offer a third of a hin of wine":

   B. Oil for mixing with the flour, wine for mixing a drink-offering.

   Form II: Intrinsic Exegesis

CVII:VII

3. A. "...a pleasing odor to the Lord":

   B. "It is a source of pleasure for me, for I have spoken and my will has been done."

   Form II: Intrinsic Exegesis

CVII:VII

4. A. "And when you prepare a bull for a burnt-offering [or for a sacrifice, to fulfil a vow or for peace-offerings to the Lord, then one shall offer with the bull a cereal-offering of three tenths of an ephah of fine flour, mixed with half a hin of oil, and you shall offer for the drink-offering half a hin of wine, as an offering by fire, a pleasing odor to the Lord]":

    B. The bull as a burnt-offering was covered by the foregoing general statements. Why then has it been singled out? It is to teach a rule governing the encompassing law, specifically:

    C. just as a bull may be brought in fulfillment of a vow or as a freewill-offering and requires drink-offerings, so whatever is brought in fulfillment of a vow or as a freewill-offering requires drink-offerings.

    D. Excluded are the sin-offering and the guilt-offering, which are not brought merely in fulfillment of a vow or as a freewill-offering and which do not require drink-offerings.

Form II: Intrinsic Exegesis

CVII:VIII

1. A. "[And when you prepare a bull] for a burnt-offering or for a sacrifice [to fulfil a vow or for peace-offerings to the Lord, then one shall offer with the bull a cereal-offering of three tenths of an ephah of fine flour, mixed with half a hin of oil, and you shall offer for the drink-offering half a hin of wine, as an offering by fire, a pleasing odor to the Lord]:"

    B. Why is this statement made?

    C. Because it is said, "as an offering by fire," if one has said, "Lo, incumbent on me is a burnt-offering, lo, incumbent on me are burnt-offerings as peace-offerings," I might infer that he may bring a single drink-offering for both of them.

    D. Scripture says, "...for a burnt-offering or for a sacrifice," so indicating that one brings drink-offerings for this one by itself and for that one by itself.

    E. Might one then maintain that even if one has said, "Lo, incumbent on me are five oxen for a burnt-offering, five oxen for peace-offerings," that he may bring a single drink-offering for all of them?

    F. Scripture says, "for a burnt-offering or for a sacrifice," so indicating that one brings drink-offerings for each one by itself.

Form II: Intrinsic Exegesis

CVII:VIII

2. A. Abba Hanin in the name of R. Eliezer says, "Why is this statement made?

    B. "For reason might have produced an error, namely:

    C. "if in a case in which the rites of a lamb brought as a burnt-offering are the same as the rites of an ox brought as peace-offerings, is it not reasonable that the drink-offerings should not be the same?

    D. "Scripture therefore says, '...for a burnt-offering or for a sacrifice,' indicating that even though the rites of an ox brought as a burnt-offering are not the same as the rites of an ox brought as peace-offerings, they are the same as to drink-offerings."

Form IV: Dialectical Exegesis: Fallacy of Logic

The exposition is identical to familiar materials and follows a single repertoire. All that changes is the context and details demanded by it.

CVII:IX

1. A. "[And when you prepare a bull for a burnt-offering or for a sacrifice, to fulfil a vow or for peace-offerings to the Lord,] then one shall offer with the bull a cereal-offering of three tenths of an ephah of fine flour, mixed with half a hin of oil, and you shall offer for the drink-offering half a hin of wine, as an offering by fire, a pleasing odor to the Lord:"

   B. The oil is for mixing with the flour, and the wine for a mixing drink-offering.

Form II: Intrinsic Exegesis

CVII:IX

2. A. "...as an offering by fire, a pleasing odor to the Lord":

   B. It is offered on grills.

   C. You say that the offering by fire is placed on grills. But perhaps it is placed directly on the flames?

   D. If you make that rule, you will turn out to put the bonfire out, while the Torah has said, *A perpetual fire will be lit on the altar, it shall not go out* (Lev. 6:6).

   E. Lo, how shall I interpret the statement of the Torah, "...as an offering by fire, a pleasing odor to the Lord"?

   F. It is to be placed on grills.

Form II: Dialectical Exegesis, Intrinsic

CVII:IX

3. A. "...as an offering by fire, a pleasing odor to the Lord":

   B. "It is a pleasure to me that I spoke and my will was carried out."

Form II: Intrinsic Exegesis

CVII:X

1. A. "Thus it shall be done for *each* bull or ram or for *each* of the male lambs or the kids, according to the number that you prepare, so shall you do with every one according to their number:"

   B. Scripture thus stresses that there is no difference between the drink-offerings brought for a calf and the drink-offerings brought for an ox.

   C. For one might have reasoned wrongly, as follows: the animal drawn from the flock requires drink-offerings, and so does one drawn from the herd. If I draw an analogy, in that the Torah has made a distinction between the drink-offerings required of a lamb and those required of a ram, so I should draw a distinction between the drink-offerings required for a calf and those required for an ox.

   D. So the Torah specifies to the contrary: "Thus it shall be done for each bull [or ram or for each of the male lambs or the kids]," indicating that the Torah has made no distinction between the drink-offerings brought for a calf and those brought for an ox.

Form II: Intrinsic Exegesis

CVII:X

2. A. Abba Hanin in the name of R. Eliezer says, "Why is this statement made? Because logic would have made us err, specifically, in a case in which the law has diminished the number of drink-offerings, it has demanded more for a ram than a lamb, in a case in which the law has demanded many drink-offerings, is it not reasonable that the law should require more for an ox than a calf?

   B. "So the Torah specifies to the contrary: 'Thus it shall be done for each bull [or ram or for each of the male lambs or the kids],' indicating that the Torah has made not demanded more drink-offerings for an ox than those to be brought for a calf."

   Form IV: Dialectical Exegesis: Fallacy of Logic

CVII:XI

1. A. "[Thus it shall be done for] each bull or ram [or for each of the male lambs or the kids, according to the number that you prepare, so shall you do with every one according to their number. All who are native shall do these things in this way, in offering an offering by fire, a pleasing odor to the Lord]:"

   B. Why is this point stressed?

   C. It is because logic would have suggested otherwise: since we find that the Torah has made a distinction between the drink-offerings required of a one year old beast and those to be brought for a two year old beast, so the Torah should distinguish the drink-offerings brought for a two year old beast from those brought for a three year old.

   D. Scripture says, "...or for each ram," indicating that even though the Torah has distinguished the drink-offerings brought for a one year old beast from those for a two year old, the Torah does not distinguish those brought for a two year old from those brought for a three year old.

   Form IV: Dialectical Exegesis: Fallacy of Logic

CVII:XI

2. A. "...or for each of the male lambs or the kids":

   B. Why is this stated?

   C. It is because logic would have suggested otherwise: since we find that the Torah has made a distinction between the drink-offerings required of lamb from those required of a ram, so the Torah should distinguish between the drink-offerings brought for a female lamb from those brought for a sheep.

   D. So Scripture states, ""...or for each of the male lambs or the kids."

   Form IV: Dialectical Exegesis: Fallacy of Logic

CVII:XII

1. A. "...according to the number that you prepare, so shall you do with every one according to their number":

   B. I know only that the law covers those listed. How do I know that the law covers beasts that are declared to be substitutes for the beasts at hand?

C. Scripture says, "...according to the number that you prepare."
Form II: Intrinsic Exegesis

CVII:XII

2. A. "'...according to the number that you prepare':
   B. "This means that one may not give less.
   C. "But is it the law that if one wants to give more, he may do so?
   D. "Scripture says, '...so shall you do with every one according to their number,'" the words of R. Josiah.
   E. R. Jonathan says, "Such a proof is not required. For lo, in any event it is said, 'All who are native shall do these things in this way.'"
   Form II: Intrinsic Exegesis

CVII:XII

3. A. "All who are native shall do these things":
   B. This means that one may not give less.
   C. But is it the law that if one wants to give more, he may do so?
   D. Scripture says, "according to their number."
   E. Or if one wants to give double, may he give double?
   F. Scripture says, "so shall you do with every one" – in accord with the number applying to each of them.
   G. On this basis sages have ruled:
   H. **The priests may mix together [and offer as one] the drink-offerings brought with oxen with those brought with other oxen, the ones brought with rams with those brought with other rams, those brought with lambs with those brought with other lambs, those brought with an animal brought by an individual and those brought with an animal offered by the community, those brought on a given day with those brought on the preceding day. But they may not mix the drink-offerings brought with lambs and those brought with oxen or those brought with rams [M. Men. 9:4].**
   I. They have further ruled:
   K. **He who says, "Lo, incumbent on me is a gift of wine," a log of wine he may not bring, two he may not bring, three he may bring. If he said four, five he may not bring, six he may bring. From that point, he may bring [any volume]. Just as the community brings wine as a matter of obligation, so an individual is permitted to make a voluntary gift of wine. [M. Men. 12:4J] They do not volunteer as a freewill-offering a single log of wine, two or five. But they volunteer as a freewill-offering three, four, or six, and any number more than six.].**
   L. "...so shall you do with every one": this serves to encompass the eleventh [beast designated as tithe of the flock].
   A-F = *Form II: Intrinsic Exegesis*
   G-L = *Form V: Scriptural Basis for a Passage of the Mishnah*

CVII:XIII

1. A. "All who are native shall do these things in this way:"
   B. Why is this said?
   C. Since it is said, *If its testicles have been crushed or bruised, torn or cut, you shall not present it to the Lord...You shall not procure any such creature from a foreigner and present it is food for your God. [Their deformity is inherent in them, a permanent defect, and they will not be acceptable on your behalf]* (Lev. 22:25),
   D. [one might have argued:] *these* you shall not acquire from them, but you may acquire from them unblemished beasts.
   E. Now that I have learned that a gentile may offer a burnt-offering, I have grounds to propose a logical argument as at the outset:
   F. An Israelite brings a burnt-offering, and a gentile brings a burnt-offering. Then just as an Israelite brings drink-offerings, so does a gentile bring drink-offerings?
   G. Scripture says, "All who are native shall do these things in this way," meaning, "These things does an Israelite do, bringing drink-offerings, but a gentile does not bring drink-offerings."
   H. Might one maintain then that his burnt-offering should not require drink-offerings at all?
   I. Scripture says, "In this way," meaning, as sages have ruled: If a gentile sent a burnt-offering from overseas and did not send the cost of drink-offerings with it, the drink-offerings are to derive from community funds.
      Form III: Dialectical Exegesis, Intrinsic

Our survey of the two *pisqaot* has produced no forms that fall outside of our original classification system, except as specified at the outset. We may now proceed to our broader survey.

We may rapidly observe that no fixed order seems to govern the use of the several forms. While it is common to commence, "Why has this statement been made," with the answer a broad-based inquiry into the relationship among a number of passages that deal with the same topic, no rule emerges. So if the document before us is cogent, the cogency must derive wholly from the resort to a fixed and limited number of formal compositions, and not from the fixed and disciplined arrangement of types of those formal compositions. I see no counterpart to the fixed rule that we shall meet in Leviticus Rabbah, and Genesis Rabbah, that one type of form nearly always comes first, another type nearly always comes last. By way of compensation, as we shall see shortly, the forms of Sifré to Numbers bear a clear statement of their own, while the forms of Leviticus Rabbah and Genesis Rabbah do not speak, through their arrangement of words, a specific message.

III

Program

To investigate the logical and topical program of our document, we turn to the rhetorical facts just now adduced and ask a fresh question: what do the formal structures of our document emphasize, and what do they ignore? Let us rapidly review them, highlighting their main traits of syllogistic discourse. Now we ask how the rhetorical plan facilitates the document's syllogistic program. This brief survey of the form therefore draws together the modes of cogent discourse, explaining how each form makes possible registering a given proposition.

1. Extrinsic Exegetical Form

The form consists of the citation of an opening verse, followed by an issue stated in terms extrinsic to the cited verse. The formal traits: [1] citation of a base-verse from Numbers, [2] a generalization ignoring clauses or words in the base-verse, [3] a further observation without clear interest in the verse at hand. The form yields a syllogism proved by a list of facts beyond all doubt.

2. Intrinsic Exegetical Form

The verse itself is clarified. The focus is on the base-verse and not on a broader issue. There are diverse versions of this exercise, some consisting only of a verse or a clause and a statement articulating the sense of the matter, others rather elaborate. But the upshot is always the same.

3. Dialectical Exegesis: Intrinsic

A sequence of arguments about the meaning of a passage, in which the focus is upon the base-verse focuses upon the meaning of the base-verse. This is the internal-exegetical counterpart to the on-going argument on whether logic works. Now logic pursues the sense of a verse, but the results of logic are tested, forthwith and one by one, against the language at hand, e.g., why is this stated? or: you say it means X but why not Y? Or, if X, then what about Y? if Y, then what about Z? All of these rather nicely articulated exegetical programs imposes a scriptural test upon the proposals of logic.

4. Dialectical Exegesis: Extrinsic

The Fallacy of Logic Uncorrected by Exegesis of Scripture

The formal indicator is the presence of the question, in one of several versions: is it not a matter of logic? The exegesis of the verse at hand plays no substantial role.

5. Scriptural Basis for a Passage of the Mishnah

What we have is simply a citation of the verse plus a law in prior writing (Mishnah, Tosefta) which the verse is supposed to sustain. The Mishnah's or the Tosefta's rule then cannot stand as originally set forth, that is, absent any exegetical foundation. On the contrary, the rule, verbatim, rests on a verse of Scripture, given with slight secondary articulation: verse, then Mishnah-sentence. That suffices, the point is made.

Let us now characterize the formal traits of Sifré to Numbers as a commentary. These, as I said in the beginning, we reduce to two classifications, based on the point of origin of the verses that are catalogued or subjected to exegesis: [1] exegesis of a verse in the book of Numbers in terms of the theme or problems of that verse, hence, intrinsic exegesis; [2] exegesis of a verse in Numbers in terms of a theme or polemic not particular to that verse, hence, extrinsic exegesis. (An equivalent taxonomy emerged in Pesiqta deRab Kahana, in reverse order, intersecting-verse/base-verse, exegesis of the components of the base-verse, or, as I named the forms of that document, propositional and exegetical forms.)

The Forms of Extrinsic Exegesis: The implicit message of the external category proves simple to define, since the several extrinsic classifications turn out to form a cogent polemic. Let me state the recurrent polemic of external exegesis.

[1] **The Syllogistic Composition:** Scripture supplies hard facts, which, properly classified, generate syllogisms. By collecting and classifying facts of Scripture, therefore, we may produce firm laws of history, society, and Israel's everyday life. The diverse compositions in which verses from various books of the Scriptures are compiled in a list of evidence for a given proposition – whatever the character or purpose of that proposition – make that one point. And given their power and cogency, they make the point stick.

[2] **The Fallibility of Reason Unguided by Scriptural Exegesis:** Scripture alone supplies reliable basis for speculation. Laws cannot be generated by reason or logic unguided by Scripture. Efforts at classification and contrastive-analogical exegesis, in which Scripture does not supply the solution to all problems, prove few and far between (and always in Ishmael's name, for whatever that is worth). This polemic forms the obverse of the point above.

So when extrinsic issues intervene in the exegetical process, they coalesce to make a single point. Let me state that point with appropriate emphasis the recurrent and implicit message of the forms of external exegesis:

Scripture stands paramount, logic, reason, analytical processes of classification and differentiation, secondary. Reason not built on scriptural foundations yields uncertain results. The Mishnah itself demands scriptural bases.

The Forms of Intrinsic Exegesis: What about the polemic present in the intrinsic exegetical exercises? This clearly does not allow for ready characterization. As we saw, at least three intrinsic exegetical exercises focus on the use of logic, specifically, the logic of classification, comparison and contrast of species of a genus, in the explanation of the meaning of verses of the book of Numbers. The internal dialectical mode, moving from point to point as logic dictates, underlines the main point already stated: logic produces possibilities,

Scripture chooses among them. Again, the question, why is this passage stated? commonly produces an answer generated by further verses of Scripture, e.g., this matter is stated here to clarify what otherwise would be confusion left in the wake of other verses. So Scripture produces problems of confusion and duplication, and Scripture – and not logic, not differentiation, not classification – solves those problems. To state matters simply: Scripture is complete, harmonious, perfect. Logic not only does not generate truth beyond the limits of Scripture but also plays no important role in the harmonization of difficulties yielded by what appear to be duplications or disharmonies. These forms of internal exegesis then make the same point that the extrinsic ones do.

In so stating, of course, we cover all but the single most profuse category of exegesis, which we have treated as simple and undifferentiated: [1] verse of Scripture or a clause, followed by [2] a brief statement of the meaning at hand. Here I see no unifying polemic in favor of, or against, a given proposition. The most common form also proves the least pointed: X bears this meaning, Y bears that meaning, or, as we have seen, citation of verse X, followed by, [what this means is].... Whether simple or elaborate, the upshot is the same.

What can be at issue when no polemic expressed in the formal traits of syntax and logic finds its way to the surface? What do I do when I merely clarify a phrase? Or, to frame the question more logically: what premises must validate my *intervention*, that is, my willingness to undertake to explain the meaning of a verse of Scripture? These seem to me propositions that must serve to justify the labor of intrinsic exegesis as we have seen its results here:

[1] My independent judgment bears weight and produces meaning. I – that is, my mind – therefore may join in the process.

[2] God's revelation to Moses at Sinai requires my intervention. I have the role, and the right, to say what that revelation means.

[3] What validates my entry into the process of revelation is the correspondence between the logic of my mind and the logic of the document.

Why do I think so? Only if I think in accord with the logic of the revealed Torah can my thought processes join issue in clarifying what is at hand: the unfolding of God's will in the Torah. To state matters more accessibly: if the Torah does not make statements in accord with a syntax and a grammar that I know, I cannot so understand the Torah as to explain its meaning. But if I can join in the discourse of the Torah, it is because I speak the same language of thought: syntax and grammar at the deepest levels of my intellect.

[4] Then to state matters affirmatively and finally: Since a shared logic of syntax and grammar joins my mind to the mind of God as revealed in the Torah, I can say what a sentence of the Torah means. So I too can amplify, clarify, expand, revise, rework: that is to say, create a commentary.

It follows that the intrinsic exegetical forms stand for a single proposition:

While Scripture stands paramount, logic, reason, analytical processes of classification and differentiation, secondary, nonetheless, man's mind joins God's mind when man receives and sets forth the Torah.

The Purpose of the Authorship of Sifré to Numbers: Can we then state in a few words and in simple language what the formal rules of the document tell us about the purpose of Sifré to Numbers? Beyond all concrete propositions, the document as a whole through its fixed and recurrent formal preferences or literary structures makes two complementary points.

[1]   Reason unaided by Scripture produces uncertain propositions.

[2]   Reason operating within the limits of Scripture produces truth.

To whom do these moderate and balanced propositions matter? Sages in particular, I think. The polemic addresses arguments internal to their circles. How do we know, and how may we be certain? If we contrast the polemic of our document about the balance between revelation and reason, Torah and logic, with the polemic of another canonical document about some other topic altogether, the contrast will tell. Then and only then shall we see the choices people faced. In that way we shall appreciate the particular choice the authorship at hand has made. With the perspective provided by an exercise of comparison, we shall see how truly remarkable a document we have in Sifré to Numbers. By itself the book supplies facts. Seen in context, the book makes points.

IV

Document

Let us now return to the main point raised in the prologue of this exercise and draw those conclusions relevant to the argument of the book:

1.   Structure: how, overall, does the document organize its materials? The framers of Sifré to Numbers, like those of Sifra, follow a clearly discernible principle or organization, citing verses one by one to amplify their sense or to join the verse to a passage of Scripture. Their document is exegetical in a strict sense: it systematically explains the meaning of verses of Scripture and it organizes its materials in line with the order of those verses.

2.   Plan: does the document at hand follow a fixed and limited plan, a repertoire of rhetorical forms? There are clearly defined rhetorical patterns, which govern throughout.

3.   Program: do these forms yield cogent and intelligible proposition(s), one(s) that, in some recurrent interest(s) or point(s) of emphasis, may make of the whole if not more than, then at least, the sum of, the parts? I have no specified what I conceive to be the syllogism that the document as a whole means to present and demonstrate.

To address the issue of defining *midrash* in its documentary context, the overall plan and program of the authorship of Sifré to Numbers do impart to the parts a cogency of rhetoric, syllogistic logic of cogent discourse, and even proposition or topic, making of the parts something that joins and therefore transcends them all. Ignoring the plan and program of the authorship of Sifré to Numbers turns into gibberish what is in fact an intelligible and cogent statement. Let us close with a reprise of the pertinent planks in Kugel's program:

> ...*midrash is an exegesis of biblical verses, not of books. The basic unit of the Bible for the midrashist is the verse: this is what he seeks to expound, and it might be said that there simply is no boundary encountered beyond that of the verse until one comes to the borders of the canon itself.*[1]

> *Our midrashic compilations are in this sense potentially deceiving, since they seem to treat the whole text bit by bit; but with the exception of certain patterns, these "bits" are rather atomistic, and, as any student or rabbinic literature knows, interchangeable, modifiable, combinable – in short, not part of an overall exegesis at all.*[2]

I am inclined to wonder whether, in forming these judgments, Kugel has paid close attention to the document before us. The exegeses of verses coalesce and are not atoms, but, at the very least, molecules. And these molecules form larger pieces of matter, as the clearcut polemic of this document, congruent to that of Sifra, suggests. I do not know where Kugel would find a document with which units of exegesis of Sifré to Numbers may be freely let alone promiscuously "interchanged, modified, or combined." Certainly, as we saw earlier, the authorship of Pesiqta deRab Kahana found useful remarkably few items of the counterpart passage in Sifré to Numbers. And these played no material role in the formation of their principal message. Nor has he surveyed the document before us (or any other, so far as I know) to determine the extent to which materials he claims may be interchanged actually have been interchanged.

---

[1] P. 93.

[2] P. 95.

Chapter Six

Genesis Rabbah

I

Structure

Like Sifra and Sifré to Numbers, Genesis Rabbah follows the sequence of verses of a biblical text and defines its principles of organization around that text.

II

Plan

Rather than a detailed analysis of a single *parashah*, let me skip that preliminary exercise and state at the outset the formal plan of Genesis Rabbah. We then shall test the hypothesis against two *parashiyyot*. Each complete *parashah* begins with its own topic. Where a topic starts, we know that discourse has begun; where the overall theme or topic changes, we know that discourse has concluded and so we have in hand a completed unit of thought. The signification of a topic for its part poses no complexity. Such a topic identifies itself because of the presence of either a verse of the book of Genesis, or a verse of another book of Scripture than Genesis, or a proposition of an abstract (essentially non-exegetical) character. The three formal modes of composition therefore aim at conveying propositions, and the formal traits dictate whether the topic at hand is (I) the interplay of the base-verse with some other verse, (II) the meaning of the base-verse, or (III) the proof of a proposition abstracted from the context established by the base-verse (that is, the book of Genesis) in particular. Our formal criterion for differentiating the first two forms is been the placement of a verse, e.g., at the beginning or at the end of a passage. The criterion for identifying form III is no more subjective, since anyone can tell that verses derive from a variety of books of Scripture and equally serve as proof for a proposition distinct from them all. So to review:

Form I: when a verse from a biblical book other than Genesis occurs at the beginning of the passage, a single formal pattern follows: exposition of that other verse, which I have called the intersecting-verse, followed by juxtaposition of the intersecting-verse with a verse of the book of Genesis.

Form **II**: when a verse from the book of Genesis occurs at the beginning of the passage, then the focus of discourse will rest upon the exposition of that verse alone.

Form **III**: when a given syllogism comes to expression at the beginning of a passage, followed by a broad range of verses, made up ordinarily as a list exhibiting fixed syntactic preferences, then the focus of discourse will require proof of the syllogism, not exposition of the verses cited in evidence for the facticity of that syllogism.

On the basis of these three purely formal criteria, we differentiate among the patterns of syntax and structure at hand:

I.   *The Intersecting-verse-Base-verse-Form*

    1.   Attribution + joining language + intersecting-verse

    2.   Exposition of the intersecting-verse

    3.   Reciprocal exposition of the base-verse and the intersecting-verse

II. *Exegesis of a Verse of Scripture*

    A.   Citation of the base-verse (which will always be a verse chosen from the larger passage subject to interpretation, not a verse chosen from some other book of the Scripture)

    B.   Comment of a given rabbi. The comment is formulated in diverse ways

    C.   Secondary, miscellaneous materials will be appended

III. *Syllogistic Composition*

    A.   Statement of a syllogism or proposition

    B.   Verses of Scripture that prove or illustrate that syollogism, listed in a catalogue of relevance evidence

    C.   Secondary expansion: miscellanies (e. g., stories) on the syllogism, providing further illustration

The formal requirement invariably is the composition of a list, a repertoire of facts ordinarily formulated in a single syntactic pattern. A syllogistic composition makes a point autonomous of the verse at hand. In this type of composition, the point of interest is in not the exposition of a verse but the proposition that is subject to demonstration, the proofs of course deriving from various verses of Scripture.

My hypothesis that Genesis Rabbah comprises three recurrent literary structures, **I.** base-verse/intersecting-verse, **II.** exegetical, and **III.** syllogistic, now requires testing. For that purpose we turn to two *parashiyyot* and undertake exactly the same procedure that produced our original hypotheses in respect to Pesiqta deRab Kahana in Chapter Three and Sifré to Numbers as well. If the proposed formal repertoire encompasses the bulk of what is before us, then we find justification to claim that the document as a whole exhibits traits of rhetorical formalization.[1] My comments on the selected *parashiyyot* focus upon form-analytical issues: why do I think a given unit of thought falls into one of the three classifications adduced to date. The upshot of what is to follow had best be stated at the outset. We shall see that our original hypothesis does encompass most of the materials of the two *parashiyyot* under study.

We do, however, find yet another principle of formulation and organization – gross aggregation – of materials, this one in no way pertinent to formal expression. Let me spell this out. While in *Parashah* I most units of thought conform to one of three patterns of formal and conventional modes of expressing ideas, in *Parashah* IV that is not the case. We shall see a long and interesting composition in which diverse completed materials – whole and comprehensible units of thought – flow together not for formal reasons but only because they speak to a common theme. In no way do they conform to a single pattern of formulating ideas on that common theme. The way in which redactors have selected and organized materials does not relate to the way in which these materials express their ideas. While in the three forms we have identified there is a correspondence between syntactical preference and mode of organizing and expressing ideas, in materials to follow we shall not identify such a concern.

Hence, very rapidly, we must identify a new species of literary principle, in addition to the formal one. This other classification is redactional, and not a matter of formal composition at all. It rests on the notion that framers have collected materials on a common theme, perhaps even offering a single syllogism or proposition, but have not imposed upon those materials a disciplined linguistic pattern. Thus we are moving into a somewhat complicated situation. We have three examples of literary structures. But we also find a formally miscellaneous but thematically cogent mode of organizing materials, one resting solely on the presence of a shared theme. That is quite another matter, so we assign to this other mode of conglomeration its own symbol. Since it cannot fall into the existing classification – form **I**, form **II**, form **III** – it will receive a letter symbol, as non-formal principle of conglomeration A.

For easy reference, I indicate at the head of each unit of thought the classification to which I assign what follows. Thus **IV:I–I** will signify that I regard IV:I as an example of form **I**. So too, **IV:II-V–A** will signify, as just stated, that the materials at hand conform to no formal rules but do form an aggregate composed in accord with a shared theme. Whether, within the materials, there also is a common proposition seems to me too subjective an issue to allow useful speculation.

---

[1] In *Comparative Midrash* I provide a survey of the formal plan of the entire document.

Genesis Rabbah Parashah Four

IV:I-I

1. A. *And God said, "Let there be a firmament in the midst of the waters"* (Gen. 1:6):

   B. It is written, *Who roofs your upper chambers with water* (Ps. 104:3).

   C. Under ordinary circumstances, when a mortal king builds a palace, he will roof it over with stones, timber, and earth.

   D. But the Holy One, blessed be He, made a roof over his world only with water, as it is said, *Who roofs your upper chambers with water* (Ps. 104:3).

   E. Thus: *And God said, "Let there be a firmament"* (Gen. 1:6).

The intersecting-verse, Ps. 104:3, clarifies the substance of the base-verse. The intersecting-verse then supplies the theme for what follows, which is the relationship between the upper and lower water. But at this point I see no further interest in the clarification of the base-verse.

IV:II-V-A

The Empty Space between Heaven and Earth

As I explained, what follows does not fall into the available categories. For the correct classification of the literary principle at hand is not formal. The intent of the compositor was simply to create a conglomerate on a subject. A single preference on syntax and morphology, whether exhibited overall or only at the beginning, does not emerge. The framer of the protracted passage has gathered diverse materials that treat a single theme. What follows for the study of the literary structures of Genesis Rabbah? It is that the following passage presents us with a new category, not in the genus of formal ones, rather, one that must be called a *redactional preference*.

Here, in what follows, we see no formal characteristics common among the compositions before us. The syntactic patterns are diverse, even at the opening of each unit, at which point, in general, we should expect to see the intervention of the hand of editors or authors interested in formal cogency. The framer of the document, IV:II-V, has drawn together a composite of materials on a single general topic. Calling the result a formally disciplined composition would constitute a gross overstatement of what is in hand. For we see a mere miscellany on a theme, not a syllogistic argument bound by considerations of form, let alone of a formally-structured argument. That is why we have to regard the present protracted passage as illustrative of yet another type of composition (again, we no longer can use the word "form" or even "literary structure"), namely, a formal miscellany on a cogent theme. The reason I dwell on the matter is that in Leviticus Rabbah I did not confront an equivalent problem; nearly all the materials collected in that compilation exhibit marks of formalization or patterning.

IV:II-V-A

1. A. [*And God said, 'Let there be a firmament...* (Gen. 1:6):] Rabbis state the matter in the name of R. Hanina, R. Phineas, R. Jacob bar Bun in the name of R. Samuel bar Nahman: "At the moment at which the Holy One, blessed be He, said, 'Let there be a firmament in the midst of the water,' the middle layer became solid, and the lower heavens and the upper heavens were made [by the residual water]."

   B. Rab said, "The works of creation were in liquid form, and on the second day they solidified: 'Let there be a firmament' is as if to say, 'Let the firmament be strengthened.'"

   C. R. Judah b. R. Simon said, "Let a lining be made for the firmament [Freedman], in line with the following verse of Scripture: *And they did beat the gold into thin plates* (Ex. 39:3)." [The word for "beat" uses the same letters as the word for "firmament."]

   D. Said R. Hanina, "Fire came forth from above and licked at the face of the firmament."

   E. When R. Yohanan would reach reach the following verse, *And by his breath the heavens were smoothed over* (Job 26:13), he would say, "Well did R. Hanina teach me."

   F. Said R. Yudan bar Simeon, "Fire came forth from on high and licked at the face of the firmament. "

2. A. R. Berekhiah, R. Jacob bar Abina in the name of R. Abba bar Kahana: "The story of the creation of the world serves to teach a lesson concerning the account of the giving of the Torah, and the same story itself is clarified: 'As when fire burns through into parts' (Is. 64:1), that is to say, they divided [Freedman: between the upper and the nether waters].

   B. "When, in fact, did the fire divide between the upper and the lower realms? Was it not in the giving of the Torah?

   C. "That was how it was when the world was created."

IV:III

1. A. R. Phineas in the name of R. Hoshayya: "Like the empty space that lies between the earth and the firmament is the empty space between the firmament and the upper water.

   B. "[That is in line with the verse]: *Let there be a firmament in the midst of the waters* (Gen. 1:6), that is to say, right in the middle, between [the water above and below]."

   C. Said R. Tanhuma, "I shall cite proof from a verse of Scripture. If the verse had stated, 'And God made the firmament and divided between the water...which is upon the firmament,' I should have concluded that it is directly upon the body of the firmament that the water is located. But when Scripture states, 'between the water which is upon the firmament,' this indicates that the upper water is suspended by a word [for the formulation, '*from* above,' which is used, bears a different meaning from the formulation, 'above.' The latter would mean, 'directly above,' while the former, which is used, bears the meaning, 'suspended above.']"

   D. Said R. Aha, "It is like the flame of a lamp, and the produce [of the water dripping through the flame] is the rain."

IV:IV

1. A. A Samaritan asked R. Meir, saying to him, "Is it possible that the upper water is suspended merely by a word?"
   B. He said to him, "Indeed so."
   C. He said to him, "Bring me a syringe [Freedman, citing Levy]." He handed him a syringe. He put a gold plate over the aperture, and the water was not stopped up. He put a silver plate over the aperture, and the water was not stopped up. When he put his finger over it, the water was stopped up.
   D. [The Samaritan] said to [Meir], "You put your finger over it [and stopped it up. But that is not comparable to holding back the upper water merely by a word.]"
   E. He said to him, "Now if I, a mere mortal, am able to stop up the water just by putting my finger [over the aperture], as to the finger of the Holy One, blessed be He, how much the more so! This proves that the upper water is suspended by a word."
   F. He said to him, "Is it really possible that he concerning whom it is written, *The heaven and the earth do I fill* (Jer. 23:24) should have talked with Moses between the two horns of the ark?"
   G. He said to him, "Bring me a convex mirror, which makes things look big." He handed him a convex mirror. He said to him, "Look at your mirror-image." He saw that it was big.
   H. "Now bring me a concave mirror, which makes things look little." He brought him a concave one. He said to him, "Look, at your mirror-image." He saw that it was little.
   I. He said to him, "If you, a mere mortal, can change your appearance however you will, he who spoke and brought the world into being – how much the more so! One must therefore say that, when he wills, is it not the case that 'Do I not fill the heaven and the earth'? But when he wills, he may speak with Moses between the horns of the ark."

2. A. Said R. Anya bar Sussai, "There are moments in which the world and all that is in it cannot hold his glory, and there are times at which he speaks with a human being from among the hairs on his head.
   B. "That is in line with the following verse of Scripture: *Then the Lord answered Job out of the whirlwind* (Job 38:1). [The word for whirlwind can be read the hair, meaning that he spoke with him] from among the hairs on his head."

3. A. [Resuming the conversation of Meir and the Samaritan, the Samaritan] said to him, "Is it possible that *the river of God has been full of water* (Ps. 65:10) from the six days of creation and as yet has not lost any [water]?"
   B. He said to him, "Go in and take a bath. But weigh yourself before you go in, and then weigh yourself after you come out [having lost the sweat that is on your body]." He went and weighed himself [as instructed] and found that he had not lost any weight.
   C. He said to him, "Did not all that sweat that went forth not come out of you?"
   D. He said to him, "Indeed so."
   E. He said to him, "Now while you, a mere mortal, found that nothing had gone forth from your fountain [since despite the loss of your sweat, now

removed in the bath, your original weight remained the same], as to the Holy One, blessed be He, how much the more so!

F. "Thus it follows that while 'the river of God has been full of water' from the six days of creation, it has not lost any water at all since that time."

4. A. Said R. Yohanan, "The Holy One, blessed be He, took all of the water present at the creation of the world and put half of the water into the firmament, and the other half into the Ocean.

B. "That is in line with this verse: 'The river...,' and the word for 'river' stands also for 'half.'"

IV:V

1. A. The firmament is like a lake, and above the lake is an arch, and on account of the evaporation of the lake, the arch drips water. It exudes thick drops, which pass through the salty water and are not mixed up with that water.

B. Said R. Yonah, "Do not let such a matter surprise you. The Jordan river passes through the Sea of Tiberias and is not mixed up with the sea.

C. "There is a miracle in a matter such as this [that the water passes through the sea but is not made salty]. If a person sifts wheat or stubble in a sieve, before the droppings have fallen two or three fingerbreadths, they are mixed together. But these flow together for many years and are not mixed together."

D. R. Yudan b. R. Simeon says, "It is because he brings them down in measure: *For he draws away the drops of water* (Job 36:27). The word for 'draw away' is used in the sense of the word as it occurs in the following verse: *And an abatement shall be made from your valuation* (Lev. 27:18). [Freedman: The sense is, 'an abatement that is calculated,' and the same sense is meant here.]"

2. A. As is the thickness of the earth, so is the thickness of the firmament: *It is he who sits above the circle of the earth* (Is. 40:22), *And he walks in the circuit of the heaven* (Job 22:14).

B. The use of the word for circle or circuit in both contexts serves to establish a comparison [between heaven and earth, with both measurements being the same].

C. R. Aha in the name of R. Hinena said, "It is as thick as a metal plate."

D. R. Joshua b. R. Nehemiah said, "It is as thick as two or three fingers."

E. Ben Pazzi said, "The upper water is more in volume than the lower water by thirty *xestes* [pints]: *Between water and water* (Gen. 1:6) [provides for an additional L before the second appearance of the word for 'water,' and the L bears a numerical value of] thirty."

F. Rabbis say, "Half and half [that is, the volume of the water is equal, above and below]."

At IV:II the theme of the base-verse, but not the language or specific allegations, accounts for the present construction. No. 1 makes its own point, on what exactly happened when the firmament was brought into existence in the midst of the water. No. 2 then carries forward the interest and theme of No. 1. But its point is critical: the Torah was given just as the world was created, so that the language used for the story of the one clarifies the language used for the description of the other. IV:III carries forward the general cosmological interest of IV:II.The reason for the inclusion of IV:IV.1-3, with No. 4 tacked on because of its relevance to the proof-text, lies in No. 1 which deals with the theme of the foregoing composition.   The entire set, therefore, was composed prior to insertion here.Both components of the passage at IV:V deal with description of the firmament. These materials are not framed as exegeses of any verse. Rather, by themselves they constitute syllogisms on the science of the firmament, with the texts of Scripture providing scientific facts for the description of the matter under discussion. But they form part of a larger composition, which, overall, does not fall into form III, for reasons amply spelled out. It remains to note that no further examples of the present phenomenon will come before us in *parashiyyot* IV or XIX.

IV:VI–II

1. A. *And God made the firmament* (Gen. 1:7):
    B. This is one of the verses of Scripture with which Ben Zoma caused an earthquake in the entire world:
    C. "[How can Scripture say,] 'And God *made?*' Did he not create the world through a word: *By the word of the Lord were the heavens made, and all the host of them by the breath of his mouth* (Ps. 33:6)! [What sort of work did God have to do, that the word 'made' has been used here?]"

2. A. Why with reference to the creation on the second day is it not written, "And it was good"?
    B. R. Yohanan, and it is repeated also in the name of R. Yose b. R. Halafta, "It is because on that day Gehenna was created: *For Tofet is ordered from yesterday* (Is. 30:33), referring to a day to which there is only a yesterday but no prior day [hence, the second day of creation]."
    C. R. Hanina said, "It is because on that day dissension was created: *And let it divide between the water [setting the upper water apart from the lower water]* (Gen. 1:7). "
    D. Said R. Tabyomi, "If, on the occasion of the creation of dissension which is [in the context at hand intended] for the good order of the world, the words, 'and it was good,' are not written, in the case of kinds of dissension which serve only for the confusion of the world, how much the more so [that nothing good can come]!"
    E. Said R. Samuel bar Nahman, "It was because the work of making the water was not yet completed. Therefore the words 'it was good' appear two times with reference to the third day. One applies to the work of creating the water [which only now had been completed], and the other to the work of creating the day."

3. A. A noble lady asked R. Yose, "Why in reference to the second day is it not written, 'And it was good'?"
    B. He said to her, "Even so, the Scripture goes and encompasses all of the days of creation at the end, for it is said *And God saw all that he had made, and lo, it was very good* (Gen. 1:31)."
    C. She said a parable to him, "If six people come to you, and you give a *mana* to each of the first five of them, and to one you give none, but then, if you go and give all of them a *mana* [shared in common], will not all of them have a *mana* and a sixth, except for this one, who will have only a sixth of a *mana* ? [So the omission of the blessing is not made

up by the inclusion of the day at the blessing given for all of the six days of creation.]"

D. He went and stated to her what R. Samuel b. Nahman had said, "It was because on the second day the entire labor of creating the water had not yet been completed. Therefore with reference to the work of the third day, two times is it written, 'For it was good,' one covering the work of creating the water, the other the work of creating the day."

4. A. R. Levi in the name of R. Tanhum bar Hanilai, "It is written, *Declaring the end from the beginning* (Is. 46:10).

B. "From the very beginning of creating the world, God foresaw Moses, who was called, *for he was good* (Ex. 2:2), and [God foresaw that] Moses would receive his punishment on account of [water, smiting the rock for water, rather than merely speaking to it], therefore with reference to water, he did not write, 'For it was good.'"

5. A. R. Simon in the name of R. Joshua b. Levi: "The matter may be compared to the case of a king who had a harsh legion. The king said, 'Since this legion is particularly harsh, let my name not be associated with it.'

B. "Along these same lines, the Holy One, blessed be He, said, 'Since this water will punish the generation of Enosh, the generation of the flood, and the generation of division, therefore let the words, 'for it was good' not be written with regard to water.'"

No. 1 provides something of an exegesis for the base-verse. We can hardly call Ps. 33:6 an intersecting-verse. Rather, what we have is an unanswered question about the formulation of the cited verse. On that basis I am justified in classifying the opening in category II. But what follows seems to me rather miscellaneous, so the arena for formalization encompasses the opening part of the passage alone.

Nos. 2, 3, 4, and 5 all deal with the omitted clause, providing a sequence of answers. What is interesting is the repeated reference to the later narrative of Genesis, e.g., the water through which the generation of the flood would be punished. Still more suggestive is the linking of Moses, "who is good," to the matter at hand. So while the treatment of the issue appears miscellaneous, a broader exegetical program guides the compositors in their selection and arrangement.

IV:VII–II

1. A. *And God called the firmament heaven* (Gen. 1:8):

B. Rab said, "The two components of the word for heaven stand for fire and water."

C. R. Abba bar Kahana in the name of Rab: "The Holy One, blessed be He, took fire and water and beat them together, and from the mixture, heaven was made."

2. A. The word for heaven uses the letters that also form the root of the word for weighing, for the heaven weighs the deeds of human beings.

B. If people have merit, *The heaven tells his righteousness* (Ps. 97:6).

C. If not, *The heaven reveals his sin* (Job 20:27).

3. A. The word "heaven" [bears the root of the word for "amazement,"] for human beings express amazement on their account, saying, "Of what is the firmament made up? Is it made of fire? Is it made of water?"

   B. R. Phineas in the name of R. Levi: "Scripture itself deals with the question: *Who lays the beams of your upper chambers in the water* (Ps. 104:3), which indicates that the firmament is made of water."

4. A. [The word for heaven may be compared to the word for] colors, some of which are blue, red, black, or white.

   B. Likewise heaven is sometimes blue, red, black, or white.

5. A. R. Isaac said, "The word for heaven, taken apart into its components, yields the meaning, 'Bear water.'

   B. "The matter may be compared to a bowl of milk. Before a drop of rennet is put into it, the milk quivers. Once a drop of rennet is put into the milk, the milk immediately congeals and stands firm.

   C. "So it is with heaven: *The pillars of heaven quiver* (Job 26:11).

   D. "Once a drop of rennet is put in: *'And there was evening and there was morning, a second day* (Gen. 1:8). "

   E. That is in line with Rab's statement, "Creation was like liquid, and only on the second day did it congeal."

The entire passage – all five components – is devoted to exegesis of the word heaven. So in formal terms, we have to regard the composition as exegetical.

Genesis Rabbah Parashah XIX

XIX:I-I

1. A. *Now the serpent was more subtle [than any other wild creature that the Lord God had made]* (Gen. 3:1):

   B. *For in much wisdom is much anger, and he who increases knowledge increases sorrow* (Qoh. 1:18).

   C. If a person increases knowledge for himself, he increases anger against himself, and because he adds to learning for himself, he adds to anguish for himself.

   D. Said Solomon, "Because I increased knowledge for myself, I increased anger against myself, and because I added learning for myself, I added anguish for myself.

   E. "Did you ever hear someone say, 'This ass went out and caught "the sun" [Freedman: ague] or "caught a fever"?'

   F. "Where are sufferings located? They are located among men."

XIX:I-A

2. A. Rabbi said, "A disciple of a sage does not require admonition [that a given act is prohibited, and if he does such an act, he will be penalized. Such a warning is required only for ordinary folk. A disciple of a sage is assumed to know the law and therefore may be penalized without prior admonition. This illustrates the point that learning increases one's exposure to anguish.]"

   B. Said R. Yohanan, "He is in the status of fine linen garments that come from Beth Shean. If they are only slightly soiled, they go to waste. But the coarse linen garments that come from Arbela, how much are they worth, and how much money does it take to buy them? [What is more valuable also can produce great loss. What is not valuable also produces no loss.]"

C.   R. Ishmael taught, "In accord with the strength of the camel is its load.

D.   "In this worldly circumstances, when two men go into a restaurant, one says, 'Bring me roast meat, white bread, and a decent wine.' The other says, 'Bring me bread and beets.' This one eats and gets a bellyache, and that one eats and does not get a bellyache. What follows is that for the one the burden is heavy, and for the other it is not."

E.   It was taught in the name of R. Meir, "Because the greatness that the snake had enjoyed was so considerable, so was the depth of his degradation: *More subtle than all* (Gen. 3:1), *More cursed than all* (Gen. 3:14). [This makes explicit the point of the foregoing observations.]"

XIX:I–II

3.   A.   *And the serpent was more subtle than any other wild creature* (Gen. 3:1):

B.   R. Hoshaiah the elder said, "He stood erect like a reed and had feet. [That is what indicated his intelligence.]"

C.   R. Jeremiah b. Eleazar said, "He was a disbeliever."

D.   R. Simeon b. Eleazar said, "He was like a camel. This world lost out on a great benefit, for if things had not happened the way they did, a man could send commerce through [a snake], who would come and go [doing his employer's business]."

No. 1 provides an appropriate intersecting-verse, in which the advantage of the virtue of intelligence is weighed against the disadvantage. That introduces the discourse at hand, reflections on the futility of learning, as illustrated by the snake, most intelligent, most cursed. No. 2 then underlines the force of the praise bestowed on the serpent. He had much to lose and he lost it all. The composition by itself of course has its own literary integrity; but we know why it has been selected and appended. Nonetheless, I have given it its own classification. That is necessary because No. 3 falls into a different classification of literary form, as indicated: exegetical, pure and simple. No. 3 specifies what sort of ability the serpent had. The exegesis now follows a single line, which is to pursue both the surface-theme, the advantages of the serpent, and the subterranean one, the sorrow of learning. No. 2 joins both themes, in pointing to the serpent's remarkable intelligence as the greatness from which he fell. This is made explicit. 3.C, D underline this same point, specifying two aspects of great intelligence, namely, the power to doubt and the ability to conduct complicated affairs.

XIX:II–III

1.   A.   "He said to the woman, 'Did God indeed say, *You shall not eat of any tree of the garden?* (Gen. 3:2):'"

B.   Said R. Hinena bar Sanesan, "There are four who opened their statements with the word 'indeed' and who perished with the word 'indeed,' and these are they:

C. "The snake, the head baker, the camp of Korach, and Haman.

D. "The snake: 'And he said to the woman, *Did God indeed say...* (Gen. 3:2).'

E. "The head baker: *Indeed, I in my dream...* (Gen. 30:16).

F. "The camp of Korach: *Indeed, you have not brought us...* (Num. 16:14).

G   "Haman: *Indeed, Esther the queen did let no man come in...* (Est. 5:12)."

The pericope omits the promised other half, the verses in which the word "indeed" opens the statement of the downfall of those named.   This is a fine example of formal classification **III**.

XIX:III–II

1. A. "And the woman said to the snake. 'We may eat of the fruit of the trees[of the garden,' but God said, *You shall not eat of the fruit of the tree which is in the midst of the garden, neither shall you touch it, lest you die* (Gen. 3:3):

    B. Where was man when this conversation was going on?

    C. Abba Halpun bar Qoriah said, "He had earlier had sexual relations, and now he was sleeping it off."

    D. Rabbis say, "God had taken him and was showing him the whole world, saying to him, 'This is what an orchard looks like, this is an area suitable for sowing grain. So it is written, *Through a land that no man had passed through, and where Adam had not dwelt* (Jer. 2:6), that is, Adam had not lived there [but there were lands Adam had seen on his tour]."

XIX:III–I

2. A. ...*of the fruit of the tree which is in the midst of the garden* (Gen. 3:3):

    B. That is in line with this verse: *Add not to his words, lest he reprove you, and you be found a liar* (Prov. 30:6). [God had said nothing about not touching the tree, but the woman said they were not to eat of the fruit of the tree or even to touch it.]

    C. R. Hiyya taught, "It is that one should not make the fence taller than the foundation, so that the fence will not fall down and wipe out the plants.

    D. "So the Holy One, blessed be He, had said, *For on the day on which you eat from it, you shall surely die* (Gen. 2:17). But that is not what she then said to the snake. Rather: 'God said,"You shall not eat from it *and you shall not touch it.*"' When the snake saw that she was lying to him, he took her and pushed her against the tree. He said to her, 'Have you now died? Just as you did not die for touching it, so you will not die from eating it.'

    E. "Rather: *For God knows that when you eat of it, your eyes will be opened and you will be like God* (Gen. 3:5)."

No. 1 provides an exegesis for the cited verse, hence falls into classification **II**, while No. 2 proceeds to introduce an intersecting-verse/base-verse composition.

XIX:IV-II

1. A. Said R. Tanhuma, "This question people asked me in Antioch: '[Could there be more than a single God, in light of the fact that *knowing good and evil* (Gen. 3:5) is given in the plural, thus, "like gods, knowing" is so constructed as to suggest a plurality of Gods.]'

   B. "I said to them, 'What is written is not, "For gods know," but rather, "For God knows."'"

2. A. R. Joshua of Sikhnin in the name of R. Levi: *[The snake] began to slander his creator, saying, 'From this tree did God eat and then he created the world. Then he told you, "You shall not eat of it* (Gen. 2:17), so that you should not create other worlds. For everyone hates the competition.'"

   B. R. Judah b. R. Simon said, "[This is what he said,] 'Whatever is created in sequence after its fellow rules over its fellow. The heaven came on the first day and the firmament on the second, and does not the firmament bear the weight of heaven [so serving it]? The firmament came on the second day and herbs on the third, and does the firmament not provide water for herbs? The herbs were created on the third day and the great lights on the fourth, the lights on the fourth and the fowl on the fifth.'"

   C. R. Judah b. R. Simon said, "The splendor of a clean bird when it flies through the heaven dims the orb of the sun."

   D. Continuing the discourse of B:] "'Yet you were created after everything else, so you should rule over everything that came before. Go ahead and eat before he creates other worlds, which will in sequence rule over you.'

   E. "That is in line with the following verse: *And the woman saw that it was good* (Gen. 3:6).

   F. "What she saw was that the statement of the snake [was good]."

No. 1 rests on the citation of the verse and its explanation. Even though in a narrative framework, the formal requirements of the structure at hand are met. The same judgment applies to No. 2. So we have in hand what appears to me to be a variation on the basic composition made up by citing a base-verse and explaining its sense or answering a question generated by the cited verse.

XIX:V-III

1. A. *[So when the woman saw] that the tree was good for food [and that it was a delight for the eyes, and that the tree was to be desired to make one wise]* (Gen. 3:6):

   B. R. Eleazar in the name of R. Yose b. Zimra: "Three statements were made concerning the tree, that it was good to eat, a delight to the eyes, and that it added wisdom,

   C "and all of them were stated in a single verse:

   D. "'So when the woman saw that the tree was good for food,' on which basis we know that it was good to eat;

   E. "'and that it was a delight to the eyes,' on which basis we know that it was a delight for the eyes,

   F. "'and that the tree was to be desired to make one wise,' on which basis we know that it added to one's wisdom.

G. "That is in line with the following verse of Scripture: *A song of wisdom of Ethan the Ezrahite* (Ps. 89:1)" [and the root for "song of wisdom" and that for "to make one wise" are the same].

XIX:V–II

2. A. *She took of its fruit and ate* (Gen. 3:6):
   B. Said R. Aibu, "She squeezed some grapes and gave him the juice."
   C. R. Simlai said, "She approached him fully prepared [with strong arguments], saying to him, 'What do you think? Is it that I am going to die, and that another woman will be created for you? [That is not possible:] 'There is nothing new under the sun' (Qoh. 1:9).
   D. "'Or perhaps you think that I shall die and you will live all by yourself? *He did not create the world as a waste, he formed it to be inhabited* (Is. 45:18)."
   E. Rabbis say, "She began to moan and weep to him."

XIX:V–II

3. A. The word "also" [*And she also gave some to her husband* (Gen. 3:6)] bears the force of a phrase of inclusion, meaning to encompass domesticated beasts, wild beasts, and fowl.
   B. Everyone obeyed her and ate of the fruit, except for one bird, which is called the phoenix.
   C. For it is written, *Then I shall die with my nest and I shall multiply my days as the phoenix* (Job 29:18).
   D. A member of the house of R. Yannai and R. Yudan bar Simeon [debated matters as follows]:
   E. A member of the house of R. Yannai said, "It lives for a thousand years, and at the end of a thousand years a fire goes forth from its nest and burns it up and leaves an egg['s bulk of ash], which goes and grows limbs and lives on."
   F. R. Yudan bar Simeon said, "It lives for a thousand years and at the end of a thousand years its body dissolves and its wings drop off, but an egg['s bulk] is left and it goes and grows parts and lives on."

Here we see a mixture of forms, **III**, then **II, II**. I think the grounds for classifying the statements in the identified forms are self-evident. No. 1 provides an obvious exegesis of the base-verse. No. 2 creates a colloquy explaining how the woman persuaded the man to follow her example. No. 3 then moves off in its own direction.

XIX:VI–II

1. A. *Then the eyes of both of them were opened* (Gen. 3:7):
   B. And had they been blind?
   C. R. Yudan in the name of R. Yohanan b. Zakkai, R. Berekhiah in the name of R. Aqiba: "The matter may be compared to the case of a villager who was walking by a glass-maker's stall. In front of him was a basket full of fine goblets and cut glass. He swung his staff and broke them all. The glass-maker went and grabbed him.

D. "He said to him, 'I know full well that I am not going to get anything of value from you [since you are so poor that you cannot pay me back]. But come and let me at least show you how much property of worth you have destroyed.'

E. "So God showed them how many generations they had destroyed [and that is the manner in which their eyes were opened]."

2. A. *And they knew that they were naked* (Gen. 3:7):

B. Even of the single religious duty that they had in hand they were now denuded. [The word "naked" is associated with "being clothed by the merit accruing from the performance of religious duties."]

3. A. *And they sewed fig leaves together and made themselves aprons* (Gen. 3:7):

B. Said R. Abba bar Kahana, "What is not written is 'an apron,' but rather 'aprons.'

C. "The sense of the plural is this: a variety of clothing, such as shirts, robes, and linen cloaks.

D. "And just as these sorts of garments are made for a man, so for a woman they make girdles, hats, and hair nets. [So the plural of the word yields the sense that they clothed themselves in a variety of garments.]"

All three parts present exegesis to the cited verse and exemplify the form quite nicely. Each of the clauses of the verse is subjected to amplification.

XIX:VII-II

1. A. *And they heard the sound of the Lord God walking in the garden in the cool of the day* (Gen. 3:8):

B. Said R. Hilpai, "We understand from the verse at hand that a sound may move [since the verse refers to the 'sound moving in the garden'], but we have not heard that fire moves.

C. "And how on the basis of Scripture do we know that fire moves? It is in the following verse: *And the fire travelled down upon the earth* (Ex. 9:23).

XIX:VII-III

2. A. Said R. Abba bar Kahana, "The word is not written, 'move,' but rather, 'walk,' bearing the sense that [the Presence of God] lept about and jumped upward.

B. "[The point is that God's presence lept upward from the earth on account of the events in the garden, as will now be explained:] The principal location of the Presence of God was [meant to be] among the creatures down here. When the first man sinned, the Presence of God moved up to the first firmament. When Cain sinned, it went up to the second firmament. When the generation of Enosh sinned, it went up to the third firmament. When the generation of the Flood sinned, it went up to the fourth firmament. When the generation of the dispersion [at the tower of Babel] sinned, it went up to the fifth. On account of the Sodomites it went up to the sixth, and on account of the Egyptians in the time of Abraham it went up to the seventh.

C. "But, as a counterpart, there were seven righteous men who rose up: Abraham, Isaac, Jacob, Levi, Kahath, Amram, and Moses. They brought the Presence of God [by stages] down to earth.

D. "Abraham brought it from the seventh to the sixth, Isaac brought it from the sixth to the fifth, Jacob brought it from the fifth to the fourth, Levi brought it down from the forth to the third, Kahath brought it down from the third to the second, Amram brought it down from the second to the first. Moses brought it down to earth."

E. Said R. Isaac, "It is written, *The righteous will inherit the land and dwell therein forever* (Ps. 37:29). Now what will the wicked do? Are they going to fly in the air? But that the wicked did not make it possible for the Presence of God to take up residence on earth [is what the verse wishes to say]."

Once more at No. 1 we have an example of form **II**. While both entries explain the word "walk, No. 2 goes its own way to make a point autonomous of the cited verse.

XIX:VIII–II

1. A. Said R. Berekhiah, "Instead of the verb, 'And they heard' [*And they heard the sound of the Lord God walking* (Gen. 3:8)], what it should say is, 'They caused to hear [with the subject of the verb being the trees, as will now be explained].

B. "They heard the sound of the trees saying, 'Lo, the thief who deceived his creator!'"

C. Said R. Hinena bar Pappa, "Instead of 'And they heard,' it should say, 'And they caused to hear.' They heard the voice of the ministering angels saying, 'The Lord is going to those in the garden.'" [This is continued at G.]

D. R. Levi and R. Isaac [concerning what the angels said]:

E. R. Levi said, "[What they heard from the angels was,] 'The one who was in the garden has died.'"

F. R. Isaac said, "[What they heard the angels say is,] 'He is taking a walk.'" [Freedman, p. 154, n. 4: When has God declared that disobedience would be followed by death? According to these interpretations the verse is rendered thus: "And they heard the voice of the angels declaring either, 'O God, man is dead and gone,' or, 'God is going to those in the garden to punish them,' or, 'O God, does man still walk about?'"]

G. [Continuing C:] "Said the Holy One, blessed be He, to them, '[He will die] but with the respite of a day [for the Hebrew translated "in the cool of the day"]. Lo, I shall provide him with the space of a day. So did I say to him, *For on the day on which you will eat it, you will surely die* (Gen. 2:17). But you do not know whether it is one day by my reckoning or one day by your reckoning. Lo, I shall give him a day by my reckoning, which is a thousand years by your reckoning. So he will live for nine hundred and thirty years and leave seventy years for his children to live in their time.' [So God's statement that man would surely die if he ate the forbidden fruit in fact did come to fruition. Adam lived a period of nine hundred thirty years. and each subsequent Adam gets seventy years.]

H. "That is in line with this verse of Scripture: *The days of our years are threescore years and ten* (Ps. 90:10)."

2. A. *In the cool of the day* (Gen. 3:8):

B. Rab said, "He judged him at the east, for 'at the cool of the day'; refers to the direction from which the day comes up, [which is to say, at the east]."

C. Zabedi b. Levi said, "It was at the west that he judged him. 'The cool of the day' refers to the direction at which the day goes down, [which is to say, at the west]."

D In the view of Rab, he treated him harshly, just as, for the time the day rises, it gets hotter.

E. In the view of Zabedi, he treated him leniently, just as, for the time that the day closes, it gets cooler.

3. A. *And the [man and his wife hid themselves from the presence of the Lord God among the trees of the garden]* (Gen. 3:8):

B. R. Aibu said, "[In hiding,] his height shrunk down and he was only a hundred cubits tall."

4. A. *Among the trees of the garden* (Gen. 3:8):

B. Said R. Levi, "This gave a foretaste of the fact that his descendants would be put into wooden coffins."

Once more we have an example of form II. Both entries explain the word "walk." How does the exegesis proceed? The effect of No. 1 is to remove the implication of a corporeal God, now by having the "sound" refer not to God's physical movements but to some other noise. No. 2 produces the same result; it is no longer "the cool of the day," but a figurative statement bearing its own message. Nos. 3 and 4 move forward in the exegesis of the verses at hand.

XIX:IX–II

1. A. "And the Lord God called to the man and said to him, *Where are you?* (Gen. 3:9):

B [The word for "where are you" yields consonants that bear the meaning,] "How has this happened to you?"

C. [God speaks:] "Yesterday it was in accord with my plan, and now it is in accord with the plan of the snake. Yesterday it was from one end of the world to the other [that you filled the earth], and now: *Among the trees of the garden* (Gen. 3:8) [you hide out]."

This seems to me nothing more than a routine exegesis of the sense of the verse.

XIX:I–III

2. A. R. Abbahu in the name of R. Yose bar Haninah: "It is written, *But they are like a man [Adam], they have transgressed the covenant* (Hos. 6:7).

B. "'They are like a man,' specifically, like the first man. [We shall now compare the story of the first man in Eden with the story of Israel in its land.]

C. "'In the case of the first man, I brought him into the garden of Eden, I commanded him, he violated my commandment, I judged him to be sent away and driven out, but I mourned for him, saying "How..."'[which begins the book of Lamentations, hence stands for a lament, but which, as we just saw, also is written with the consonants that also yield, 'Where are you'].

D. "'I brought him into the garden of Eden,' as it is written, *And the Lord God took the man and put him into the garden of Eden* (Gen. 2:15).

E. "'I commanded him,' as it is written, *And the Lord God commanded...* (Gen. 2:16).

F. "'And he violated my commandment,' as it is written, *Did you eat from the tree concerning which I commanded you* (Gen. 3:11).

G. "'I judged him to be sent away,' as it is written, *And the Lord God sent him from the garden of Eden* (Gen. 3:23).

H. "'And I judged him to be driven out.' *And he drove out the man* (Gen. 3:24).

I. "'But I mourned for him, saying, "How...".' 'And he said to him, "Where are you"' (Gen. 3:9), and the word for 'where are you' is written, 'How....'

J. "'So too in the case of his descendants, [God continues to speak,] I brought them into the Land of Israel, I commanded them, they violated my commandment, I judged them to be sent out and driven away but I mourned for them, saying, "How...."'

K. "'I brought them into the Land of Israel.' *And I brought you into the land of Carmel* (Jer. 2:7).

L. "'I commanded them.' *And you, command the children of Israel* (Ex. 27:20). *Command the children of Israel* (Lev. 24:2).

M. "'They violated my commandment.' *And all Israel have violated your Torah* (Dan. 9:11).

N. "'I judged them to be sent out.' *Send them away, out of my sight and let them go forth* (Jer 15:1).

O. "'....and driven away.' *From my house I shall drive them* (Hos. 9:15).

P. "'But I mourned for them, saying, "How...."' *How has the city sat solitary, that was full of people* (Lam. 1:1)."

No. 2 presents a proposition, not spelled out but nonetheless clear, comparing Adam and Israel. That is why I classify this item as exemplary of form III. From a redactional viewpoint, of course, No. 1 certainly sets the stage for No. 2 and the whole must be regarded as a single, thoughtful composition.

XIX:X-II

1. A. *And he said, 'I heard the sound of you in the garden, and I was afraid, because I was naked, and I hid himself.' He said, 'Who told you [that you were naked? Have you eaten of the tree of which I commanded you not to eat?']* (Gen. 3:10-11):

B. Said R. Levi, "The matter may be compared to the case of a woman who wanted to borrow a little yeast, who went in to the house of the wife of a snake-charmer. She said to her, 'What does your husband do with you? [How does he treat you?]'

C. "She said to her, 'Every sort of kindness does he do with me, except for the case of one jug filled with snakes and scorpions, of which he does not permit me to take charge.'

D. "She said to her, 'The reason is that that is where he has all his valuables, and he is planning to marry another woman and to hand them over to her.'

E. "What did the wife do? She put her hand into the jug [to find out what was there]. The snakes and scorpions began to bite her. When her husband got home, he heard her crying out. He said to her, 'Could you have touched that jug?'

F. "So: *Have you eaten of the tree of which I commanded you not to eat?* (Gen. 3:11)."

The parable serves as an exegesis of the cited verses. At a more sophisticated stage of the work, people may wish to differentiate among the forms and types of exegeses, but, at this stage, it suffices to classify the item as exemplary of form II. Why so? As I see it, the parable spells out the obvious sense of the discourse of Scripture.

XIX:XI–III

1. A. "The man said, *The woman whom you gave to be with me gave me fruit of the tree, and I ate* (Gen. 3:12):"

B. There are four on whose pots the Holy One, blessed be He, knocked, only to find them filled with piss, and these are they: Adam, Cain, the wicked Balaam, and Hezekiah.

C. Adam: "The man said, *The woman whom you gave to be with me gave me fruit of the tree and I ate* (Gen. 3:12)."

D. Cain: "And the Lord said to Cain, *Where is Abel, your brother?* (Gen. 4:9)."

E. The wicked Balaam: "And God came to Balaam and said, *What men are these with you?* (Num. 22:9)"

F. Hezekiah: "Then came Isaiah the prophet to king Hezekiah and said to him, *What did these men say?* (2 Kgs. 20:14)."

G. But Ezekiel turned out to be far more adept than any of these: *Son of man, can these bones live? And I said, O Lord God, you know* (Ez. 37:3).

H. Said R. Hinena bar Pappa, "The matter may be compared to the case of a bird that was caught by a hunter. The hunter met someone who asked him, 'Is this bird alive or dead?'

I. "He said to him, 'If you want, it is alive, but if you prefer, it is dead.' So: '"Will these bones live?" And he said, "Lord God, you know."'"

The list proves a point, hence a fine instance of form III. Those who turned out to be pisspots did not reply in a humble way.

XIX:XII–I

1. A. [*The man said, 'The woman whom you gave to be with me gave me fruit of the tree, and I ate'* (Gen. 3:12):] That is in line with the following

verse of Scripture: *Then would I speak and not fear him, for I am not so with myself* (Job 9:35).

B. Said Job, "I am not like him who said, *The woman whom you gave to be with me gave me the fruit of the tree* (Gen. 3:21) [and further, *Because you have listened to the voice of your wife* (Gen. 3:17)]. He obeyed his wife's instructions, but I did not obey my wife." [We shall shortly see a more important contrast between Job and Adam, also showing the degradation of Adam.]

2. A. Said R. Abba bar Kahana, "Job's wife was Dinah, to whom he said, *You speak as one of the vile women speaks* (Job 9:10). *What? shall we accept good at the hand of God and shall we not accept evil?* (Job 9:10)."

   B. Said R. Abba, "What is written is not, 'I shall receive,' but 'We shall receive.' The sense of the statement then is this: 'Are we going to be fit people when it comes to what is good and not fit people when it comes to what is bad?'"

3. A. *For all this did not Job sin with his lips* (Job 9:10):

   B. Said R. Abba, "With his lips he did not sin, but in his heart he sinned."

4. A. Said R. Abba, "What is written [at Gen. 3:12] is not, 'and I did eat,' but, 'I did eat and *I will eat* .'"

   B. Said R. Simeon b. Laqish, "The first man was separated from the garden of Eden only after he had actually blasphemed and cursed. That is in line with what is written: *And he looked that it should bring forth grapes, and it brought forth wild grapes* (Is. 5:2)."

XIX:XII–II

5. A. *The woman said, 'The serpent beguiled me, and I ate'* (Gen. 3:13):

   B. "He incited, incriminated, beguiled me" [Freedman].

   C. *He incited me: The enemy shall not incite him* (Ps. 89:23).

   D. *He incriminated me: When you lend to your neighbor* (Deut. 24:10) [making him liable for repayment, here: making me liable to punishment (Freedman, p. 58, n. 2)].

   E. *He beguiled me: Now therefore let not Hezekiah beguile you* (2 Chr. 32:15).

XIX:XII.1-3 + 4 introduce Job in the clarification of the passage at hand, and the initial phase of the composition follows form **I**. No. 5 then proceeds to the exegesis of the cited verses, also following a single formal pattern. No. 5 moves on to the next verse. So Nos. 1-4 present an intersecting-verse, and those components provide a fairly substantial exposition of the intersecting-verse before returning to the base-verse. On that basis the opening component of the composition falls into the classification of form **I**, the concluding, form **II** (for self-evident reasons).

The three hypothetical forms encompass most, though not all, of the materials of *parashiyyot* IV and XIX. The other items are joined together into classification A: thematic composites, lacking distinctive formal traits. The present result justifies our turning to the document as a whole. We proceed to survey Genesis Rabbah with two questions in hand, one on the literary forms of the work, the other about the organization of the forms in particular order.

In the aggregate Genesis Rabbah conforms to two important literary patterns. First of all, forms: we are able to classify the bulk of its completed units of thought among three forms or patterns, as specified. Second, the ordering of forms: we can demonstrate that the formal types of units of discourse will be arranged in accord with a single set of preferences. The redactors preferred overall to commence discourse with forms of type **I** and to conclude with forms of type **II**. It follows that Genesis Rabbah, viewed overall, presents an orderly, not a random and unsystematic, picture of its literary traits, both formal and redactional. Materials are formulated in accord with a limited set of patterns. They then are laid out in accord with a clearly defined set of rules of ordering types of units of discourse. We discover a dual taxonomy, one formal, the other redactional. Formally and redactionally, therefore, Genesis Rabbah conforms to patterns to be discerned through simple inductive inquiry.

III

Program

Let me repeat what I have offered elsewhere as an overall characterization of the syllogistic program of Genesis Rabbah.[2] The mode by which this characterization has been reached is spelled out in other studies, and for our purposes it suffices simply to summarize the matter. The authorship of Genesis Rabbah focuses its discourse on the proposition that the book of Genesis speaks to the life and historical condition of Israel, the Jewish people. The entire narrative of Genesis is so formed as to point toward the sacred history of Israel, the Jewish people: its slavery and redemption; its coming Temple in Jerusalem; its exile and salvation at the end of time. The powerful message of Genesis in the pages of Genesis Rabbah proclaims that the world's creation commenced a single, straight line of events, leading in the end to the salvation of Israel and through Israel all humanity. Therefore a given story will bear a deeper message about what it means to be Israel, on the one side, and what in the end of days will happen to Israel, on the other.

If I had to point to the single most important proposition of Genesis Rabbah, it is that, in the story of the beginnings of creation, humanity, and Israel, we find the message of the meaning and end of the life of the Jewish people. The deeds of the founders supply signals for the children about what is going to come in the future. So the biography of Abraham, Isaac, and Jacob also constitutes the history of Israel later on. If the sages could announce a single syllogism and argue it systematically, that is the proposition on which they would insist. The sages understood that stories about the progenitors, presented in the book of Genesis, define the human condition and proper conduct for their children, Israel in time to come. Accordingly, they systematically asked

---

[2]*Genesis and Judaism: The Perspective of Genesis Rabbah. An Analytical Anthology* (Atlanta, 1986: Scholars Press for Brown Judaic Studies).

Scripture to tell them how they were supposed to conduct themselves at the critical turnings of life. In a few words let me restate the conviction of the framers of Genesis Rabbah about the message and meaning of the book of Genesis:

> We now know what will be in the future. How do we know it? Just as Jacob had told his sons what would happen in time to come, just as Moses told the tribes their future, so we may understand the laws of history if we study the Torah. And in the Torah, we turn to beginnings: the rules as they were laid out at the very start of human history. These we find in the book of Genesis, the story of the origins of the world and of Israel.
>
> The Torah tells us not only what happened but why. The Torah permits us to discover the laws of history. Once we know those laws, we may also peer into the future and come to an assessment of what is going to happen to us – and, especially, of how we shall be saved from our present existence. Because everything exists under the aspect of a timeless will, God's will, and all things express one thing, God's program and plan, in the Torah we uncover the workings of God's will. Our task as Israel is to accept, endure, submit, and celebrate.

Now Kugel and his friends may fairly claim that the message at hand derives from a broad range of rabbinic documents of late antiquity, medieval, and modern times. They may therefore point to that message as evidence for their view that documentary distinctions make no considerable difference in the interpretation of midrash-exegesis. For a document that presents no distinctive message does not define an arena for discourse at all, just as Kugel maintains in his definitions. What transcends documentary lines also obliterates those lines. That seems to me a fair question. Comparison between two or more documents, however, shows that what appears visible to the naked eye upon closer inspection presents traits and features requiring further differentiation. Things are by no means what they seem. I shall now show that Genesis Rabbah's documentary proposition does constitute a distinctive and definitive trait of that document in particular.[3]

That closer inspection in the present case takes the form of comparison. Specifically, we shall see that the present message is *distinctive* – but not unique – to the authorship of Genesis Rabbah when we compare what they wished, in compiling their document, to say with what another authorship advanced as its prinicpal proposition in compiling *its* document. We now ask ourselves a simple question: is the message of Sifré to Numbers the same as that of Genesis

---

[3]I underline *distinctive*, not unique. No one claims that a given document says nothing that we do not find in any other document. On the contrary, documents bearing unique messages do not comprise a canon, and – more than by definition, but by intrinsic traits and implicit syllogisms, every rabbinic document forms part of the canon of the dual Torah. The distinctions I made in the opening chapter between autonomy, connection, and continuity come into play here.

Rabbah? The answer is obvious. No, these are different books. They make different points in answering different questions. In plan and in program they yield more contrasts than comparisons. Why does that fact matter to my argument? Since these *are* different books, which *do* use different forms to deliver different messages, it must follow that there is nothing routine or given or to be predicted about the point that the authorship of Sifré to Numbers wishes to make. Why not? Because it is not a point that is simply "there to be made." It is a striking and original point. How, again, do we know it? The reason is that, when the sages who produced Genesis Rabbah read Genesis, they made a different point from the one at hand. So contrasting the one composition with the other shows us that each composition bears its own distinctive traits – traits of mind, traits of plan, traits of program.

The upshot is simple. Once we characterize the persistent polemic of Sifré to Numbers and then compare that polemic to the characteristic point of argument of Genesis Rabbah (and, as it happens, Leviticus Rabbah as well), we see that our document has chosen forms to advance its own distinctive, substantive argument. Its exegetical program points, explicitly in extrinsic exegesis, implicitly in intrinsic exegesis, to a single point, and that point is made on every page.

Let us now return to the main point raised in the prologue of this exercise and draw those conclusions relevant to the argument of the book:

1.   Structure: how, overall, does the document organize its materials? The framers follow a clearly discernible principle or organization, citing verses one by one to amplify their sense or to join the verse to a passage of Scripture. The document is not exegetical but essentially syllogistic. That is, while in a strict sense it organizes its materials in line with the order of verses, it does not comment on all of the verses or even most of them. It works out a different formal exercise, invoking verses from other documents in order to clarify the sense and message of the verses of the book of genesis.

2.   Plan: does the document at hand follow a fixed and limited plan, a repertoire of rhetorical forms? There is a limited rhetorical repertoire, which governs throughout.

3.   Program: do these forms yield cogent and intelligible proposition(s), one(s) that, in some recurrent interest(s) or point(s) of emphasis, may make of the whole if not more than, then at least, the sum of, the parts? We can discern at least one important polemic, and, beyond that, we see a systematic picture of the sense and meaning of the cited passage. There is nothing random or casual about the propositional program of the document.

Chapter Seven

Leviticus Rabbah

I

Structure

While Leviticus Rabbah focuses the discourse of each of its thirty-seven parashiyyot on a verse of the book of Leviticus, these verses in no way are sequential, e.g., Lev. 1:1, then Lev. 1:2, in the way in which the structure of Genesis Rabbah dictates exegesis of the verses of the book of Genesis, read in sequence. The document's *parashiyyot* work out theses on a sequence of themes, for example, the evils of gossip or of drink, the unique character of Moses, and the like. But the respective themes cover a variety of propositions, and a *parashah* ordinarily displays and demonstrates more than a single cogent syllogism. In this regard, as we shall see in Chapter Eight, Pesiqta deRab Kahana differs, since the framers of its twenty-eight *pisqaot* clearly propose to announce and demonstrate the validity of twenty-eight implicit syllogisms, which we can readily identify and state on our own.

Seen in sequence, the three documents, Genesis Rabbah, Leviticus Rabbah, and Pesiqta deRab Kahana therefore show us three developing stages in the history of syllogistic discourse within the midrash-compilations. The first makes a variety of points, not cogent with one another in sequence but entirely cogent seen as a whole, and allows those points to unfold every which way as the sequence of verses dictates. The second makes a variety of points, but the order of verses plays no role in the spelling out of those propositions; the unit of discourse is the complete *parashah*, thematically composed, rather than the individual component of a *parashah* centered on a given verse of Scripture. The third then resorts to the framework of a complete pisqa (=*parashah*) to make a single point, that is, to display and demonstrate a single syllogism. Any notion that documents constitute no independent variable, that the base-unit of midrash-exegesis is formed by the statement of a verse and its meaning, and that we may disregard the lines of documentary discourse, seems to me to contradict the facts before us.

II

Plan

Let us begin with the parashah as a whole and then proceed to the work of classifying its units of discourse and explaining the order in which units of each classification are presented.

Leviticus Rabbah Parashah Five

V:I

1. A. *If it is the anointed priest who sins, [thus bringing guilt on the people, then let him offer to the Lord for the sin which he has committed a young bull without blemish]* (Lev. 4:3).
    B. *When he is quiet, who can condemn? When he hides his face, who can set him right [RSV: behold him] [whether it be a nation or a man? that a godless man should not reign, that he should not ensnare the people]* (Job 34:29-30).
    C. R. Meir interpreted [the matter] [Gen. R. 36:1], "'When he is quiet' – in his world, 'when he hides his face' – in his world.
    D. "The matter may be compared to the case of a judge who draws a veil inside and so does not see what goes on outside.
    E. *So the people of the generation of the flood thought: 'The thick clouds cover him, so he will not see [what we do]'* (Job 22:14).
    F. They said to him, "That's enough from you, Meir."
2. A. Another interpretation: *When he is quiet, who can condemn? When he hides his face, who can set him right?* (Job 34:29)
    B. When he gave tranquility to the generation of the flood, who could come and condemn them?
    C. What sort of tranquility did he give them? *Their children are established in their presence, and their offspring before their eyes. [Their houses are safe from fear, and no rod of God is upon them]* (Job 21:8).
    D. R. Levi and rabbis:
    E. R. Levi said, "A woman would get pregnant and give birth in three days. [How do we know it?] Here, the word, 'established,' is used, and elsewhere: *Be establshed in three days* (Ex. 19:15). Just as the word, 'established,' used there involves a span of three days, so the word, 'established,' used here means three days."
    F. Rabbis say, "In a single day a woman would get pregnant and give birth.
    G. "Here, the word, 'established,' is used, and elsewhere: *And be established in the morning* (Ex. 34:2). Just as the word 'established' stated there involves a single day, so the word 'established' used here involves a single day."
3. A. "And their offspring before their eyes" – for they saw children and grandchildren.
    B. *They send forth their little ones like a flock, [and their children dance]* (Job 21:11).
    C. [The word for "children" means] "their young."
    D. Said R. Levi, "In Arabia for children they use the word 'the young.'"
4. A. *And their children dance* (Job 21:11) –
    B. ["they dance"] like devils.

C. That is in line with the following verse of Scripture: *And satyrs will dance there* (Is. 13:21).

5. A. They say: When one of them would give birth by day, she would say to her son, "Go and bring me a flint, so I can cut your umbilical cord."

B. If she gave birth by night, she would say to her son, "Go and light a lamp for me, so I can cut your umbilical cord."

C. M'SH B: A woman gave birth by night and said to her son, "Go and light a lamp for me, so I can cut your umbilical cord."

D. [In Aramaic:] When he went out to fetch it, a devil, Ashmadon [Asmodeus], head of the spirits, met him. While the two were wrestling with one another, the cock crowed. [Ashmadon] said to him, "Go, boast to your mother that my time has run out, for if my time had not run out, I could have killed you."

E. He said to him, "Go, boast to your mother's mother that my mother had not cut my umbilical cord, for if my mother had cut my umbilical cord, I would have beaten you."

F. This illustrates that which is said: *Their houses are safe from fear* (Job 21:9) – from destroying spirits.

6. A. "And no rod of God is upon them" – [for their houses are free from suffering.

B. [And this further] illustrates that which is said: *[When he is quiet, who can condemn,] when he hides his face, who can put him right* (Job 34:30).

C. When [God] hides his face from them, who can come and say to him, "You have not done right."

D. And how, indeed, did he hide his face from them? When he brought the flood on them.

E. That is in line with the following verse of Scripture: *And he blotted out every living substance which was upon the face of the earth* (Gen. 7:23).

7. A. *Whether it be to a nation [or a man together]* (Job 34:29) – this refers to the generation of the flood.

B. "Or to a man" – this refers to Noah.

C. "Together" – he had to rebuild his world from one man, he had to rebuild his world from one nation.

On the surface, the sole point of contact between the base-verse and the intersectingverse, Lev. 4:3 and Job 34:29-30, is in the uncited part of the passage of Job, "that he should not ensnare the people." The anointed priest has sinned and in so doing has brought guilt on the entire people. If, however, that is why the entire assembly of exegeses of Job has been inserted here, that theme plays no rule in making the collection of materials on Job. For at no point in the present unit (or in the next one) does the important segment of the passage of Job come under discussion. The interpretation of Job 34:29 in light of the story of the flood predominates here. No. 1 has Meir's view that the entire passage refers to God's failure to intervene, with special reference to the flood. No. 2 pursues the same line of thought. No. 3 illustrates the notion that their children "are established in their presence," and Nos. 3-4 continue to spell out the phrase by phrase exegesis of the same verse. No. 5 pursues the same line of thought. No. 6 shifts the ground of interpretation. Now God is "quiet," but later, in "hiding his face," he brings punishment on them. No. 7 completes the exegesis of the cited passage of Job in line with the view that Job was a contemporary of Noah and spoke of his ties. Noah might then serve as the counterpart and opposite of the priest who brings guilt on the people. But that is by no means the clear intent of the passage at hand.

V:II

1. A. Another interpretation: *When he is quiet, who can condemn* (Job 34:29).
   B. When he gave tranquility to the Sodomites, who could come and condemn them?
   C. What sort of tranquility did he give them?
   D. *As for the earth, out of it comes bread, but underneath it is turned up as by fire. Its stones are the place of sapphires, and it has dust of gold* (Job 28:5-6).

2. A. *That path no bird of prey knows, and the falcon's eye has not seen it* (Job 28:7).
   B. R. Levi in the name of R. Yohanan bar Shahina: "The falcon [bar hadayya-bird] spots its prey at a distance of eighteen mils."
   C. And how much is its portion [of food]?
   D. R. Meir said, "[A mere] two handbreadths."
   E. R. Judah said, "One handbreadth."
   F. R. Yose said, "Two or three fingerbreadths."
   G. [In Aramaic:] And when it stood on the trees of Sodom, it could not see the ground because of the density of [the foliage of] the trees.

3. A. "When he hides his face, who can put him right?" –
   B. When he hid his face from them, who comes to say to him, "You did not do rightly"?
   C. And when did he hide his face from them?
   D. When he made brimstone and fire rain down on them.
   E. That is in line with the following verse of Scripture: *Then the Lord made brimstone and fire rain on Sodom and Gomorrah* (Gen. 19:24).

The second unit simply carries forward the exercise of reading Job 28:5ff., now in line with the story of Sodom and Gomorrah, rather than the Generation of the Flood.

V:III

1. A. Another interpretation of *When he is quiet, who can condemn? When he hides his face, who can set him right?* (Job 34:29).
   B. When he gave tranquility to the ten tribes, who could come and condemn them?
   C. What sort of tranquility did he give them? *Woe to those who are at ease in Zion, and to those who feel secure on the mountain of Samaria, the notable men of the first of the nations, to whom the house of Israel to come* (Amos 6:1).

2. A. "Woe to those who are at ease in Zion" refers to the tribe of Judah and Benjamin.

B. "Those who feel secure on the mountain of Samaria" refers to the ten tribes.

C. "The notable men of the first of the nations" who derive from the two noteworthy names, Shem and Eber.

D. When the nations of the world eat and drink, they pass the time in nonsense-talk, saying, "Who is a sage, like Balaam! Who is a hero, like Goliath! Who is rich, like Haman!"

E. And the Israelites come after them and say to them, "Was not Ahitophel a sage, Samson a hero, Korah rich?"

3. A. *Pass over to Calneh and see, [and thence go to Hamath the great, then go down to Gath of the Philistines. Are they better than these kingdoms? Or is their territory greater than your territory?]* (Amos 6:2).

B. [Calneh] refers to Ctesiphon.

C. "Hamath the great" refers to Hamath of Antioch.

D. "And go down to Gath of the Philistines" refers to the mounds of the Philistines.

E. "Are they better than these kingdoms? Or is their territory greater than your territory?"

F. *O you who put far away the evil day* (Amos 6:3) [refers to] the day on which they would go into exile.

4. A. *And bring near the seat of violence?* (Amos 6:3). This refers to Esau.

B. "Did you bring yourselves near to sit next to violence" – this refers to Esau.

C. That is in line with the following verse of Scripture: *For the violence done to your brother Jacob, [shame shall cover you]* (Obad. 1:40).

5. A. *[Woe to] those who lie upon beds of ivory* (Amos 6:4) – on beds made of the elephant's tusk.

B. *And stink on their couches* (Amos 6:4) – who do stinking transgressions on their beds.

C. *Who eat lambs from the flock [and calves from the midst of the stall]* (Amos 6:4).

D. They say: When one of them wanted to eat a kid of the flock, he would have the whole flock brought before him, and he would stand over it and slaughter it.

E. When he wanted to eat a calf, he would bring the entire herd of calves before him and stand over it and slaughter it.

6. A. *Who sing idle songs to the sound of the harp [and like David invent for themselves instruments of music]* (Amos 6:5).

B. [They would say that] David provided them with musical instruments.

7. A. *Who drink wine in bowls* (Amos 6:6).

B. Rab, R. Yohanan, and rabbis:

C. Rab said, "It is a very large bowl" [using the Greek].

D. R. Yohanan said, "It was in small cups."

E. Rabbis say, "It was in cups with saucers attached."

F. Whence did the wine they drink come?

G. R. Aibu in the name of R. Hanina said, "It was wine from Pelugta, for the wine would entice (PTH) the body."

H. And rabbis in the name of R. Hanina said, "It was from Pelugta' [separation], since, because of their wine-drinking, the ten tribes were enticed [from God] and consequently sent into exile."

8. A. *And anoint themselves with the finest oils* (Amos 6:6).

   B. R. Judah b. R. Ezekial said, "This refers to oil of unripe olives, which removes hair and smooths the body."

   C. R. Haninah said, "This refers to oil of myrrh and cinnamon."

9. A. And [in spite of] all this glory: *They are not grieved over the ruin of Joseph* (Amos 6:6).

   B. *Therefore they shall now be the first of those to go into exile, [and the revelry of those who stretch themselves shall pass away]* (Amos 6:7).

   C. What is the meaning of "the revelry of those who stretch themselves"?

   D. Said R. Aibu, "They had thirteen public baths, one for each of the tribes, and one additional one for all of them together.

   E. "And all of them were destroyed, and only this one [that had served all of them] survived.

   F. "This shows how much lewdness was done with them."

10. A. *When he hides his face, who can set him right?* (Job 34:29).

    B. When he hid his face from them, who then could come and say to him, "You did not do right"?

    C. How did he hide his face from them? By bringing against them Sennacherib, the king of Assyria.

    D. That is in line with the following verse of Scripture: *In the fourteenth year of King Hezekiah, Sennacherib, king of Assyria, came up [against all the fortified cities of Judah and took them]* (Is. 36:1).

11. A. What is the meaning of, "and took them"?

    B. Said R. Abba b. R. Kahana, "Three divine decrees were sealed on that day.

    C. "The decree against the ten tribes was sealed, for them to fall into the hand of Sennacherib; the decree against Sennacherib was sealed, for him to fall into the hand of Hezekiah; and the decree of Shebna was sealed, to be smitten with leprosy.

12. A. *Whether it be a nation [or a man]* (Job 34:29) – this refers to Sennacherib, as it is said, *For a nation has come up upon my land* (Joel 1:6).

    B. *...or a man* (Job 34:29) – this refers to Israel: *For you, my sheep, the sheep of my pasture, are a man* (Ez. 34:31).

    C. *Together* (Job 34:29) – this refers to King Uzziah, who was smitten with leprosy.

    D. That is in line with the following verse of Scripture: *And Uzziah the King was a leper until the day he died* (2 Chr. 26:21).

13. A. [Margulies: What follows treats *...whether it be a nation or a man together* (Job 34:29):] Now the justice of the Holy One, blessed be He, is not like man's justice.

    B. A mortal judge may show favor to a community, but he will never show favor to an individual.

    C. But the Holy One, blessed be He, is not so. Rather: *If it is the anointed priest who sins, [thus bringing guilt on the people,] then let him offer [for the sin which he has committed] a young bull [without blemish to the Lord as a sin-offering]* (Lev. 4:3-4).

    D. "[If the whole congregation of Israel commits a sin unwittingly, and the thing is hidden from the eyes of the assembly, and they do any one of the things which the Lord has commanded not to be done and are guilty,

when the sin which they have committed becomes known,] the assembly
shall offer a young bull for a sin-offering" (Lev. 4:13-14). [God exacts
the same penalty from an individual and from the community and does
not distinguish the one from the other. The anointed priest and the
community both become subject to liability for the same offering, a
young bull.]

Finally, at No. 13, we come to the verse with which we began. And we
find a clear point of contact between the base-verse and the intersecting one, Job
34:29, as Margulies explains. Still, there is no clear reason for including a
sustained exegesis of Amos 6:3ff. No. 1 completes the original exegesis by
applying the cited verse to the ten tribes, first tranquil, then punished, as at V:I,
II. 1.C then links Amos 6:1 to the present context. Once Amos 6:1 makes its
appearance, we work through the elements of Amos 6:1-7. That massive
interpolation encompasses Nos. 2-9. No. 10 resumes where No. 1 left off. No.
11 is tacked on to 10.D, and then Nos. 12, 13 continue the exegesis in terms of
Israelite history of Job 34:29. Then, as I said, No. 13 stands completely
separate from all that has gone before in V:I-III.12.

What then is the primary intent of the exegete? It is to emphasize the
equality of anointed priest and ordinary Israelites. The expiation demanded of the
one is no greater than that of the other. Considering the importance of the
anointed priest, the ceremony by which he attains office, the sanctity attached to
his labor, we cannot miss the polemic. What the anointed priest does
unwittingly will usually involve some aspect of the cult. When the community
commits a sin unwittingly, it will not involve the cult but some aspect of the
collective life of the people. The one is no more consequential than the other;
the same penalty pertains to both. So the people and the priest stand on the
same plane before God. And the further meaning of the verse of Job then cannot
be missed. When God hides his face, in consequence of which the people suffer,
it is for a just cause. No one can complain; he is long-suffering but in the end
exacts his penalties. And these will cover not unwitting sin, such as Leviticus
knows, but deliberate sin, as with the Generation of the Flood, Sodom, and the
Ten Tribes. There would then appear to be several layers of meaning in the
exegetical construction, which we must regard as a sustained and unified one, a
truly amazing achievement.

V:IV

1. A. Said R. Abbahu, "It is written, *Take heed that you do not forsake the
   Levite [as long as you live in your land]* (Deut. 12:19). What follows
   thereafter? *When the Lord your God enlarges your territory [as he has
   promised you]* (Deut. 12:20).
   B. "What has one thing got to do with the other?
   C. "Said the Holy One, blessed be He, 'In accord with your gifts will they
   enlarge your [place].'"

D. R. Huna in the name of R. Aha, "If a slave brings as his offering a young bull, while his master brings a lamb, the slave takes precedence over his master.

E. "This is in accord with what we have learned in the Mishnah: *If the young bull of the anointed priest and the young bull of the community are waiting [sacrifice], the young bull of the anointed priest takes precedence over the young bull of the community in all aspects of the sacrificial rite* (M. Hor. 3:6)."

2. A. *A man's gift makes room for him and brings him before great men* (Prov. 18:16).

B. M'SH B: R. Eliezer, R. Joshua, and R. Aqiba went to the harborside of Antioch to collect funds for the support of sages.

C. [In Aramaic:] A certain Abba Yudan lived there.

D. He would carry out his religious duty [of philanthropy] in a liberal spirit, but had lost his money. When he saw our masters, he went home with a sad face. His wife said to him, "What's wrong with you, that you look so sad?"

E. He repeated the tale to her: "Our masters are here, and I don't know what I shall be able to do for them."

F. His wife, who was a truly philanthropic woman – what did she say to him? "You only have one field left. Go, sell half of it and give them the proceeds."

G. He went and did just that. When he was giving them the money, they said to him, "May the Omnipresent make up all your losses."

H. Our masters went their way.

I. He went out to plough. While he was ploughing the half of the field that he had left, the Holy One, blessed be He, opened his eyes. The earth broke open before him, and his cow fell in and broke her leg. He went down to raise her up, and found a treasure beneath her. He said, "It was for my gain that my cow broke her leg."

J. When our masters came back, [in Aramaic:] they asked about a certain Abba Yudan and how he was doing. They said, "Who can gaze on the face of Abba Yudan [which glows with prosperity] – Abba Yudan, the owner of flocks of goats, Abba Yudan, the owner of herds of asses, Abba Yudan, the owner of herds of camels."

K. He came to them and said to them, "Your prayer in my favor has produced returns and returns on the returns."

L. They said to him, "Even though someone else gave more than you did, we wrote your name at the head of the list."

M. Then they took him and sat him next to themselves and recited in his regard the following verse of Scripture: *A man's gift makes room for him and brings him before great men* (Prov. 18:16).

3. A. R. Hiyya bar Abba called for charity contributions in support of a school in Tiberias. A member of the household of Siloni got up and pledged a litra of gold.

B. R. Hiyya bar Abba took him and sat him next to himself and recited in his regard the following verse of Scripture: *A man's gift makes room for him and brings him before great men* (Prov. 18:16).

4. A. [In Aramaic:] R. Simeon b. Laqish went to Bosrah. A certain Abba [Lieberman deletes: Yudan], "the Deceiver," lived there. It was not –

Heaven forfend – that he really was a deceiver. Rather, he would practice [holy] deception in doing the religious duty [of philanthropy].

B.   [In Aramaic:] He would see what the rest of the community would pledge, and he would then pledge to take upon himself [a gift equivalent to that of the rest of the] community.

C.   R. Simeon b. Laqish took him and sat him next to himself and recited in his regard the following verse of Scripture: *A man's gift makes room for him and brings him before great men* (Prov. 18:16).

We find neither a base-verse nor an intersecting one. Rather, what will be the secondary verse – Prov. 18:16 – comes in the distant wake of a problem presented by the information of Lev. 4. Specifically, we find reference to the sacrifice of the young bulls of the high priest, of the community, and of the ruler. The issue then naturally arises, which one comes first? The Mishnah answers that question, at M. Hor. 3:6. Reflection upon that answer generates the observation that the anointed priest comes first, as in Scripture's order, in particular when the offerings are of the same value. But if one offering is more valuable than the other, the more valuable offering takes precedence. Then comes secondary reflection on the fact that a person's gift establishes his rank even if it is on other grounds lower than what he otherwise would attain. No. 1 does not pursue that secondary reflection, but invites it at 1.C. The invocation of Prov. 18:16 then is not on account of Lev. 4 at all. It must follow that Nos. 2-4 would better serve a compilation of materials on Deut. 12:19-20 than the present passage. What follows No. 1 serves a purpose in no way closely connected either to the sense or to the syntax of our passage. The entire complex, Nos. 2-4, occurs at Y. Hor. 3:4. It is lifted whole, attached because of the obvious relevance to No. 1. We find no pretense, then, that these stories relate in any way to Lev. 4.

For the story-teller at No. 2, the climax comes at L-M, the sages' recognition that their placing of Abba Yudan at the head of the list had made possible the serendipitous accident. Nos. 3 and 4 omit the miraculous aspect entirely.

V:V

1.   A.   Reverting to the base-text (GWPH): *If it is the anointed priest who sins* (Lev. 4:3).

     B.   This refers to Shebna.

2.   A.   *[Thus says the Lord, God of hosts,] "Come, go to this steward (SKN), to Shebna, who is over the household, [and say to him, 'What have you to do here and whom have you here, that you have hewn here a tomb for yourself, you who hew a tomb on the height and carve a habitation for yourself in the rock? Behold, the Lord will hurl you away violently, O you strong young man! He will seize firm hold on you, and whirl you round and round and throw you like a ball into a wide land; there you shall die, and there shall be your splendid chariots, you shame of your master's house. I will thrust you from your office and you will be cast down from your station]"* (Is. 22:15-19).

B. R. Eliezer said, "He was a high priest."

C. R. Judah b. Rabbi said, "He was steward."

D. In the view of R. Eliezer, who said he was a high priest, [we may bring evidence from Scripture,] for it is written, *And I will clothe him with your robe [and will bind your girdle on him and will commit your authority into his hand]* (Is. 22:21).

E. In the view of R. Judah b. Rabbi, who said he was steward, [we may bring evidence from Scripture,] for it is written, *And I will commit your authority to his hand* (Is. 22:21).

F. R. Berekiah said, "What is a 'steward' (SWKN)? It is one who comes from Sikhni.

3 . A. And he went up and was appointed komes opsarion [the Greek for chief cook] in Jerusalem.

B. That is in line with the prophet's condemnation, saying to him, *What have you to do here, and whom have you here* (Is. 22:16).

C. "You exile, son of an exile! What wall have you built here, what pillar have you put up here, and what nail have you hammered in here?!"

D. R. Eleazar said, "A person has to have a nail or a peg firmly set in a synagogue so as to have the right to be buried in that place [in which he is living]."

E. "And have you hewn here a tomb for yourself?" (Is. 22:16). He made himself a kind of a dovecote and put his tomb on top of it.

F. *You who hew a tomb on the height* (Is. 22:16) –

G. R. Ishmael in the name of Mar Uqba, "On the height the decree was hewn out concerning him, indicating that he should not have a burial place in the land of Israel."

H. *You who carve a habitation for yourself in the rock* (Is. 22:16) – a stone coffin.

I. *Behold, the Lord will hurl you away violently* (Is. 22:17) – one rejection after another.

J. "...hurl away violently (GBR)" – [since the word GBR also means cock:] said R. Samuel b. R. Nahman, "[In Aramaic:], it may be compared to a cock which is driven and goes from place to place."

K. *He will seize a firm hold on you* (Is. 22:17), [since the words for "firm hold" may also be translated, "wrap around," thus: "And he will wrap you around"] the meaning is that he was smitten with sara'at, in line with that which you find in Scripture, *And he will wrap his lip around* (Lev. 13:45).

L. *And whirl you round and round [and throw you like a ball]* (Is. 22:18) – exile after exile.

M. "Like a ball" – just as a ball is caught from hand to hand and does not fall to the ground, so [will it be for him].

N. *Into a wide land* (Ezra 8:17)– this means Casiphia .

O. *There you shall die and there shall be your splendid chariots* (Is. 22:18) –

4 . A. In accord with the position of R. Eliezer, who said that Shebna had been a high priest, [the reference to the splendid chariots implies] that he had been deriving personal benefit from the offerings.

B. In accord with the view of R. Judah b. Rabbi, who said that he had been steward, [the reference to the splendid chariots implies] that he had derived personal benefit from things that had been consecrated for use in the upkeep of the sanctuary.

C. *You shame of your master's house* (Is. 22:18).

D. In accord with the position of R. Eliezer, who said that Shebna had been a high priest, [the shame was] that he had treated the offerings in a disgraceful way.

E. In accord with the view of R. Judah b. Rabbi, who said that he had been steward, [the shame was] that he had treated both of his masters disgracefully, that is Hezekiah, on the one side, Isaiah on the other.

5. A. R. Berekhiah in the name of R. Abba b. R. Kahana: "What did Shebna and Joahaz [2 Kngs. 18:18] do? They wrote a message and attached it to an arrow and shot it to Sennacherib through the window. In the message was written the following: "We and everyone in Jerusalem want you, but Hezekiah and Isaiah don't want you."

B. Now this is just what David had said [would happen]: *For lo, the wicked bend the bow, they have fitted their arrow to the string* (Ps. 11:2).

C. "For lo, the wicked bend the bow" – this refers to Shebna and Joahaz.

D. "They have fitted their arrow to the string" – on the bowstring.

E. *To shoot in the dark at the upright in heart* (Ps. 11:2) – at two upright in heart, Hezekiah and Isaiah.

What the exegete contributes to the explanation of Lev. 4:3 is simply the example of how an anointed priest may sin. The rest of the passage is a systematic exposition of the verses about Shebna. But the entire matter of Shebna belongs here only within Eliezer's opinion that he was a high priest. That is a rather remote connection to the present passage of Leviticus. So because of the allegation that Shebna was high priest, the entire passage – fully worked out on its own – was inserted here. The redactor then appeals to theme, not to content, in drawing together the cited verses of Leviticus and Isaiah. Nos. 2, 4 are continuous with one another. No. 3 inserts a systematic, phrase by phrase exegesis of Is. 22:15ff. No. 5 then complements the foregoing with yet further relevant material. So the construction, apart from No. 1, is cogent and well-conceived. Only linkage to Lev. 4:3 is farfetched.

V:VI

1. A. *If it is the anointed priest who sins* (Lev. 4:3).

B. [What follows occurs at T. Hor. 2:4, explaining M. Hor. 3:4, cited above at V:IV.1.E:] [If] the anointed high priest must atone [for a sin] and the community [SBWR for SRYK] must be atoned for [in line with Lev. 4:13], it is better that the one who [has the power to] make atonement take precedence over the one for whom atonement is made,

C. As it is written, *And he will atone for himself and for his house* (Lev. 16:17).

D. ["His house"] refers to his wife.

2. A. *If it is the anointed priest who sins* (Lev. 4:3) –

B. Will an anointed priest commit a sin!

C. Said R. Levi, "Pity the town whose physician has gout [and cannot walk to visit the sick], whose governor has one eye, and whose public defender plays the prosecutor in capital cases."

3. A. *[If it is the anointed priest who sins,] thus bringing guilt (L'SMT) [on the people, then let him offer for the sin which he has committed a young bull...]* (Lev. 4:3).

   B. Said R. Isaac, "It is a case of death (MWT) by burning ('S) [inflicted on one who commits sacrilege by consuming offerings from the altar]."

   C. "The matter may be compared to the keeper of a bear, who ate up the rations of the bear. The king said, 'Since he went and ate up the bear's rations, let the bear eat him.'

   D. "So does the Holy One, blessed be He, say, 'Since Shebna enjoyed benefit from things that had been consecrated to the altar [for burning], let fire consume him.'"

4. A. Said R. Aibu [Y. Ter. 8:3, A.Z. 2:3], "M'SH B: Once there was a butcher in Sepphoris, who fed Israelites carrion and torn-meat. On the eve of the Day of Atonement he went out drinking and got drunk. He climbed up to the roof of his house and fell off and died. The dogs began to lick him.

   B. "[In Aramaic:] They came and asked R. Hanina the law about moving his corpse away from the dogs [on the Day of Atonement].

   C. *"He said to him, 'You will be holy people to me, therefore you shall not eat any meat that is torn of beasts in the field, you shall cast it to the dogs'* (Ex. 22:30).

   D. "This man robbed from the dogs and fed carrion and torn-meat to Israelites. Leave him to them. They are eating what belongs to them."

5. A. *He shall bring the bull to the door of the tent of meeting before the Lord, [and lay his hand on the head of the bull and kill the bull before the Lord]* (Lev. 4:4).

   B. Said R. Isaac, "The matter may be compared to the case of a king, one of whose admirers paid him honor by giving him a handsome gift and by offering him lovely words of praise. The king then said, 'Set this gift at the gate of the palace, so that everyone who comes and goes may see [and admire] it,'

   C. "as it is said, 'And he shall bring the bull [to the door of the tent of meeting].'"

The opening units, Nos. 1-4, form a kind of appendix of miscellanies to what has gone before. No. 1 reaches back to V:IV, explaining the passage of the Mishnah cited there. No. 2 is joined to No. 3, which relates to the cited passage to Shebna. So Nos. 2-3 complete the discussion of V:V. It seems to me that No. 4 is attached to No. 3 as an illustration of the case of a public official who abuses his responsibility. No. 5 provides a fresh point, moving on to a new verse. There is no intersecting verse; the exegesis is accomplished solely through a parable.

V:VII

1. A. *[If the whole congregation of Israel commits a sin unwittingly and the thing is hidden from the eyes of the assembly, and they do any one of the things which the Lord has commanded not to be done and are guilty, when the sin which they have committed becomes known, the assembly shall offer a young bull for a sin-offering and bring it before the tent of*

meeting;] and the elders of the congregation shall lay their hands [upon the head of the bull before the Lord] (Lev. 4:13-15).

B. [Since, in laying their hands (SMK) on the head of the bull, the elders sustain (SMK) the community by adding to it the merit they enjoy,] said R. Isaac, *The nations of the world have none to sustain them, for it is written, 'And those who sustain Egypt will fall'* (Ez. 30:6).

C. "But Israel has those who sustain it, as it is written: *And the elders of the congregation shall lay their hands [and so sustain Israel]* (Lev. 4:15)."

2. A. Said R. Eleazar, "The nations of the world are called a congregation, and Israel is called a congregation.

B. "The nations of the world are called a congregation: *For the congregation of the godless shall be desolate* (Job 15:34).

C. "And Israel is called a congregation: *And the elders of the congregation shall lay their hands* (Lev. 4:15).

D. "The nations of the world are called sturdy bulls and Israel is called sturdy bulls.

E. "The nations of the world are called sturdy bulls: 'The congregation of [sturdy] bulls with the calves of the peoples' (Ps. 68:31).

F. "Israel is called sturdy bulls, as it is said, *Listen to me, you sturdy [bullish] of heart* (Is. 46:13).

G. "The nations of the world are called excellent, and Israel is called excellent.

H. "The nations of the world are called excellent: *You and the daughters of excellent nations* (Ex. 32:18).

I. "Israel is called excellent: *They are the excellent, in whom is all my delight* (Ps. 16:4).

J. "The nations of the world are called sages, and Israel is called sages.

K. "The nations of the world are called sages: *And I shall wipe out sages from Edom* (Ob. 1:8).

L. "And Israel is called sages: *Sages store up knowledge* (Prov. 10:14).

M. "The nations of the world are called unblemished, and Israel is called unblemished.

N. "The nations of the world are called unblemished: 'Unblemished as are those that go down to the pit' (Prov. 1:12).

O. "And Israel is called unblemished: *The unblemished will inherit goodness* (Prov. 28:10).

P. "The nations of the world are called men, and Israel is called men.

Q. "The nations of the world are called men: *And you men who work iniquity* (Ps. 141:4).

R. "And Israel is called men: *To you who are men I call* (Prov. 8:4).

S. "The nations of the world are called righteous, and Israel is called righteous.

T. "The nations of the world are called righteous: *And righteous men shall judge them* (Ez. 23:45).

U. "And Israel is called righteous: *And your people – all of them are righteous* (Is. 60:21).

V. "The nations of the world are called mighty, and Israel is called mighty.

W. "The nations of the world are called mighty: *Why do you boast of evil, O mighty man* (Ps. 52:3).

X. "And Israel is called mighty: *Mighty in power, those who do his word* (Ps. 103:20).

We see two distinct types of exegeses, one to which the base-passage is central, the other to which it is peripheral. Yet the two passages belong together, and we have every reason to suppose that they were made up as a single cogent statement. No. 1 focuses upon the double meaning of the word SMK, one, lay hands, the other, sustain, drawing the contrast stated by Isaac. Once such a contrast is drawn, a catalogue of eight further contrasts will be laid out. Since the opening set, 2.A-B, depends upon the passage at hand, we must accept the possibility that Eleazar's statement has been constructed to work its way through the contrast established by Isaac. For both authorities make the same point. Even though the nations of the word are subject to the same language as is applied to Israel, they still do not fall into the same classification. For language is dual. When a word applies to Israel, it serves to praise, and when the same word applies to the nations, it underlines their negative character. Both are called congregation, but the nations' congregation is desolate, and so throughout, as the context of the passage cited concerning the nations repeatedly indicates. The nations' sages are wiped out; the unblemished nations go down to the pit; the nations, called men, only work iniquity. Now that is precisely the contrast drawn in Isaac's saying, so, as I said, the whole should be deemed a masterpiece of unitary composition. Then the two types of exegesis – direct, peripheral – turn out to complement one another, each making its own point.

V:VIII

1. A. R. Simeon b. Yohai taught, "How masterful are the Israelites, for they know how to find favor with their creator."
   B. Said R. Yudan, [in Aramaic:], "It is like the case of Samaritan [beggars]. The Samaritan [beggars] are clever at begging. One of them goes to a housewife, saying to her, 'Do you have an onion? Give it to me.' After she gives it to him, he says to her, 'Is there such a thing as an onion without bread?' After she gives him [bread], he says to her, 'Is there such a thing as food without drink?' So, all in all, he gets to eat and drink."
   C. Said R. Aha [in Aramaic:], "There is a woman who knows how to borrow things, and there is a woman who does not. The one who knows how to borrow goes over to her neighbor. The door is open, but she knocks [anyhow]. Then she says to her neighbor, 'Greetings, good neighbor. How're you doing? How's your husband doing? How're your kids doing? Can I come in? [By the way], would you have such-and-such a utensil? Would you lend it to me? [The neighboring housewife] says to her, 'Yes, of course.'
   D. "But the one who does not know how to borrow goes over to her neighbor. The door is closed, so she just opens it. She says [to the neighboring housewife], 'Do you have such-and-such a utensil? Would you lend it to me?' [The neighboring housewife] says to her, 'No.'"
   E. Said R. Hunia [in Aramaic:], "There is a tenant-farmer who knows how to borrow things, and there is a tenant-farmer who does not know how to borrow. The one who knows how to borrow combs his hair, brushes off

his clothes, puts on a good face, and then goes over to the overseer of his work to borrow from him. [The overseer] says to him, 'How's the land doing?' He says to him, 'May you have the merit of being fully satisfied with its [wonderful] produce.' 'How are the oxen doing?' He says to him, 'May you have the merit of being fully satisfied with their fat.' 'How are the goats doing?' 'May you have the merit of being fully satisfied with their young.' 'And what would you like?' Then he says, 'Now if you might have an extra ten denars, would you give them to me?' The overseer replies, 'If you want, take twenty.'

F. "But the one who does not know how to borrow leaves his hair a mess, his clothes filthy, his face gloomy. He too goes over to the overseer to borrow from him. The overseer says to him, 'How's the land doing?' He replies, 'I hope it will produce at least what [in seed] we put into it.' 'How are the oxen doing?' 'They're scrawny.' 'How are the goats doing?' 'They're scrawny too.' 'And what do you want?' 'Now if you might have an extra ten denars, would you give them to me?' The overseer replies, 'Go, pay me back what you already owe me!'"

G. Said R. Hunia, "David was one of the good tenant-farmers. To begin with, he starts a psalm with praise [of God], saying, 'The heavens declare the glory of God, and the firmament shows his handiwork' (Ps. 19:2). The Heaven says to him, 'Perhaps you need something?' 'The firmament shows his handiwork.' The firmament says to him, 'Perhaps you need something?'

H. "And so he would continue to sing: *Day unto day utters speech, and night to night reveals knowledge* (Ps. 19:3).

I. "Said to him the Holy One, blessed be He, 'What do you want?'

J. "He said before him, *Who can discern errors?* (Ps. 19:13).

K. "'What sort of unwitting sin have I done before you?'

L. "[God] said to him, 'Lo, this one is remitted, and that one is forgiven you.'

M. *"And cleanse me of hidden sins* (Ps. 19:13). '...from the secret sins that I have done before you.'

N. "He said to him, 'Lo, this one is remitted, and that one is forgiven to you.'

O. "'Keep back your servant also from deliberate ones.' This refers to transgressions done in full knowledge.

P. *"That they may not have dominion over me. Then I shall be faultless* (Ps. 19:14). This refers to the most powerful of transgressions.

Q. *"And I shall be clear of great transgression* (Ps. 19:14)."

R. Said R. Levi, "David said before the Holy One, blessed be He, *Lord of the age[s], you are a great God, and, as for me, my sins are great too. It will take a great God to remit and forgive great sins: For your name's sake, O Lord, pardon my sin, for [your name] is great* (Ps. 25:11)."

Once more the construction appears from beginning to end to aim at a single goal. The opening statement, 1.A, makes the point, and the closing construction, Gff., illustrates it. In the middle come three apt narratives serving as similes, all told in Aramaic, and all following exactly the same pattern. Then the systematic account of a passage of Scripture is provided to make exactly the same point. I cannot state the exact sense of the passage on the heaven and the firmament, G, but from that point, the discourse is pellucid. Q-R should be separated from G-P, since what Levi's statement does is simply augment the primary passage. The unity of theme and conception accounts for the drawing together of the entire lot. To be sure, B-F can serve other purposes. But since Hunia's statement, E-F, introduces his exegesis of Ps. 19, the greater likelihood is that a single hand has produced the entire matter (possibly excluding Q-R) to make a single point. Why has the redactor thought the passage appropriate here? The offering for unwitting sin of Lev. 4, to which K makes reference in the progression through the types of sins, from minor to major, for which David seeks forgiveness, certainly accounts for the inclusion of the whole. Then whoever made up the passage did not find the stimulus in Lev. 4. For the rather general observation of 1.A states the framer's message. That message pertains to diverse contexts, as the exposition of Ps. 19 makes clear; nothing would compel someone to make up a passage of this sort to serve Lev. 4 in particular.

Let us now turn to the classification of the units of discourse of which the *parashah* is composed. What we want to know is the structure of the *parashah* as a whole, where its largest subunits of thought begin and end and how they relate to one another. How shall we recognize a complete unit of thought? It will be marked off by the satisfactory resolution of a tension or problem introduced at the outset. A complete unit of thought may be made up of a number of subdivisions, many of them entirely spelled out on their own. But the composition of a complete unit of thought always will strike us as cogent, the work of a single conception on how a whole thought should be constructed and expressed. While that unitary conception drew upon already available materials, the main point is made by the composition as a whole, and not by any of its (ready-made) parts.

In the first classification we take up the single most striking recurrent literary structure of Leviticus Rabbah. It is what we may call the base-verse/intersecting-verse construction, already familiar from Pesiqta deRab Kahana. In such a construction, a base-verse, drawn from the book of Leviticus, is juxtaposed to an intersecting-verse, drawn from any book other than a pentateuchal one. Then this intersecting-verse is subjected to systematic exegesis. On the surface the exegesis is out of all relationship with the base-verse. But in a stunning climax, all of the exegeses of the intersecting-verse are shown to relate to the main point the exegete wishes to make about the base-verse. What that means is that the composition as a whole is so conceived as to impose meaning and order on all of the parts, original or ready-made parts, of which the author of the whole has made use. For the one example in *Parashah* 5, the base-verse is Lev. 4:3 and the intersecting-verse Job 34:29-30. Here is the outline of the first three subdivisions of the *parashah.*

V:I.1.C-F   Lev. 4:3, Job 34:29-30 and the generation of the flood
V:I.2.A-C   Lev. 4:3, Job 34:29-30 and the generation of the flood

V:I.2.E-G	Lev. 4:3, Job 34:29-30 and the generation of the flood
V:I.3.A	Lev. 4:3, Job 34:29-30 and the generation of the flood
V:I.3.B-D	Job 21:11
V:I.4	Job 21:11
V:I.5.A-B	Generation of the flood
V:I.5.C-F	Ma'aseh
V:I.6.A-E	Job 34:29-30, Gen. 7:23. Relevance: Reference to God's hiding his face.
V:I.7.A-C	Job 34:29. Refers to Noah.
V:II.1	Job 34:29. Refers to Sodomites. First comes tranquility, then punishment. Job 28:7
V:II.2	Further exegesis of Job 28:7.
V:II.3	God hid his face from Sodomites (Job 34:29) and then punished them (Gen. 19:24).
V:III.1	Job 34:29. Refers to Ten Tribes, first tranquility, then punishment. Amos 6:1.
V:III.2	Further comment on Amos 6:1
V:III.3	Further comment on Amos 6:2
V:III.4	Amos 6:3
V:III.5	Amos 6:4
V:III.6	Amos 6:5
V:III.7	Amos 6:6
V:III.8	Amos 6:6
V:III.9	Amos 6:6, 7. All of the units on Amos simply comment on clauses of verses.
V.III.10	Job 34:29. How God hid his face from the Ten Tribes. Isaiah 36:1.
V:III.11	Isaiah 36:1
V:III.12	Job 34:29. Refers to Sennacherib (Joel 6) and Israel (Ez. 34:31).
V:III.13	Job 34:29 linked to Lev. 4:3-4. God exacts the same penalty from an individual or a community, so Job 34:29 and also Lev. 4:13-14.

As we saw when we followed the text in detail, the composition moves with striking cogency over its chosen examples: the Generation of the Flood, the Ten Tribes, Sennacherib and Israel. So three large-scale illustrations of Job 34:29-30 are laid out, and then the entire composition reverts to Lev. 4:3ff. to make a single point about all that has gone before.

Another form is the intersecting-verse/base-verse construction. Secondary in size and in exegetical complexity to the one just now surveyed, here the intersecting-verse is worked out, then comes the base-verse, given a simple exemplification. Just as in the first type, the exegete may assemble passages on that exemplificatory entry. We have two instances. The first example is V:V. Since Lev. 4:3 refers to the sin of an anointed priest, the exegete wishes to show us how an anointed priest may sin and so he invokes the name of Shebna. The rest follows.

V:V.1	Lev. 4:3. Refers to Shebna.
V:V.2	Shebna (Is. 22:15-19)
V:V.3	Shebna (Is. 22:16-18)
V:V.4	Shebna and Joahaz

The second example is somewhat more subtle. Here we have a play on a word used in the base-verse. Then a whole series of verses will be adduced to make a point based on that play on words. These proof-texts cannot be called intersecting-verses in the way in which, in the earlier classification and in the first example of the present one, the cited verses intersect with, but take over discourse from, the base-verse. Quite to the contrary, the base-verse generates a point, which then is richly expanded by the cited verses. Nonetheless, I should regard the present example as a variation on the foregoing. The reason is that, in a strictly formal sense, the pattern remains what we have seen to this point: a set of illustrative verses that make the main point the exegete wishes to associate with or about the base-verse, given at the end.

V:VII.1-2   Lev. 4:13-15. Exegesis of the verse, with special attention to a word-play. The upshot is that Israel is distinguished from the nations. Then a long catalogue of such distinctions is appended.

A third classification derives from the clause by clause type of exegesis of the base-verse, with slight interest in intersecting-verses or in illustrative materials deriving from other books of the Scripture. The base-verse in this classification defines the entire frame of discourse, either because of its word choices or because of its main point. Where verses of other passages are quoted, they serve not as the focus of discourse but only as proof-texts or illustrative-texts. They therefore function in a different way from the verses adduced in discourse in the first two classifications, for, in those former cases, the intersecting-verses form the center of interest. As we see at V:VI, we deal with the subject-matter of Lev. 4:3-4, on the one side, and we also explain the derivation of words used in the cited verse, on the other. These are distinct modes of exegesis – ideational, philological – but the difference is slight in determining the classification at hand. It is simply exegesis of verses of Leviticus, item by item. Here are examples of the exegetical type of unit of discourse.

V:VI.1   Lev. 4:3. Precedence in atonement rite.

V:VI.2   Lev. 4:3. How can an anointed priest sin?

V:VI.3   Lev. 4:3. Explanation of a word used in the cited verse.

V:VI.4   Lev. 4:3 and Shebna. Illustration.

V:VI.5   Lev. 4:4. Why bring the bell to the tent of meeting as Lev. 4:4
            specifies.

The category of miscellanies and how they are joined now demands
attention. By a "miscellany," I mean a construction that does not relate to any
base-verse in Leviticus 4 or to the cited intersecting-verses; that does not address
any theme or principle pertinent to the base-verse or to its larger context; and
that appears to have been formed for purposes entirely distinct from the
explanation or amplification of a passage of the book of Leviticus. One such
example is at V:IV.1-4, at which, as we see, the general theme of Lev. 4:3 – the
sacrifices of several officials, in order – triggers the inquiry into which offering
comes first. But at issue is the principle that whoever sacrifices proportionately
more in terms of his means is the one who gets the more credit. That notion is
unrelated to Lev. 4:3. The passage is cogent. Here is the outline, which, as we
see, deals with Prov. 18:16 and provides anthology of rather coherent materials
for that verse.

V:IV.1   God recognizes the value of a gift to the cult, e.g., in accord with
            the donor's sacrifice. Deut. 12:19, 20; M. Hor. 3:6.

V:IV.2   "A man's gift makes room for him" (Prov. 18:16) and long
            illustrative story.

V:IV.3   Prov. 18:16

V:IV.4   Prov. 18:16

A second example, drawn from Parashah 5, serves Ps. 19:2-3, 13-14, and the
reason for its inclusion with reference to Lev. 4 is not entirely clear.

V:VIII.1   Israel knows how to placate God. The point is joined to Ps.
            19:23, 13-14. This construction does not belong to Lev. 4.

We therefore discern three categories of units of discourse, illustrated by
generally rather sizable subunits. These are, first, the (complex) base-
verse/intersecting-verse construction (I); second, the (simple) intersecting-
verse/base-verse construction (II); and, third, the clause-by-clause exegetical
construction (III). We note, finally, the category of miscellanies (IV), always
marked by the simple trait of irrelevance to the concrete context at hand.

Can we discern an order followed by the several types of units of discourse?

1. Base-verse/intersecting-verse construction: V:I-III
2. Intersecting-verse/base-verse construction: V:V, V:VII
3. Clause by clause exegetical construction: V:VI
4. Miscellanies: V:IV, V:VIII

The obvious problem is at V:V-VII. Can we account for the insertion of V:VI between V:V and V:VII? We certainly can. V:VI.1-4 form an appendix to V:V – pure and simple. The organizer of the whole had no choice but to insert his appendix behind the materials supplemented by his appendix. The same sort of reasoning then accounts for the insertion of miscellanies, e.g., V:IV after V:I-III. What V:IV does is simply carry forward the problem of which beast comes first when a number of beasts are awaiting offering for the purposes of atonement for various officials. That issue is very important to the author of V:III. So the first of the two cases in which we have miscellanies turns out to exemplify a rather careful mode of arranging materials. Where a major point carries in its wake exemplificatory materials, these will be inserted before the parashah moves on to new matters. There is no difficulty in explaining why the arranger of the whole has placed V:VIII at the end; what we do not know is why, to begin with, he selected that unit of discourse. But that issue need not detain us.

We emerge with two hypotheses, one firm, the other less so. The first is the hypothesis that the units of discourse are framed in accord with conventions that define and distinguish three recurrent literary structures: (1) base-verse/intersecting-verse construction; (2) intersecting-verse/base-verse construction; (3) clause by clause exegetical construction (invoking a broad range of intersecting-verses only for narrowly-illustrative purposes). We noted, in addition, a category we called "miscellaneous."

The second hypothesis is that the categories of units of discourse also explain the order of arrangement of types of units of discourse. First will come the (I) base-verse/intersecting-verse construction; then will come (II) intersecting-verse/base-verse construction; finally we shall have (III) clause-by-clause exegetical constructions. If we were to assign cardinal numbers to these types of constructions I, II, and III, we should also be able to use ordinal numbers, first, second, third. Why? Because in accord with the stated hypothesis, type I will come first, type II second, and type III third. Type IV encompasses miscellanies.

Rather than proceed to two further *parashiyyot,* let me simply state the formal characteristics of Leviticus Rabbah as a whole. I count, in all of Leviticus Rabbah, 304 entries in four catalogues of types of units of discourse:

I	38	12.5%
II	84	27.6%

III	94	30.9%
IV	88	28.9%

The three defined taxa thus cover 71% of the whole. The two truly distinctive patterns, types **I** and **II**, cover a sizable part of the whole – 40%.

As to the order of types of units of discourse, the following complete survey states the simple facts:

Type **I** comes in first position in	31/37	83.7%
Type **II** comes in first position in	5/37	13.5%
Type **III** comes in first position in	0/37	0.0%
Type **IV** comes in first position in	1/37	2.7%
Type **I** comes in second position in	13/37	35.1%
Type **II** comes in second position in	21/37	56.7%
Type **III** comes in second position in	1/37	2.7%
Type **IV** comes in second position in	2/37	5.4%
Type **I** comes in last position in	0/37	0.0%
Type **II** comes in last position in	0/37	0.0%
Type **III** comes in last position in	16/37	43.2%
Type **IV** comes in last position in	21/37	56.7%

The framer of a passage ordinarily began with a base-verse/intersecting-verse construction. He very commonly proceeded with an intersecting-verse/base-verse construction. Then he would provide such exegeses of pertinent verses of Leviticus as he had in hand. He would conclude either with type **III** or type **IV** constructions, somewhat more commonly the latter than the former. So the program of the authors is quite simple. They began with types **I** and **II** – 100% of the first and second position entries, proceeded with type **III**, and concluded with type **III** or **IV**.

III

Program

The message of Leviticus Rabbah is that the laws of history may be known, and that these laws, so far as Israel is concerned, focus upon the holy life of the community. If Israel then obeys the laws of society aimed at Israel's sanctification, then the foreordained history, resting on the merit of the ancestors, will unfold as Israel hopes. So there is no secret to the meaning of the events of the day, and Israel, for its part, can affect its destiny and effect salvation.

The distinctive mode of thought in Leviticus Rabbah (and, self-evidently, in other documents of the same sort, that is, appealing to a variation of the intersecting-verse/base-verse rhetorical pattern) appeals to metanoymic and metapohoric thinking. Reading one thing in terms of something else, the builders of the document systematically adopted for themselves the reality of the Scripture, its history and doctrines. They transformed that history from a sequence of one-time events, leading from one place to some other, into an ever-present mythic world. No longer was there one Moses, one David, one set of happenings of a distinctive and never-to-be-repeated character. Now whatever happens, of which the thinkers propose to take account, must enter and be absorbed into that established and ubiquitous pattern and structure founded in Scripture. It is not that biblical history repeats itself. Rather, biblical history no longer constitutes history as a story of things that happened once, long ago, and pointed to some one moment in the future. Rather it becomes an account of things that happen every day – hence, an ever-present mythic world, as I said.

That is why, in Leviticus Rabbah, Scripture as a whole does not dictate the order of discourse, let alone its character. In this document they chose in Leviticus itself a verse here, a phrase there. These then presented the pretext for propositional discourse commonly quite out of phase with the cited passage. The verses that are quoted ordinarily shift from the meanings they convey to the implications they contain, speaking about something, anything, other than what they seem to be saying. So the as-if frame of mind brought to Scripture brings renewal to Scripture, seeing everything with fresh eyes. And the result of the new vision was a reimagining of the social world envisioned by the document at hand, I mean, the everyday world of Israel in its Land in that difficult time. For what the sages now proposed was a reconstruction of existence along the lines of the ancient design of Scripture as they read it. What that meant was that, from a sequence of one-time and linear events, everything that happened was turned into a repetition of known and already experienced paradigms, hence, once more, a mythic being. The source and core of the myth, of course, derive from Scripture – Scripture reread, renewed, reconstructed along with the society that revered Scripture.

So the mode of thought that dictated the issues and the logic of the document, telling the thinkers to see one thing in terms of something else, addressed Scripture in particular and collectively. And thinking as they did, the framers of the document saw Scripture in a new way, just as they saw their own circumstance afresh, rejecting their world in favor of Scripture's, reliving Scripture's world in their own terms. That, incidentally, is why they did not write history, an account of what was happening and what it meant. It was not that they did not recognize or appreciate important changes and trends reshaping their nation's life. They could not deny that reality. In their apocalyptic reading of the dietary and leprosy laws, they made explicit their close encounter with the history of the world as they knew it. But they had another mode of responding to history. It was to treat history as if it were already known and readily understood. Whatever happened had already happened. Scripture dictated the contents of history, laying forth the structures of time, the rules that prevailed and were made known in events. Self-evidently, these same thinkers projected into Scripture's day the realities of their own, turning Moses and David into rabbis, for example. But that is how people think in that mythic, enchanted world in which, to begin with, reality blends with dream, and hope projects onto future and past alike how people want things to be.

Let us turn, now, from these somewhat abstract observations to a concrete account of what happened, in particular, when the thinkers at hand undertook to reimagine reality – both their own and Scripture's. Exactly how did they think about one thing in terms of another, and what did they choose, in particular, to recognize in this rather complex process of juggling unpalatable present and unattainable myth? We turn to the specifics by reverting to the tried and true method of listing all the data and classifying them. Exactly what did the framers of Leviticus Rabbah learn when they opened the book of Leviticus? To state the answer in advance, when they read the rules of sanctification of the priesthood, they heard the message of the salvation of all Israel. Leviticus became the story of how Israel, purified from social sin and sanctified, would be saved.

Let us turn, then, to the classifications of rules that sages located in the social laws of Leviticus. The first, and single paramount, category takes shape within the themes associated with the national life of Israel. The principal lines of structure flow along the fringes: Israel's relationships with others. These are (so to speak) horizontal, with the nations, and vertical, with God. But, from the viewpoint of the framers of the document, the relationships form a single, seamless web, for Israel's vertical relationships dictate the horizontals as well; when God wishes to punish Israel, the nations come to do the work. The relationships that define Israel, moreover, prove dynamic, not static, in that they respond to the movement of the Torah through Israel's history. When the Torah governs, then the vertical relationship is stable and felicitous, the horizontal one secure, and, when not, God obeys the rules and the nations obey God. So the first and paramount, category takes shape within the themes associated with the national life of Israel. The principal lines of structure flow along the fringe, Israel's relationships with others. The relationships form a single, seamless web, for Israel's vertical relationships dictate the horizontals as well; when God wishes to punish Israel, the nations come to do the work. The relationships that define Israel, moreover, prove dynamic, not static, in that they respond to the movement of the Torah through Israel's history. When the Torah governs, then the vertical relationship is stable and felicitous, the horizontal one secure, and, when not, God obeys the rules and the nations obey God.

We now catalogue and classify all of the propositions emerging from the paragraphs of thought of Leviticus Rabbah. My effort is to state, as simply and accurately as I can, what the framer of a given paragraph wished to express, either directly or through rich illustrative materials.

The National Life of Israel: Israel, God, and the Nations

I:XI	Torah is life to Israel, poison to nations.
I:XII	Gentiles have no prophets.
I:XIII	Gentile prophets are inferior.
II:I	Israel is precious to God.
II:IV-V	God gave Israel many laws so as to express his love and ongoing concern. This was because they enthroned God at the Red Sea.
II:VI	Scripture is so worded as to treat Israel with respect.
V:II	God punishes Israel's sins by placing gentile rulers over them, e.g., Sennacherib.
V:VII	Virtues of Israel are vices for nations [see I:XI, XIII].
VI:I	Israel are God's witnesses.
VI:V	Israel violated its oath at Sinai, but God forgave Israel. [Also: VII:I.]
VII:IV	God is concerned not to waste Israel's resources.
X:I-III	God favors prophets and priests who justify Israel.
XII:II	God meets Israel in the tent of meeting.
XIII:II	Israel alone was worthy to receive the Torah. By observing food taboos, Israel shows its special position. [Also: XIII:III.]
XIII:IV-V	Food taboos symbolize Israel's fate among the nations. The four kingdoms as exemplary of food laws.
XV:IX	Skin ailments symbolize Israel's fate among the nations. The four kingdoms.
[XVI:I	Leprosy as punishment for social sins, e.g., gossip.]
XVII:I	Israel is singled out to be punished for specific sins. Others suffer at last judgment.
XVII:V	If Israel sins in the Land, it will be punished as Canaan was.
XVII:VI	Canaanites hid their treasures, and by afflicting the houses, God revealed the hiding place.
XVII:VII	The Temple's affliction is symbolized by the leprosy disease affecting houses.
XVIII:II	Individuals and nations cause their own punishment. [Also: XVIII:III.]
XVIII:IV	Israel was unafflicted at Sinai. After they sinned, various afflictions appeared.

XVIII:V	God governs Israel the same way kings govern kingdoms. But God heals with that with which he punishes.
XIX:IV	Israel's sins provoke punishment.
XX:VIII-IX	Sins in the cult caused death of Nadab and Abihu.
XX:X	Social sins and the death of Nadab and Abihu. Snootiness, pride.
XXI:XI	Israel is sustained by merits of the patriarchs.
XXII:VIII	God permitted sacrifice as an antidote to sin.
XXIII:I-III	Israel is the rose, the nations, the thorns. Various circumstances in Israel's history at which that fact was shown.
XXIII:V	Israel among the nations is steadfast in loyalty to God and will be redeemed.
XXIII:VI	Israel was created only to do religious duties and good deeds.
XXIII:VII	Israel must be different from gentiles, particularly in sexual practices. [Also XXIII:IX, XXIII:XIII.]
XXIV:I-II	When God exalts a people, it is done justly and so his act endures.
XXV:I	The Torah is what protects Israel.
XXV:IV	God kept his promises to the patriarchs to favor their descendants.
XXVII:V	God favors the victim.
XXVII:VI	God shows Israel special favor, which disappoints the nations. He does not demand much from Israel. [Also: XXVII:VIII.]
XXVII:IX	The animals used in the cult stand for the meritorious ancestors.
XXVII:XI	God will ultimately save Israel even from its cruelest enemies.
XXVIII:III	God asks very little of Israel.
XXVIII:IV	Merely with prayer Israel is saved, not with weapons.
XXVIII:VI	The merit of the religious duty of the sheaf of first fruits causes Israel to inherit the land, peace is made, Israel is saved.
XXIX:II	Israel's suffering among the nations is due to Jacob's lack of faith.
XXIX:V	Israel is redeemed because of keeping commandments. [Also: XXIX:VIIIB.]
XXIX:VII	Israel is saved through the merit of the patriarchs. [Also: XXIX:VIII, XXIX:X.]
XXX:I	Israel serves Esau [Rome] because of insufficient devotion to Torah study.
XXX:II	Israel's victory is signified by palm branches.
XXX:IX-XII	The symbols of Sukkot stand for God, the patriarchs, Israel's leaders, Israel. [Also: XXX:XIV.]
XXXI:III	God wants from Israel something he surely does not need, e.g., lamp, and that is the mark of God's love. [Also: XXXI:IV, XXXII:VIII.]
XXXII:I	Israel is reviled among the nations but exalted by God.

The recurrent messages may be stated in a single paragraph.

God loves Israel, so gave them the Torah, which defines their life and governs their welfare. Israel is alone in its category (*sui generis*), so what is a virtue to Israel is a vice to the nation, life-giving to Israel, poison to the gentiles. True, Israel sins, but God forgives that sin, having punished the nation on account of it. Such a process has yet to come to an end, but it will culminate in Israel's complete regeneration. Meanwhile, Israel's assurance of God's love lies in the many expressions of special concern, for even the humblest and most ordinary aspects of the national life: the food the nation eats, the sexual practices by which it procreates. These life-sustaining, life-transmitting activities draw God's special interest, as a mark of his general love for Israel. Israel then is supposed to achieve its life in conformity with the marks of God's love. These indications moreover signify also the character of Israel's difficulty, namely, subordination to the nations in general, but to the fourth kingdom, Rome, in particular. Both food laws and skin diseases stand for the nations. There is yet another category of sin, also collective and generative of collective punishment, and that is social. The moral character of Israel's life, the treatment of people by one another, the practice of gossip and small-scale thuggery – these too draw down divine penalty. The nation's fate therefore corresponds to its moral condition. The moral condition, however, emerges not only from the current generation. Israel's richest hope lies in the merit of the ancestors, thus in the Scriptural record of the merits attained by the founders of the nation, those who originally brought it into being and gave it life.

The world to come is so portrayed as to restate these same propositions. Merit overcomes sin, and doing religious duties or supererogatory acts of kindness will win merit for the nation that does them. Israel will be saved at the end of time, and the age, or world, to follow will be exactly the opposite of this one. Much that we find in the account of Israel's national life, worked out through the definition of the liminal relationships, recurs in slightly altered form in the picture of the world to come.

Israel and the world to come. Salvific doctrines and symbols

II:II	In this world and in the world to come, Israel, Levites, priesthood, heave offerings, firstlings, Land, Jerusalem, etc., will endure.
III:I	Israel will be redeemed on the Sabbath.
VII:III	Israel will be redeemed through the merit of Torah study.
IX:I	The thanksgiving-offering will continue in the world to come. [Also: IX:VIII.]
X:IX	Jerusalem in the world to come.
XI:II	Rebuilding of Jerusalem in the world to come.
XVII:VII	Temple will be rebuilt.
XXI:I-IV	Israel is saved because of the merit of the people at various turnings in their history, e.g., at the Red Sea. Also through merit of atonement.
XXI:V-VI	Religious duties counteract sin.
XXIII:V	Israel will be saved through its steadfast faith.
XXIII:VI	Israel will be redeemed when Esau no longer rules.
XXX:XVI	Through merit of lulab, Temple will be rebuilt.
XXXI:XI	Merit of eternal light brings messiah.

The world to come will right all presently unbalanced relationships. What is good will go forward, what is bad will come to an end. The simple message is that the things people revere, the cult and its majestic course through the year, will go on; Jerusalem will come back, so too the Temple, in all their glory. Israel will be saved through the merit of the ancestors, atonement, study of Torah, practice of religious duties. The prevalence of the eschatological dimension at the formal structures, with its messianic and other expressions, here finds its counterpart in the repetition of the same few symbols in the expression of doctrine. The theme of the moral life of Israel produces propositions concerning not only the individual but, more important, the social virtues that the community as a whole must exhibit.

The Laws of Society for Israel's Holy Community

I:X	Israel became punishable for violating divine law only after the Torah was taught to them a second time in the tent of meeting.
II:VII	Offerings should not derive from stolen property. [Also: III:IV.]
III:I	Not expiating sin through an inexpensive offering is better than doing so through an expensive one. Better not sin at all. [Also: IX:I, IX:V, IX:VIII.]
III:II-III	God will not despise a meager offering of a poor person. [Also: III:V, VIII:IV.]
IV:I	God punishes with good reason and not blindly.

IV:II	The soul wants to do ever more religious duties.
IV:III	Unwitting sin is caused by haste.
IV:IV-V	Soul and body are jointly at fault for sin.
IV:VI	Israelites are responsible for one another.
IV:VIII	Soul compared to God.
V:IV	Philanthropy makes a place for the donor.
V:VIII	Israel knows how to please God.
VI:III	False oath brings terrible punishment.
VII:II	If one repents sin, it is as if he made an offering in the rebuilt Temple.
VII:II	God favors the contrite and penitent. [Also: VII:VI, VIII:I, IX:I, IV, VI, God favors the thanksgiving-offering.]
IX:III	God favors those who bring peace even more than those who study Torah.
IX:IX	Peace is the highest value.
X:V	Repentance and prayer effect atonement for sin.
X:VI	Priests' acts effect atonement.
XI:V	God responds to human virtue by acting in the same way.
XII:I, IV	Wine leads to poverty, estrangement.
XIV:V	Even the most pious person has a sinful side to his nature.
XV:IV	Gossip causes a specific ailment. God punishes Israel because he cares about Israel's moral condition.
XV:V	Sin of mother effects embryo.
XV:VI	Correspondence of sin and punishment. People get what they deserve.
XVI:I	Leprosy punishes gossip, other sins. [Also: XVI:II, XVII:III, XVIII:IV.]
XVI:V	Sinning through speech – general principle and particular examples.
XVI:VI	Skin disease and gossip. [Also: XVI:VII.]
XVI:VIII	People cause their own ailments through sin.
XVII:II	Diseases afflicting a house and the sin of the owner.
XVII:IV	God penalizes first property, then the person.
XXII:VI	Thievery is tantamount to murder.
XXII:X	For each prohibition there is a release.
XXIII:X-XI	God rewards those who avoid sin.
XXIII:XII	Adultery may be in one's mind.
XXIV:VI	Sanctification is through avoiding sexual misdeed.

XXIV:VII	Israel must remain holy if God is to be in its midst. [Also: XXIV:VIII.]
XXV:III	People are like God when they plant trees.
XXVI:II	God's pure speech versus humanity's gossip.
XXVII:I	God seeks justice, but it may be fully worked out only in the world to come. [Also: XXVII:II.]
XXX:V	One cannot serve God with stolen property. [Also: XXX:VI.]
XXXII:V	Israel keeps itself sexually pure.
XXXIII:I	What people say has the power of life and death.
XXXIV:II	God repays generosity.
XXXIV:V	People should not envy one another.
XXXIV:VIII	God rewards generosity. [Also: XXXIV:IX, XXXIV:X, XXXIV:XI.]
XXXV:VII	If Israel keeps the commandments, it is as if they made them.
XXXVII:I	It is unwise to vow.

First of all, the message to the individual constitutes a revision, for this context, of the address to the nation: humility as against arrogance, obedience as against sin, constant concern not to follow one's natural inclination to do evil or to overcome the natural limitations of the human condition. Israel must accept its fate, obey and rely on the merits accrued through the ages and God's special love. The individual must conform, in ordinary affairs, to this same paradigm of patience and submission.

Great men and women, that is, individual heroes within the established paradigm, conform to that same pattern, exemplifying the national virtues. Among these, of course, Moses stands out; he has no equal. The special position of the humble Moses is complemented by the patriarchs and by David, all of whom knew how to please God and left as an inheritance to Israel the merit they had thereby attained.

If we now ask about further recurring themes or topics, there is one so commonplace that we should have to list the majority of paragraphs of discourse in order to provide a complete list. It is the list of events in Israel's history, meaning, in this context, Israel's history solely in scriptural times, down through the return to Zion. The one-time events of the generation of the flood, Sodom and Gomorrah, the patriarchs and the sojourn in Egypt, the exodus, the revelation of the Torah at Sinai, the golden calf, the Davidic monarchy and the building of the Temple, Sennacherib, Hezekiah, and the destruction of northern Israel, Nebuchadnezzar and the destruction of the Temple in 586, the life of Israel in Babylonian captivity, Daniel and his associates, Mordecai and Haman – these events occur over and over again. They turn out to serve as paradigms of sin and atonement, steadfastness and divine intervention, and equivalent lessons. We find, in fact, a fairly standard repertoire of scriptural heroes or villains, on the one side, and conventional lists of Israel's enemies and their actions and downfall, on the other. The boastful, for instance, include (VII:VI) the generation of the flood, Sodom and Gomorrah, Pharaoh, Sisera, Sennacherib, Nebuchadnezzar, the wicked empire (Rome) – contrasted to Israel, "despised and humble in this world." The four kingdoms recur again and again, always ending, of course, with Rome, with the repeated message that after Rome will come Israel. But Israel has to make this happen through its faith and submission to God's will. Lists of enemies ring the changes on Cain, the Sodomites, Pharaoh, Sennacherib, Nebuchadnezzar, Haman.

Accordingly, the mode of thought brought to bear upon the theme of history remains exactly the same as before: list making, with data exhibiting similar taxonomic traits drawn together into lists based on common monothetic traits or definitions. These lists then through the power of repetition make a single enormous point. They prove a social law of history. The catalogues of exemplary heroes and historical events serve a further purpose. They provide a model of how contemporary events are to be absorbed into the biblical paradigm. Since biblical events exemplify recurrent happenings, sin and redemption, forgiveness and atonement, they lose their one-time character. At the same time and in the same way, current events find a place within the ancient, but eternally present, paradigmatic scheme. So no new historical events, other than exemplary episodes in lives of heroes, demand narration because, through what is said about the past, what was happening in the times of the framers of Leviticus Rabbah would also come under consideration. This mode of dealing with biblical history and contemporary events produces two reciprocal effects. The first is the mythicization of biblical stories, their removal from the framework of ongoing, unique patterns of history and sequences of events and their transformation into accounts of things that happen all the time. The second is that contemporary events too lose all of their specificity and enter the paradigmatic framework of established mythic existence. So (1) the Scripture's myth happens every day, and (2) every day produces re-enactment of the Scripture's myth.

Salvation and sanctification join together in Leviticus Rabbah. The laws of the book of Leviticus, focused as they are on the sanctification of the nation through its cult, in Leviticus Rabbah indicate the rules of salvation as well. The message of Leviticus Rabbah attaches itself to the book of Leviticus, as if that book had come from prophecy and addressed the issue of the meaning of history and Israel's salvation. But the book of Leviticus came from the priesthood and spoke of sanctification. The paradoxical syllogism – the as-if reading, the opposite of how things seem – of the composers of Leviticus Rabbah therefore reaches simple formulation. In the very setting of sanctification we find the promise of salvation. In the topics of the cult and the priesthood we uncover the national and social issues of the moral life and redemptive hope of Israel. The repeated comparison and contrast of priesthood and prophecy, sanctification and salvation, turn out to produce a complement, which comes to most perfect union in the text at hand.

The focus of Leviticus Rabbah and its laws of history is upon the society of Israel, its national fate and moral condition. Indeed, nearly all of the *parashiyyot* of Leviticus Rabbah turn out to deal with the national, social condition of Israel, and this in three contexts: (1) Israel's setting in the history of the nations, (2) the sanctified character of the inner life of Israel itself, (3) the future, salvific history of Israel. So the biblical book that deals with the holy Temple now is shown to address the holy people. Leviticus really discusses not the consecration of the cult but the sanctification of the nation – its conformity to God's will laid forth in the Torah, and God's rules. So when we review the document as a whole and ask what is that something else that the base-text is supposed to address, it turns out that the sanctification of the cult stands for the salvation of the nation. So the nation now is like the cult then, the ordinary Israelite now like the priest then. The holy way of life lived now, through acts to which merit accrues, corresponds to the holy rites then. The process of metamorphosis is full, rich, complete. When everything stands for something else, the something else repeatedly turns out to be the nation. This is what our document spells out in exquisite detail, yet never missing the main point.

IV

Document

The documentary distinctiveness of Leviticus Rabbah strikes most forcefully when we compare that composition to its closest friend and neighbor, Genesis Rabbah. The framers of Leviticus Rabbah treat topics, not particular verses. They make generalizations that are freestanding. They express cogent propositions through extended compositions, not episodic ideas. Earlier, in Genesis Rabbah, as we have seen, things people wished to say were attached to predefined statements based on an existing text, constructed in accord with an organizing logic independent of the systematic expression of a single, well-framed idea. That is to say, the sequence of verses of Genesis and their contents played a massive role in the larger-scale organization of Genesis Rabbah and expression of its propositions. Now the authors of Leviticus Rabbah so collected and arranged their materials that an abstract proposition emerges. That proposition is not expressed only or mainly through episodic restatements, assigned, as I said, to an order established by a base-text (whether Genesis or Leviticus, or a Mishnah-tractate, for that matter). Rather it emerges through a logic of its own. What is new is the move from an essentially exegetical mode of logical discourse to a fundamentally philosophical one. It is the shift from discourse framed around an established (hence old) text to syllogistic argument organized around a proposed (hence new) theorem or proposition. What changes, therefore, is the way in which cogent thought takes place, as people moved from discourse contingent on some prior principle of organization to discourse autonomous of a ready-made program inherited from an earlier paradigm.

Let us now return to the main point raised in the prologue of this exercise and draw those conclusions relevant to the argument of the book:

1.   Structure: how, overall, does the document organize its materials? The framers follow a clearly discernible principle or organization which tells them how to frame their ideas in systematic statements and then how to order those statements by their distinct types.

2.   Plan: does the document at hand follow a fixed and limited plan, a repertoire of rhetorical forms? We have seen a fixed and limited selection of available forms.

3.   Program: do these forms yield cogent and intelligible proposition(s), one(s) that, in some recurrent interest(s) or point(s) of emphasis, may make of the whole if not more than, then at least, the sum of, the parts? Not only do the framers of Leviticus Rabbah follow a well-composed set of forms, but the character of these forms turns out, upon close inspection, to state, in its way, the very message of a theological character that the propositions of those same forms delivers in its way. Ignoring the plan and program of the authorship of Leviticus Rabbah renders incomprehensible what is in fact an intelligible and thoroughly cogent statement.

Chapter Eight

Pesiqta deRab Kahana

I

Structure

The single definitive trait of Pesiqta deRab Kahana derives from its structure, which generates the fundamental principle of organization and topical selection, and, as I shall show in due course, the distinctive and differentiating traits of rhetoric – therefore also of logic of cogent discourse and syllogistic composition – to begin with are generated by the topical program of this writing. Our initial definition of Pesiqta deRab Kahana therefore begins with a simple account of the things the document's framers have chosen as the structure for laying out the program of their twenty-eight *pisqaot*, or propositions. The facts come before the interpretation.

In the catalogue of *pisqaot* that follows, by Torah-lection I mean that a passage is read in the synagogue on a specified Sabbath. By prophetic-lection I mean the same thing. The Sabbath that is so distinguished is then indicated as to its occasion. What we shall now see is that the structure of the document derives not from Scripture at all, but from the unfolding of the liturgical calendar of the synagogue and its lections on special occasions in particular. These are the facts:

Pisqa Base-verse

    Topic or Occasion

1. *On the day Moses completed* (Num. 7:1)

   Torah-lection for the Sabbath of Hanukkah

2. *When you take the census* (Ex. 30:12)

   Torah-lection for the Sabbath of Sheqalim first of the four Sabbaths prior to the advent of Nisan, in which Passover falls

3. *Remember Amalek* (Deut. 25:17-19)

   Torah-lection for the Sabbath of Zakhor second of the four Sabbaths prior to the advent of Nisan, in which Passover.falls

4. *Red heifer* (Num. 19:1ff.)

    Torah-lection for the Sabbath of Parah third of of the four Sabbaths prior to the advent of Nisan, in which Passover falls

5. *This month* (Ex. 12:1-2)

    Torah-lection for the Sabbath of Hahodesh, fourth of the four Sabbaths prior to the advent of Nisan, in which Passover falls

6. *My offerings* (Num. 28:1-4)

    Torah-lection for the New Moon which falls on a weekday[1]

7. *It came to pass at midnight* (Ex. 12:29-32)

    Torah-lection for the first day of Passover

8. *The first sheaf* (Lev. 23:11)

    Torah-lection for the second day of Passover on which the first sheaves of barley were harvested and waved as an offering[2]

9. *When a bull or sheep or goat is born* (Lev. 22:26)

    Lection for Passover

10. *You shall set aside a tithe* (Deut. 14:22)

    Torah-lection for Sabbath during Passover in the Land of Israel or for the eighth day of Passover outside of the Land of Israel[3]

11. *When Pharaoh let the people go* (Ex. 13:17-18)

    Torah-lection for the Seventh Day of Passover

12. *In the third month* (Ex. 19:1ff.)

    Torah-lection for Pentecost

13. *The words of Jeremiah* (Jer. 1:1-3)

    Prophetic-lection for the first of three Sabbaths prior to the Ninth of Ab

14. *Hear* (Jer. 2:4-6)

    Prophetic-lection for the second of three Sabbaths prior to the Ninth of Ab

15. *How lonely sits the city* (Lam. 1:1-2)

    Prophetic-lection for the third of three Sabbaths prior to the Ninth of Ab

16. *Comfort* (Is. 40:1-2)

    Prophetic-lection for the first of three Sabbaths following the Ninth of Ab

---

[1]Abraham Goldberg, Pesiqta deRab Kahana, *Qiryat Sefer* 1967: 43:69, cited by Braude and Kapstein, p. 124, n. 1.

[2]Braude and Kapstein, p.154, n. 1.

[3]*Ibid.*, p. 186, n. 1.

17. *But Zion said* (Is. 49:14-16)

Prophetic-lection for the second of three Sabbaths following the Ninth of Ab

18. *O afflicted one, storm tossed* (Is. 54:11-14)

Prophetic-lection for the third of three Sabbaths following the Ninth of Ab

19. *I even I am he who comforts you* (Is. 51:12-15)

Prophetic-lection for the fourth of three Sabbaths following the Ninth of Ab

20. *Sing aloud, O barren woman* (Is. 54:1ff.)

Prophetic-lection for the fifth of three Sabbaths following the Ninth of Ab

21. *Arise, shine* (Is. 60:1-3)

Prophetic-lection for the sixth of three Sabbaths following the Ninth of Ab

22. *I will greatly rejoice in the Lord* (Is. 61:10-11)

Prophetic-lection for the seventh of three Sabbaths following the Ninth of Ab

23. *The New Year*

No base-verse indicated. The theme is God's justice and judgment.

24. *Return O Israel to the Lord your God* (Hos. 14:1-3)

Prophetic-lection for the Sabbath of Repentance between New Year and Day of Atonement

25. *Selihot*

No base-verse indicated. The theme is God's forgiveness.[4]

26. *After the death of the two sons of Aaron* (Lev. 16:1ff.)

Torah-lection for the Day of Atonement

27. *And you shall take on the first day* (Lev. 23:39-43)

Torah-lection for the first day of the Festival of Tabernacles

28. *On the eighth day* (Num. 29:35-39)

Torah-lection for the Eighth Day of Solemn Assembly

This catalogue draws our attention to three eccentric *pisqaot*, distinguished by their failure to build discourse upon what I have called (for the sake of the initial analysis) the base-verse. These are No. 4, which may fairly claim that its topic, the red cow, occurs in exact verbal formulation in the verses at hand; No. 23, the New Year, and No. 25, *Selihot*. The last-named may or may not take an integral place in the structure of the whole. But the middle item, the New Year,

---

[4]Goldberg, *op. cit.*, cited by Braude and Kapstein, links the Pisqa at hand to the Fast of Gedaliah, on the third of Tishre, or to one of the days between New Year's Day and the Day of Atonement when the Torah is read.

on the very surface is essential to a structure that clearly wishes to follow the line of holy days onward through the the Sabbath of Repentance, the Day of Atonement, the Festival of Tabernacles, and the Eighth Day of Solemn Assembly. So while we may claim that No. 4 is no exception to the formal pattern and No. 25 may sustain more than a single explanation for its inclusion, therefore may come late in the formation of the document,[5] No. 23 forms an essential component of the pattern, therefore the statement, of the generative authorship and cannot be dismissed as a possible accretion later on. The rhetorically idiosyncratic traits of the *pisqa* therefore draw our attention and will provide a fundamental fact in the inductive examination of intrinsic evidence, which we now undertake.

Let us now address to the internal evidence at hand a simple set of inductive questions, answered solely out of the facts before us. Is Pesiqta deRab Kahana organized around a text? The criterion is whether or not the authorship persistently refers to data outside of its own framework, appeals to an authority beyond itself.

The answer on the surface is affirmative, in that the authorship quotes Scripture as its authority. We know that fact (as if we had to say so) because of the persistent pattern of invoking the language of citation, *as it is said, as it is written,* and the like, a powerful form of internal evidence. It is affirmative in a more profound sense, a sense deriving from the structure of language, syntax and sentence-formation. The authorship builds its cogent discourses (*pisqaot*) not on the foundation of syllogisms stated in the language and terms of the authorship alone, but rather, on the basis of syllogisms that refer to or borrow from another, prior writing. That writing we may call *the text* selected by the authorship of Pesiqta deRab Kahana for the foundation for a commentary. But I make that statement only with the proviso that the word *text* may refer to a variety of structures, not solely to Scripture. Each *pisqa* repeatedly refers to data clearly outside the frame of discourse of the authorship and treated as authoritative within that same frame. The liturgical calendar dictates lections and themes that also govern the organization of our document in particular.

The *pisqaot* that link up with holy days, moreover, tell us to why the document does the things it does do: *why this*, not only *why not that*. Comparison with other documents furthermore highlights the importance of the internal traits on which I have laid emphasis. For other authorships prior to the one at hand,[6] moreover, did precisely what ours did *not* do, and none built a cogent unit of sustained and protracted discourse on the basis chosen by our authorship, that is, the character and theme of a holy day. The framers of Sifra and Sifré to Numbers and Sifré to Deuteronomy follow the verses of Scripture and attach to them whatever messages they wish to deliver. The authorship of

---

[5]Here is where manuscript evidence extending over many centuries would prove helpful.

[6]In the final part of this chapter I outline the sequence of documents and identify the appropriate place of ours.

Genesis Rabbah follows suit, though less narrowly guided by verses and more clearly interested in their broader themes. The framers of Leviticus Rabbah attached rather broad, discursive and syllogistic statements to verses of the book of Leviticus, but these verses do not follow in close sequence, one, then the next, as in Sifra and its friends. That program of exposition of verses of Scripture read in or out of sequence, of organization of discourse in line with biblical books, parallel to the Tosefta's and Talmuds' authorships exposition of passages of the Mishnah, read in close sequence or otherwise, we see, defines what our authorship has not done.

The structure of Pesiqta deRab Kahana derives not from passages of the Pentateuchal books, or from passages of Prophetic books but from passages selected because – it is unanimously held – synagogue liturgy identified them with particular Sabbath and festival occasions, as follows:

Adar-Nisan-Sivan

Passover-Pentecost: *Pisqaot* 2-12

[possible exception: *Pisqa* 6]

Tammuz-Ab-Elul

The Ninth of Ab: *Pisqaot* 13-22

Tishri

Tishre 1-22: *Pisqaot* 23-28

Only *Pisqa* 1 (possibly also *Pisqa* 6) falls out of synchronic relationship with a long sequence of special occasions in the synagogual-lections.

To conclude, Pesiqta deRab Kahana follows the synagogual-lections from early spring through fall, in the Western calendar, from late February or early March through late September or early October, approximately half of the solar year, 27 weeks, and somewhat more than half of the lunar year. On the very surface, the basic building block is the theme of a given lectionary Sabbath – that is, a Sabbath distinguished by a particular lection – and not the theme dictated by a given passage of Scripture, let alone the exposition of the language or proposition of such a scriptural verse. The topical program of the document may be defined very simply: expositions of themes dictated by special Sabbaths or festivals and their lections.

II

Plan

Chapter Three contains ample evidence that Pesiqta deRab Kahana follows a rhetorical plan that we may define on the basis of inductive evidence. The document as a whole follows the formal plan presented there. In the interests of economy, therefore, we proceed directly to the matter of program.

III

Program

Rhetorical analysis has yields the proposition that Pesiqta deRab Kahana consists of twenty-eight syllogisms, each presented in a cogent and systematic way by one of the twenty-eight *pisqaot*, respectively. Each *pisqa* contains an implicit proposition, and that proposition may be stated in a simple way. It emerges from the intersection of an external verse with the base-verse that recurs through the *pisqa,* and then is restated by the systematic dissection of the components of the base-verse, each of which is shown to say the same thing as all the others. Let me now specify as these form a coherent statement the implicit proposition of each of the *pisqaot* of Pesiqta deRab Kahana. May we state in a few simple words the recurrent and cogent syllogism of our document? I see these three propositions:

1. *God loves Israel, that love is unconditional, and Israel's response to God must be obedience to the religious duties that God has assigned, which will produce merit.*

Israel's obedience to God is what will save Israel. That means doing the religious duties as required by the Torah, which is the mark of God's love for – and regeneration of – Israel. The tabernacle symbolizes the union of Israel and God. When Israel does what God asks above, Israel will prosper down below. If Israel remembers Amalek down below, God will remember Amalek up above and will wipe him out. A mark of Israel's loyalty to God is remembering Amalek. God does not require the animals that are sacrificed, since man could never match God's appetite, if that were the issue, but the savor pleases God [as a mark of Israel's loyalty and obedience]. The first sheaf returns to God God's fair share of the gifts that God bestows on Israel, and those who give it benefit, while those who hold it back suffer. The first sheaf returns to God God's fair share of the gifts that God bestows on Israel, and those who give it benefit, while those who hold it back suffer. Observing religious duties, typified by the rites of The Festival, brings a great reward of that merit that ultimately leads to redemption. God's ways are just, righteous and merciful, as shown by God's concern that the offspring remain with the mother for seven days. God's love for Israel is so intense that he wants to hold them back for an extra day after The Festival in order to spend more time with them, because, unlike the nations of the world, Israel knows how to please God. This is a mark of God's love for Israel.

2. *God is reasonable and when Israel has been punished, it is in accord with God's rules. God forgives penitent Israel and is abundant in mercy.*

The good and the wicked die in exactly the same circumstance or condition. Laughter is vain because it is mixed with grief. A wise person will not expect too much joy. But when people suffer, there ordinarily is a good reason for it.

That is only one sign that God is reasonable and God never did anything lawless and wrong to Israel or made unreasonable demands, and there was, therefore, no reason for Israel to lose confidence in God or to abandon him. God punished Israel to be sure. But this was done with reason. Nothing happened to Israel of which God did not give fair warning in advance, and Israel's failure to heed the prophets brought about her fall. And God will forgive a faithful Israel. Even though the Israelites sinned by making the golden calf, God forgave them and raised them up. On the New Year, God executes justice, but the justice is tempered with mercy. The rites of the New Year bring about divine judgment and also forgiveness because of the merit of the fathers. Israel must repent and return to the Lord, who is merciful and will forgive them for their sins. The penitential season of the New Year and Day of Atonement is the right time for confession and penitence, and God is sure to accept penitence. By exercising his power of mercy, the already-merciful God grows still stronger in mercy.

3. *God will save Israel personally at a time and circumstance of his own choosing. Israel may know what the future redemption will be like, because of the redemption from Egypt.*

The paradox of the red cow, that what imparts uncleanness, namely touching the ashes of the red cow, produces cleanness is part of God's ineffable wisdom, which man cannot fathom. Only God can know the precise moment of Israel's redemption. That is something man cannot find out on his own. But God will certainly fulfil the predictions of the prophets about Israel's coming redemption. The Exodus from Egypt is the paradigm of the coming redemption. Israel has lost Eden – but can come home, and, with God's help, will. God's unique power is shown through Israel's unique suffering. In God's own time, he will redeem Israel. The lunar calendar, particular to Israel, marks Israel as favored by God, for the new moon signals the coming of Israel's redemption, and the particular new moon that will mark the actual event is that of Nisan. When God chooses to redeem Israel, Israel's enemies will have no power to stop him, because God will force Israel's enemies to serve Israel, because of Israel's purity and loyalty to God. Israel's enemies are punished, and what they propose to do to Israel, God does to them. Both directly and through the prophets, God is the source of true comfort, which he will bring to Israel. Israel thinks that God has forsaken them. But it is Israel who forsook God, God's love has never failed, and will never fail. Even though he has been angry, his mercy still is near and God has the power and will to save Israel. God has designated the godly for himself and has already promised to redeem them. He will assuredly do so. God personally is the one who will comfort Israel. While Israel says there is no comfort, in fact, God will comfort Israel. Zion/Israel is like a barren woman, but Zion will bring forth children, and Israel will be comforted. Both God and Israel will bring light to Zion, which will give light to the world. The rebuilding of Zion will be a source of joy for the entire world, not for Israel alone. God will rejoice in Israel, Israel in God, like bride and groom.

IV

Document

Let me conclude by answering the broad question, does the document at hand deliver a particular message and viewpoint or does it merely serve as a repository for diverse, received materials? The answer is the former.

There is a profoundly cogent statement made through the composition of this document, and this is the message of Pesiqta deRab Kahana: God loves Israel, that love is unconditional, and Israel's response to God must be obedience to the religious duties that God has assigned, which will produce merit. God is reasonable and when Israel has been punished, it is in accord with God's rules. God forgives penitent Israel and is abundant in mercy. God will save Israel personally at a time and circumstance of his own choosing. Israel may know what the future redemption will be like, because of the redemption from Egypt. Pesiqta deRab Kahana therefore has been so assembled as to exhibit a viewpoint, a purpose of its particular authorship, one quite distinctive, in its own context (if not in a single one of its proipositions!) to its framers or collectors and arrangers.

Such a characteristic literary purpose is so powerfully particular to one authorship that nearly everything at hand can be shown to have been chosen and much has furthermore been arranged and even (re)shaped for the ultimate purpose of the authorship at hand. These then are collectors and arrangers who demand the title of authors. Do the materials cohere, or are they merely miscellaneous? In form and in polemic, in plan and in program, the materials assembled in Pesiqta deRab Kahana do cohere, to such a degree that on the basis of traits of cogency we can differentiate materials in Pesiqta deRab Kahana that are original to Leviticus Rabbah from those distinctive to Pesiqta deRab Kahana. Not only so, but the program, the framing of a position on the role of logic and reason in the mind of sages, and the plan, the defining of recurrent rhetorical forms and patterns,join into a single statement. And since they do cohere, we may conclude that the framers of the document indeed have followed a single plan and a program. That justifies my claim that the framers of Pesiqta deRab Kahana have carried out a labor not only of conglomeration, arrangement and selection, but also of genuine authorship or composition in the narrow and strict sense of the word.

Pesiqta deRab Kahana emerges from authors, not merely arrangers and compositors. They come to Israel with a particular (if not distinctive) message, and this they deliver through powerful and purposeful discourse. Focusing upon the document they created, seen whole, complete, and in its three dimensions of rhetoric, logic, and topic, we recognize the primary of documentary discourse. In

Pesiqta deRab Kahana we take up not a composite but a composition, a work of integrity, a message addressed to a particular place, time, and circumstance by a distinct and singular authorship. Their message derives from Sinai: Israel is in the hands of a loving and forgiving God, who will save Israel in his own good time. But their chosen medium of organization and proportion, sense and meaning, appealing as it does for proportion and sense to the orderly and reliable passage of the seasons testifies to the pertinence of their message. And that choice is original, not received but invented, and very much their own.

Part Four

THE PRIMACY OF DOCUMENTARY DISCOURSE

Chapter Nine

Context and Contents:
The Centrality of the Canonical Process

I

Kugel's "Two Introductions" and the Documentary Facts

We have found difficulty in locating evidence in support of Kugel's propositions. Indeed, the preponderance of evidence pointed to precisely the opposite conclusions. Since Kugel clearly has worked hard on the study of midrash-exegeses, readily invoking what everybody knows as proof for his premises or positions ("as any student or rabbinic literature knows"), we must conclude that – as in the case of all mortals – his strength is his weakness. What he knows he knows in one way, rather than in some other. Having spent a great deal of effort to explain how a given verse has precipitated a received exegesis, he quite reasonably concluded that exegeses begin with the problems of verses. Having reached that position, furthermore, he appears not to have spent a great deal of time in the analysis of rhetoric, on the one side, or in the inquiry into the principles of logical cogency and intelligible discourse, on the other. This has further discouraged him from asking whether a document as a whole proposes to make a point or to register a syllogism or a set of syllogisms. I suppose that, if one works in a pickle factory all day long, everything for supper will taste like pickles.

And yet, I think there is a deeper premise than the one defined by scholarly habits, both bad and good. The clue lies in Kugel's explicit recognition of the category of canon: "there simply is no boundary encountered beyond that of the verse until one comes to the borders of the canon itself." That is another way of saying that the Torah is one and seamless, or that Judaism is Judaism. And so it is – at the end.

But the problem of how diverse documents, with their premises and their distinct syllogisms, fit together is not solved merely by saying it is solved. Precisely how the diverse documents constitute a canon, where, when, and why a given document and its message made its way into the canon – these are questions Kugel and those he represents do not address. They treat as the premise of their literary critical reading of midrash-exegeses what in fact defines the most profound and difficult problem in the reading of all of the documents that, today, after the fact, constitute the canon, or the Torah.

In the academy we do not frame our hypotheses out of the detritus of theological conviction. In the sectarian world of seminary and yeshiva, people do just that. Kugel stands for a position – not limited to Orthodox Judaism by any means – that everything is one thing and bounded only at the outer limits. That is correct theology. But it is bad scholarship. The reason is not merely that, as a matter of fact, it is wrong. Bad scholarship treats as a premise what is in fact the issue; it begs the question.

Kugel is a man of intelligence, sensibility, learning and industry. I am confident that, as he reflects on the case made here, he will learn to construct his argument and introduce midrash by framing hypotheses and testing them, questions and exploring them, rather than, as he does here, by defining axioms and repeatedly illustrating them. Then, I am certain, he will find greater motivation than he has exhibited to date to study the work of others who have pursued the same inquiries.

II

The Propositions One By One

A very brief reprise suffices to state the upshot of this sustained study of documents and their properties.

1. *Midrash stands for Judaic biblical interpretation in general:*
   I shall deal with this prosition in the concluding section.

2. *Midrash is precipitated by the character of the verse subject to exegesis:*

   ...midrash's precise focus is most often what one might call surface irregularities in the text: a good deal of the time, it is concerned with...*problems.*[1]

In detail, Kugel may well be right. That is to say, once an exegete has chosen the verse and knows what he wishes, in general, to prove, then a set of the properties of a given verse may attract attention. Why one type of property, rather than some other, why one issue, not another – these are questions to which the discrete exegesis of a verse on its own does not respond. And, as we have seen, in the comparison of such midrash-compilations as the two families we have examined, Sifra and Sifré to Numbers, on the one side, Genesis Rabbah, Leviticus Rabbah, and Pesiqta deRab Kahana, on the other, we can propose theses in response to those questions – the ones of why this, not that? – and we can test those theses against the traits of rhetoric, logic, and even topic.

In all, I do not register a one-sided disagreement with the position represented by Kugel that the traits of a given verse register in the formation of

---

[1]P. 92.

an exegesis of that verse. I am certain that the received exegetical literature, the thousand-year tradition of reading the midrash-exegeses precisely the way Kugel and others wish to read them, enjoys ample proof in result in detail. But it begs the question to conclude *post hoc, ergo propter hoc*, as Kugel and his friends do.

3.   *Midrash is an exegesis of biblical verses, not of books:*

...midrash is an exegesis of biblical verses, not of books. The basic unit of the Bible for the midrashist is the verse: this is what he seeks to expound, and it might be said that there simply is no boundary encountered beyond that of the verse until one comes to the borders of the canon itself.[2]

What I have already said applies here. It is simply false to claim that there is no boundary between midrash-exegesis of a single verse and the entirety of the canon of Judaism. The opposite is the fact.

And yet here too, Kugel is not completely wrong. As I said in the preface and Chapter One, some materials do travel freely from document to document, though apart from verses of Scripture, nothing known to me appears in every document of the dual Torah in its repertoire of late antiquity, through the Talmud of Babylonia. Hyman's *Torah hekketubah vehammesurah*, which lists pretty much all places in the corpus in which a given verse comes under discussion, sustains that judgment, as a rapid survey will show. Nonetheless, the peripatetic sayings and stories do journey hither and yon. So Kugel is talking about facts, if not (in proportion to the whole) a great many, and if not (in weight of evidence) probative ones.

But why they are accepted here and not there (where – to argue imaginatively, as Kugel and his friends do so elegantly – they *might have* appeared), what a given authorship has chosen to accomplish through citing a passage they have found in an earlier document, we cannot explain for the documents of late antiquity merely by saying things move from here to there. If a document's authorship exhibits a cogent program, as do the five authorships we have consulted, then we should be able to explain why they have used a peripatetic saying or story or exegesis of a verse of Scripture in the way they have. Or, we should be able to state, we do not know what, if anything, they proposed to accomplish in resorting to the passage at hand. Or we should ask about the history of a composite unit of materials prior to the authorship's selecting it, for at least some travelling materials were composed into a larger conglomerate prior to their insertion in some of the several documents in which they occur. So the reason a given midrash-exegesis recurs may well be found in the history of the larger composite of which it forms a part. That proposition is fairly easy to demonstrate, as a matter of fact. And it calls into question the

---

[2]P. 93.

notion that authorships compose their documents essentially through free association.[3]

4. *The components of midrash-compositions are interchangeable:*

> Our midrashic compilations are in this sense potentially deceiving, since they seem to treat the whole text bit by bit; but with the exception of certain patterns, these "bits" are rather atomistic, and, as any student or rabbinic literature knows, interchangeable, modifiable, combinable – in short, not part of an overall exegesis at all.[4]

Kugel is wrong. He does not demonstrate that the components of midrash-exegesis are mere atoms, readily interchanged, modified, combined in diverse ways. In his defense, I point to what I said at the third proposition. Some (few) midrash-exegeses do occur in a number of passages. Characterizing all of them as Kugel does, however, violates the facts of something on the order of 80-90% of the midrash-exegeses in the documents we have examined.

But there is another line of argument in support of Kugel's contention. The midrash-documents of medieval times are highly imitative, borrowing and arranging and rearranging whole tracts of received materials. The authorships intervene in various ways, in some cases making up exegeses and assigning them to named authorities of a thousand years earlier. They succeed because of their power of imitation. Now if Kugel wishes to propose that the pseudepigraphic character of the midrash-compilations of medieval and early modern times – the making of collections/*yalquts* continued into the nineteenth century! – demonstrates the interchangeable character of the received materials, I believe he can make a solid case. But that case testifies to the taste of the imitators and pseudepigraphs, rather than to the historical setting and point of origin of the earlier documents. Usefulness to later authorships tells us about the enduring appeal of the creations of earlier ones. It does not tell us that everything is everywhere interchangeable – unless as our premise we take the facticity of attributions, on the one side,[5] and the fundamental irrelevance of context and circumstance of the original formation of the document, on the

---

[3]The conception that authorships play an active role in the formation of what they include in their documents is not new to me or particular to my school. It is in fact a routine inquiry, one that has produced interesting results for diverse scholars. I call attention, for example, to Steven Fraade, "Sifré Deuteronomy 26 (and Deut. 3:23): How Conscious the Composition," *Hebrew Union College Annual* 1983, 54:245-302. Despite his certainty on these matters, I can find in Kugel's notes no reference to, or argument with, Fraade. My own debate with Fraade is in my *Religious Studies of Judaism. Description, Analysis, and Interpretation* (Lanham, 1986: University Press of America *Studies in Judaism* series) I:93-128, in particular, pp. 104-108, "Fraade vs. Fraade." But Fraade in his HUCA paper is certainly on the right track.

[4] P. 95

[5]I shall refer to Kugel's history of midrash in a moment.

other. But, as a matter of fact, Kugel and his friends build on both of these premises.

5. *Midrash is the way every Jew reads Scripture:*

> Forever after, one cannot think of the verse or hear it recited without also recalling the solution to its problematic irritant – indeed, remembering it in the study-house or synagogue, one would certainly pass it along to others present, and together appreciate its cleverness and erudition. And so midrashic explications of individual verses no doubt circulated on their own, independent of any larger exegetical context. Perhaps in this sense it would not be inappropriate to compare their manner of circulating to that of jokes in modern society; indeed, they were a kind of joking, a learned and sophisticated play about the biblical text, and like jokes they were passed on, modified, and improved as they went, until a great many of them eventually entered into the common inheritance of every Jew, passed on in learning with the text of the Bible itself.[6]

Kugel does not prove that "every Jew" has received this "common inheritance," though as a matter of religious faith he may hold that every Jew should accept it. He does not demonstrate that we deal with "a kind of joking," and nothing in the propositions and syllogisms I have outlined in Part Three justifies his rather jejune characterization of this literature. How this literary judgment, which I regard as unproved and probably groundless, accords with the theological position at hand I cannot say. What I find stunning in the midrash-compilations as well as in their contents, the midrash-exegeses is the urgency and immediacy of matters, not the cleverness and erudition demonstrated therein. Israel, the people of God, turned with deep anxieties about salvation to Genesis, Leviticus, and the sacred calendar. I find nothing amusing, merely clever, or particularly erudite in what the sages found there. In my description, analysis, and interpretation of the midrash-compilations, I find messages of self-evident truth in response to questions of life and death.

As a believing Jew, I too have a position to express. In this judgment of Kugel's I find no merit, since it treats as trivial and merely personal what is in fact a monumental theological statement of the founders of Judaism. Our sages were not scholars, mere clever erudites. They were holy men and they gave God's judgment, through the Torah, oral and written, to suffering Israel – then and now. As a religious Jew, that is my deepest conviction, on account of which I cannot find redeeming arguments in behalf of Kugel's amazing judgment.

---

[6]P. 95.

III

From Mishmash to Midrash

Taking *midrash-meaning-exegesis* out of the documentary context, that is, *midrash-meaning-a-document* that organizes and presents midrash turns *midrash* into *mishmash*. That is not because of errors of judgment about trivialities, let alone because he does not know what he is talking about, but because of a fundamental error in the reading of the literature. Since, as I said, Kugel has evidently read the documents atomistically, he claims that they are made up only of atoms. When he works his way through complete compilations of midrash-exegeses and gives us his judgment on whether or not they form mere scrapbooks or purposely statements, documents of integrity, as I have done in *The Integrity of Leviticus Rabbah*, we shall see whether or not he maintains the view he announces in the statement under discussion here.

Still, before concluding, I hasten to say a word in Kugel's defense. It would be an altogether too harsh judgment to conclude that Kugel is merely making things up as he goes along, though a certain distance does appear to have opened up between Kugel's allegations about the literature he purports to interpret and the actual character of documents of that same literature. I believe he has conscientiously done his best to represent things he has studied as well as he can. But it would be a bit generous to concede that he has done his homework awfully well. Since my description of the documents is accurate and available for all to study if they wish, and since that literary judgment on matters of rhetoric, logic, and topic stands at complete variance with Kugel's premises, I think we shall have to conclude that he has some considerable gaps in his mastery of the sources – at least the five important samples discussed here. And yet, by stating in a forthright and unabashed way the convictions of Orthodox Judaism as well as a fair part of ethnic Judaic scholarship concerning midrash, Kugel deserves our thanks for precipitating a fruitful debate. We in the academic sector of Judaic studies welcome that debate and intend to pursue it most vigorously.

Now let us turn to the upshot of the matter, Kugel's claim to give us two introductions to midrash. Kugel's two introductions yield not even one definition. Midrash in his definition is pretty much the same thing as "Jewish creativity itself." Let us return to Kugel's most general statement of the matter:

> At bottom midrash is not a genre of interpretation but an interpretative stance, a way of reading the sacred text...The genres in which this way of reading has found expression include...translations of the Bible such as the early Aramaic targumim; retellings of biblical passages and books such as the "Genesis Apocryphon"...; sermons, homilies, exegetical prayers and poems, and other synagogue pieces; and of course the great standard corpora of Jewish exegesis..., in short, almost all of what constitutes classical and much of medieval Jewish writing....for at heart

midrash is nothing less than the foundation stone of rabbinic Judaism and it is as diverse as Jewish creativity itself.[7]

Kugel does not tell us what midrash is, when he says it is "a way of reading the sacred text." For until he explains precisely what *way* it is – and what way it is not – he has clarified nothing. And definition requires comparison, for when we define we exclude just as we include. But in this statement, Kugel encompasses everything Jews wrote as midrash. To me in this definition, midrash is pretty much a mishmash.

And it is a mishmash of Judaisms, in the sense that "Jewish creativity" encompasses everything any Jew wrote anywhere (at least, within the canon of contemporary Orthodox Jewish scholarship). In making this bizarre judgment, Kugel not only declines to define midrash. He also fails to differentiate among the different groups behind the writings to which he makes reference. The Genesis Apocryphon is not a document produced and preserved by the same people who wrote and handed on Genesis Rabbah ("rabbinic Judaism" indeed!), for example, and no one has demonstrated the rabbinic provenience of the Targumim (except for Onqelos). Many have shown the opposite. So I do not exaggerate in concluding that Kugel homogenizes everything every Jew every wrote, so to speak, into one Judaism.

A further aspect of his "Two Definitions of Midrash" requires passing attention at this point, his history of midrash.[8] In that history, Kugel takes at face value all attributions of sayings and most of books, so that if a given figure, rabbinical or otherwise, is assigned a statement, Kugel takes as fact that the man made that statement at the time at which he is supposed to have lived. Kugel furthermore invokes for his history of interpretation of Scripture works that rest upon the same gullible position, e.g., p. 100, n. 6: "For the historical setting of this transition and parallels to the inspired interpreter outside the rabbinic tradition see D. Patte, *Early Jewish Hermeneutic in Palestine.*" Patte at that stage in his work took for granted and at face value pretty much everything he read in the rabbinic literature, so presenting a picture of the fourth century B.C. out of writings of the fifth century A.D., a mere nine hundred years later. On that basis Kugel presents us with his linear, incremental, and unitary picture of the history of midrash within Judaism: everything everybody ever wrote, more or less. That introduces nothing.

Accordingly, I believe that the authorships of the five documents we have analyzed will have found puzzling many aspects of Kugel's introduction and description of their work. The source of his misrepresentation of the literature is not trivial, and he has not made minor mistakes to be blown up out of all

---

[7]*Op. cit.* pp. 91-2.

[8]See pp. 80-90, which I have neglected, and, especially, the repertoire of scholarly authorities cited in those pages. This is the connection to my *Reading and Believing: Ancient Judaism and Contemporary Gullibility.*

proportion into an indictment of the integrity of the man and his scholarship. On the contrary, no one doubts his scholarly ethics, his learning, his character, commitment, and conscience – only his critical judgment *on the issue at hand.* And the issue is not one of orthodoxy or heresy, but merely one of introduction: the accurate description, analysis, and interpretation of some old books. I think he has not accomplished an accurate description, because he read the parts but not the whole. I think he has not accomplished a rigorous analysis because he has read acutely but has not undertaken a program of comparison and contrast. I think he has not given us a plausible interpretation – that is, an introduction, a definition – because he has thought deeply but not worked inductively on the basis of intrinsic evidence and, alas, also has brought a set of convictions, I have shown of a theological character, that are inappropriate to the secular work of literary analysis.

Appendix

One Definition of Midrash

Gary G. Porton

University of Illinois, Urbana

In 1979 I wrote that "the scholarly study of midrash is in its infancy."[1] Recent years have seen the study of midrash move into its early childhood as a number of scholars have turned their attention to this topic. However, most of these projects have posed the same old questions and gone over old ground. Few investigations have exhibited a fresh approach to the subject or explored new territory.[2] In addition many of the "new" studies simply "re-invent the wheel" instead of improving it, for often "new" definitions of midrash or "new" approaches to the topic ignore what have preceded them. In an effort to encourage the new generation of scholars of midrash to build on the past work of others instead of merely repeating it, I take this opportunity to repeat the conclusions of my earlier studies.[3] I hope that this essay will encourage those interested in the topic of rabbinic midrash to move forward in their work by improving on what has already been done and by producing fresh, new results in their investigations.

In 1979 I defined midrash as "a type of literature, oral or written, which has its starting point in a fixed, canonical text, considered the revealed word of God

---

[1] Gary G. Porton, "Midrash: The Palestinian Jews and the Hebrew Bible in the Greco-Roman Period" in Hildegard Temporini and Wolfgang Haase (eds.), *Aufstieg und Niedergang der romischen Welt* (Berlin & New York, 1979), II.19.2, 104. See also my "Defining Midrash" in Jacob Neusner (ed.), *The Study of Ancient Judaism I: Mishnah, Midrash, Siddur* (New York: 1981), 55-92, *Understanding Rabbinic Midrash: Text and Commentary* (New York: 1985), and my forthcoming entry on Midrash in the *Anchor Bible Dictionary*.

[2] Among the very few who have posed new questions and applied new methods to the problem of rabbinic midrash is Jacob Neusner. I call special attention to the following works: *The Evidence of Leviticus Rabbah* (Chicago: 1985), *The Integrity of Leviticus Rabbah* (Chicago: 1985), *Midrash in Context: Exegesis in Formative Judaism* (Philadelphia: 1983), *Genesis Rabbah: The Judaic Commentary to the Book of Genesis, A New American Translation* (Atlanta: 1985), 3 vols., *Sifre to Numbers: An American Translation and Explanation* (Atlanta: 1986), 2 vols, *Comparative Midrash: The Plan and Program of Genesis and Leviticus Rabbah* (Atlanta: 1986), and with Roger Brooks, *Sifra: The Rabbinic Commentary on Leviticus, An American Translation* (Atlanta: 1985).

[3] In the present essay I merely repeat my conclusions; those interested in my arguments and supports for these conclusions are referred to the works listed in note 1.

by the midrashist and his audience, and in which this original verse is explicitly cited or clearly alluded to." Although I still find this a workable definition, in 1985 I simplified it and wrote "midrash refers to statements, comments or remarks that are juxtaposed to the accepted authoritative Jewish Scriptures." The point of both definitions is the same: For something to be considered midrash it must have a clear relationship to the accepted canonical text of Revelation. Midrash is a term given to a Jewish activity which finds its locus in the religious life of the Jewish community.[4] While others exegete their revelatory canons and while Jews exegete other texts, only Jews who explicitly tie their comments to the Bible engage in Midrash.[5]

Many Israelites have exegeted their canonical Revelation in a variety of ways, and different members of the community have considered different documents to be authoritative. In my original study I identified four different types of midrashic activity in addition to rabbinic midrash. 1) Many have drawn attention to the midrashic activity found within the Bible itself. Different scholars have pointed to Deuteronomy's rewriting of Exodus, Numbers, and Leviticus, the titles of some of the Psalms, and the books of Chronicles as examples of early midrashic activity. While it is difficult to determine whether or not the "biblical midrashists" considered the texts they exegeted as canonical, there is no doubt that we have a good deal of inter-biblical exegesis and commentary. 2) Translations of the Bible are another example of non-rabbinic midrashic activity. Because I have found no proof that the earliest *targumin* were composed by rabbis, I have listed the creation of these texts as a non-rabbinic midrashic activity. Of course, there is a wide disparity among the Aramaic translations of the Hebrew Bible, and some of them are more expansive and interpretive than others; however, few would deny that the very activity of translating a text from one language to another is a form of commenting on the original texts. 3) A third form of non-rabbinic midrash from the turn of the eras is the rewriting of the biblical narrative. Such works as the *Liber Antiquitatum Biblicarum* of Pseudo-Philo, the *Genesis Apocryphon,* and *Jubilees* fall into this category. If we could establish that the early sections of Josephus' *Antiquities* and Philo's many allegories and his *Life of Moses* were written for communities which accepted the authority of the biblical texts upon which these writers built, these too could be fit into this category. 4) The *pesharim* found among the writings from Qumran represent yet another type of ancient Jewish midrash, for its apocalyptic tone and its exclusive concern with the history of the Dead Sea Community set it apart from the other examples of ancient Jewish exegetical

[4]I distinguish between midrash and exegesis only by assigning the former word to activity within the Israelite community. However, it should be clear that there may be extensive parallels between midrash which occurs within an Israelite context and exegesis which occurs in other religious and cultural systems.

[5]For examples of the same rabbinic comments appearing as midrashic statements and non-midrashic statements see *Understanding Rabbinic Midrash*, 6-8.

activity. Some have suggested that another type of midrashic activity can be found in the liturgy which developed in ancient Judaism and was finally codified in the Gaonic period. This is an interesting question; however, sufficient work has not been done in uncovering the relationship between the liturgy and Scripture to allow us to reach a final decision on this matter.

Rabbinic midrash represents an independent phenomenon, for the rabbis are a distinct class within the Jewish community of Late Antiquity. The definitive characteristic of the ancient rabbi was his knowledge and how he attained it. What a rabbi knew distinguished him from the rest of the Jewish community, and the fact that he had gained his information by studying with another rabbi who participated in a chain of tradition which stretched back to God and Moses on Mount Sinai also set him apart in his larger environment. A rabbi's knowledge began with the Written Torah, the five books of Moses, the public record of the perfect revelation from the perfect God, and from there it moved into the Oral Torah, that part of revelation which had been handed down from God to Moses our Rabbi and from Moses our Rabbi, through an unbroken chain, to the rabbis of Late Antiquity. The Oral Torah is the record of rabbinic attempts to solve problems encountered in the Written Torah, for among other things it filled in the details, explained unclear matters and expanded upon enigmatic passages found in the Written Torah. The Oral Torah also offered the rules and methods according to which the Written Torah was to be interpreted and upon which an understanding of it should be based. In short, the Oral Torah provided the guidelines that made possible the understanding of and the application of Scripture's lessons in contemporary life. The Oral Torah was the key to unlocking the mysteries of the Written Torah, and the rabbis were the only ones who possessed this key. Because the rabbis alone knew the entirety of Revelation, the Oral and Written Torah, they acted differently from the rest of the community; they ate different foods, wore different clothes, and even spoke their own jargon. Thus, Rabbinic midrash is the type of midrash produced by this small segment of the Jewish population of Palestine and Babylonia during the first seven centuries of the common era.

Rabbinic midrash is based on several presuppositions. The rabbis believed that the Written Torah was the accurate and complete public record of a direct revelation from the One, Unique, and Perfect God to His people; therefore, nothing in the Bible was unimportant or frivolous. Every letter, every verse, and every phrase contained in the Bible was important and written as it was for a specific reason. The Bible contained no needless expressions, no "mere" repetitions, and no superfluous words or phrases. The assumption that every element of the biblical text was written in a specific way in order to teach something underlies the midrashic activity of the rabbis. Furthermore, the rabbis believed that everything contained in Scriptures was interrelated. Often, one verse is explained by reference to another verse. A section of the Prophets may be used to explain a verse from the Torah, or a portion of the Torah may explain a passage from the Writings. In addition, the rabbis believed that any given biblical verse was open to more than one possible interpretation. Taken as a whole, the rabbinic midrashic collections offer a wide variety of explanations of the same verses, the Hebrew Bible. Even within a single collection we often find contradictory midrashic statements standing side by side. Moreover, especially in the earlier collections of rabbinic midrash, we find attempts to prove that reason unaided by revelation is fallible. A common midrashic activity is to refute a reasonable or logical conclusion merely by citing a verse from Scripture. The midrashic activity was important, for without it, people might not act in proper ways and might misunderstand the realities of the world, man and God. Therefore, the midrashic activity represents the other side of the coin from the mishnaic activity of the rabbinic class. A fifth assumption of the rabbis who engaged in the production of midrash was that their activity was a religious, God-centered enterprise. While other peoples in Late Antiquity interpreted their ancient documents and even created many of the techniques which the rabbis used and which were codified in the lists of midrashic rules attributed to Hillel, Ishmael, and Eliezer b. Yosi the Galilean, the rabbis alone believed that their activity was related to the word of the One and Only God. For the rabbis, the Hebrew Bible contained all the secrets of the universe, and it was the ultimate source of all knowledge and wisdom. Rabbinic Midrash was thus one means of discovering these secrets, of attaining true knowledge and wisdom. The Bible was the only true guide for human action; it was the standard against which one measured one's deeds, the final arbiter of true and false, right and wrong. Rabbinic Midrash expounds only one document, and that text was not of human origin. With the passing of time and the development and refinement of rabbinic thought, the study of the Torah became the most holy task possible to humans, and thus, the goal of a well-led life. Its rewards were received in this world; but more importantly, they were bestowed fully in the world-to-come. The rabbis were not merely interested in explaining difficult words or obscure passages, in identifying unknown places, in solving problems within an ancient text. Their interpretation and study led to salvation, nor only for the Jews, but for the whole world. Midrash as a product of rabbinic theology which focused on the Word of the One and Only God who had created this world, revealed His will on Mount Sinai, and would eventually perfect His creation.

While I have spoken of the presuppositions of "the rabbis" and "rabbinic midrash," these are oversimplifications. Each collection of rabbinic midrash develops from these presuppositions in its own way. Each has its own plan, agenda, and integrity. Just as we cannot accurately portray what the "rabbis" believed or taught, we cannot speak of "rabbinic midrash" as a single phenomenon. There were many rabbis who taught a variety of things. Some rabbis taught some things, others taught about other things. The individual sages agreed and disagreed with their colleagues and might, as individuals be pictured as holding inconsistent and contradictory opinions. Similarly, we have a variety of midrashic texts. Each is unique and in some ways different from the others, while at the same sharing similarities with the other collections. What is important is that each collection be studied on its own terms as well as part of the larger phenomenon of rabbinic midrash. Neusner[6] and I[7] independently have demonstrated that the various midrashic documents must be studied as integrated units before they are dealt with as part of the larger category of rabbinic midrash. Neusner has shown that comparative midrash means comparing whole documents of midrash, and I have demonstrated that each rabbinic midrashic collection exhibits its own style of exegesis, while at the same time sharing themes and concerns with other midrashic collections.

The activity of producing rabbinic midrash is one aspect of the agenda of the sages in Late Antiquity. It derives from their theological concerns, their world-view, and their place in the Jewish community. Rabbinic midrash is different from other types of midrashic activity in Late Antiquity because the rabbis were different from other types of Israelites and non-Israelites of this period. Thus, the study of rabbinic midrash offers us insight into not only the exegetical activity of the rabbis but also into the larger questions of rabbinic Judaism and the thought of the rabbinic class. Rabbinic midrash is one element in the complex whole of Judaism in Late Antiquity, and it must be understood both as a unique phenomenon made up of discrete elements and as part of a larger whole.

[6]See the works listed above in note 2, especially *Comparative Midrash*, 1-19.

[7]This is demonstrated in *Understanding Rabbinic Midrash*.

Index